MILITARY HISTORY
FROM PRIMARY SOURCES

SEA BATTLES IN THE AGE OF SAIL

JAMES GRANT

EDITED AND INTRODUCED
BY BOB CARRUTHERS

Pen & Sword
MARITIME

This edition published in 2012 by
Pen & Sword Maritime
An imprint of
Pen & Sword Books Ltd
47 Church Street
Barnsley
South Yorkshire
S70 2AS

First published in Great Britain in 2011 in digital format by
Coda Books Ltd.

Copyright © Coda Books Ltd, 2011
Published under licence by Pen & Sword Books Ltd.

ISBN 978 1 78159 162 8

This book contains an extract from 'British Battles on Land and Sea' by James Grant.
Published by Cassell and Company Limited, 1894.

Printed and bound by CPI Group (UK) Ltd, Croydon, CR0 4YY

Pen & Sword Books Ltd incorporates the Imprints of Pen & Sword Aviation, Pen & Sword
Family History, Pen & Sword Maritime, Pen & Sword Military, Pen & Sword Discovery, Pen
& Sword Politics, Pen & Sword Atlas, Pen & Sword Archaeology, Wharncliffe Local History,
Wharncliffe True Crime, Wharncliffe Transport, Pen & Sword Select, Pen & Sword Military
Classics, Leo Cooper, The Praetorian Press, Claymore Press, Remember When, Seaforth
Publishing and Frontline Publishing

For a complete list of Pen & Sword titles please contact
PEN & SWORD BOOKS LIMITED
47 Church Street, Barnsley, South Yorkshire, S70 2AS, England
E-mail: enquiries@pen-and-sword.co.uk
Website: www.pen-and-sword.co.uk

CONTENTS

INTRODUCTION
BY BOB CARRUTHERS

The Author

James Grant (1822-1887) was a prolific Scottish author. Born in Edinburgh, Scotland, he was a distant relation of Sir Walter Scott. Writing some 90 books, including many yellow-backs, titles included Adventures of an Aide-de-camp, One of "The six hundred", The Scottish musketeers and The Scottish cavalier.

Development of England's Navy

The strength of the fleets of the united Kingdom of England was an important element in the kingdom's power in the 10th century. At one point Aethelred II had an especially large fleet built by a national levy of one ship for every 310 hides of land, but it is uncertain whether this was a standard or exceptional model for raising fleets. During the period of Danish rule in the 11th century the authorities maintained a standing fleet by taxation, and this continued for a time under the restored English regime of Edward the Confessor (reigned 1042-1066), who frequently commanded fleets in person.

The Battle of Sluys

English naval power seems to have declined as a result of the Norman conquest. Medieval fleets, in England as elsewhere, were almost entirely composed of merchant ships enlisted into naval service in time of war. From time to time a few "king's ships" owned by the monarch were built for specifically warlike purposes, but unlike some European states England did not maintain a small permanent core of warships in peacetime. England's naval organisation was haphazard and the mobilisation of fleets when war broke out was slow.

With the Viking era at an end, and conflict with France largely confined to the French lands of the English monarchy, England faced little threat from the sea during the 12th and 13th centuries, but in the 14th century the outbreak of the Hundred Years War dramatically increased the French menace. Early in the war French plans for an invasion of England failed when Edward III of England destroyed the French fleet in the in 1340. Major fighting was thereafter confined to French soil and England's naval capabilities sufficed to transport armies and supplies safely to their continental destinations. However, while subsequent French invasion schemes came to nothing, England's naval forces could not prevent frequent raids on the south-coast ports by the French and their Genoese and Castilian allies; such raids halted finally only with the occupation of northern France by Henry V Rodger calls Edward III's own claim to be the "Sovereign of the Seas" into question, arguing there was hardly any Royal Navy before the reign of Henry V (1413-22). Rodger also argues that for much of the fourteenth century, the French had the upper hand, apart from Sluys in 1340 and, perhaps, off Winchelsea in 1350. (reigned 1413-1422).

The standing Navy Royal, with its own secretariat, dockyards and a permanent core of purpose-built warships, was created in the 16th century during the reign of Henry VIII. Under Elizabeth I England became involved in a war with Spain, which saw privately-owned ships combining with the Navy Royal in highly profitable raids against Spanish commerce and colonies. In 1588 Philip II of Spain sent the Spanish Armada against England in order to end English support for Dutch rebels, to stop English corsair activity and to depose the Protestant Elizabeth I. The Spaniards sailed from Lisbon, planning to escort an invasion force from the Spanish Netherlands but the plan failed due to poor planning, English harrying, blocking action by the Dutch and mainly as a result of an extremely bad weather.

- C H A P T E R   I -

EXPLOITS OF SIR FRANCIS DRAKE

B Y SEA, the attempts of Elizabeth to humble the Spaniards were much more successful and brilliant - than in the Low Countries. America was regarded as the chief source of the great wealth of Philip II., as well as the most defenceless portion of his vast dominions; and as a breach had now been made with him, Elizabeth was resolved not to leave him unmolested in that quarter. The great success of the Spaniards and Portuguese in both Indies had excited the emulation of the English; and as the progress of commerce - still more that of colonies - is slow, it was fortunate that a war at this critical period had opened a more flattering object to ambition and to avarice, by tempting England to engage in naval enterprises.

Drake and Hawkins were at this time in the zenith of their fame; but accounts differ very much as to the naval force of England. Some assert that the navy about the year 1578 consisted of 146 sail, whose guns varied from forty to six. Campbell, in his "Lives of the Admirals," discredits this statement; and the most accurate accounts we seem to have of the navy in the year named make it to consist of only twenty-four ships - the largest being the *Triumph*, of 1,000 tons, and the smallest the *George*, 60 tons. "The whole number of ships in England," says Captain Schomberg, R.N., "was estimated at this time at 135, from 100 tons upwards, and 650 from 40 to 100 tons." The queen dined on board the ship, the *Golden Hind*, in which Sir Francis Drake sailed round the world, and gave orders that it should be preserved as a lasting monument of his own and of England's glory; but in process of years she was broken up, and nothing now remains of her but a chair, which was presented to the University of Oxford.

The dinner occurred at Deptford, on the 4th of April, 1584, and on that occasion she knighted him. Drake, one of England's most eminent naval heroes, was born of humble parents, near Tavistock, in 1545. He was one of the twelve sons of Edmund Drake, a poor seaman, and in his nineteenth year was captain of the *Judith*, when he fought so gallantly under Sir John Hawkins, at San Juan de Ulloa, in the Gulf of Mexico.

Under Sir Francis, a fleet of twenty-one sail was prepared for an expedition to the West Indies. Besides the seamen, 2,300 soldiers, under Christopher, Earl of Carlisle, were put on board. Many of the latter were volunteers of spirit and enterprise, and all were led by well-trained officers; for, like the navy, the army was now becoming a regular profession. The land officers were Captain Anthony Powel, sergeant-major; Captains Morgan and Sampson, "corporals of the field;" and ten other captains. Drake's own ship was named the *Elizabeth Bonaventure*, Captain William Fenner. The *Great Galleon* was under Rear-Admiral Francis Knollys; Carlisle, lieutenant-general, was in the *Tiger*.

This expedition left England in March, 1585; and the reader may be able to form some idea of the names, dimensions, and weight of the cannon-shot, and powder of the ancient English ordnance from Sir William Morison, in his "Naval Tracts," written in the time of Elizabeth and James I. (See table on following page).

Bombardes were greatly used by the Spaniards and Portuguese on board of their great caracks; and M. Blondel, in his "Art de Jetter des Bombes," says, they were first used for shelling purposes in land war against Wachtendonck, in Gueldreland, in 1588.

The use of the explosive shell had at this time been known to the English for more than forty years. Stow tells us that, about 1543, Ralph Hogge, the Sussex gun - founder, brought over a certain Fleming, named Peter Van Collet, who "devised, or caused to be made, certain mortar pieces, being at the mouth from eleven to nine inches wide, for the use whereof the said Peter caused to be made certain hollow shot to be stuffed with fyrework, whereof the bigger sort for the same has screws of iron to receive a match to carry fyre, to break in small pieces the said hollow shot, whereof the smallest piece hitting a man would kill or spoil him."

Drake's first exploit in this voyage was to plunder Vigo, to the amount of 30,000 ducats, including a cross from the cathedral, of silver double gilt. His next was the surprise and capture of St. Jago, near the Cape de Verde. There he found plenty of provisions but no treasure, and after setting the town on fire he bore on for the West Indies; and after losing 300 men by disease at Dominica, in January, 1586, he was off the island of Hispaniola.

He landed with 1,200 pike-men and musketeers, and 200 seamen, within ten miles of the city of San Domingo, and when he drew near it there came forth 150 Spanish gentlemen, all well mounted and armed, to oppose him, but they were speedily

Name	Bore (Inches)	Weight of gun (lbs.)	Weight of shot (lbs.)	Weight of powder (lbs.)
Cannon-royale	8.5	8,000	66	30
Cannon	8	6,000	60	27
Serpentine	7	5,500	53.5	25
Bastard-Cannon	7	4,500	41	20
Demi-Cannon	6.75	4,000	30.5	18
Culverin	5.5	4,500	17.5	12
Basilisk	5	400	15	10
Saker	3.5	1,400	5.5	5.5
Falcon	2.5	660	2	3.5

Information taken from Sir William Morison's "Naval Tracts".

repulsed; and then the English advanced towards the two gates of the city, which then faced the sea. These barriers the Spaniards were resolved to defend, and had manned them both well.

In front of each they had planted some pieces of cannon, and placed arquebusiers in ambush on each side of the way; but Sir Francis Drake and a captain named Powell, each leading one-half of the force landed, marched resolutely against both gates at once, vowing that, "with God's assistance, they would not give over till they met each other in the market-place."

Sir Francis, having received the fire of both the cannon in front and the ambush on his flank, charged furiously to prevent them reloading. He captured the guns, put the Spaniards to flight, and entering the gate with the fugitives, pell-mell, soon cut a passage, as he had sworn, to the market - place, where Captain Powell, whose success at the other gate was exactly similar, met him soon after, with the survivors of his command.

There they barricaded themselves, because the town was too large to be overrun by a force so small as theirs; and about midnight they attacked the gate of the castle, upon which the Spaniards instantly abandoned it. Some of the garrison were made prisoners, and the rest fled seaward in boats. The English having now possession of the fortress, enlarged their quarters, and remained in San Domingo for a month. They were completely masters of the place, which an eye-witness of the expedition, whose narrative is preserved, describes as a city of great extent and magnificence, but which Drake wasted with fire and sword during the whole of January.

During that time he sent a negro boy with a flag of truce to the Spaniards. He was met by some officers of a galley which Drake had taken in the harbour, and one of them barbarously ran him through the body with his sword. The boy lived to crawl back and acquaint Sir Francis with this outrage, and then expired at his feet.

Upon this, in a very questionable spirit, Drake ordered his provost-marshal to hang two Spanish friars he had taken prisoners j and sent another to inform the Spanish officers that "until they delivered up to him the officer who murdered his messenger, he would hang two Spanish prisoners every day." The Spaniards thereupon found themselves compelled to send the officer; and Sir Francis forced the escort who brought him to hang him instantly in his presence.

These stern measures greatly terrified and exasperated the inhabitants of San Domingo, to whom he sent commissioners to treat about the ransom of the whole city from destruction; and, to make matters more speedy, as there was some delay in the transaction, he employed 200 seamen in the task of deliberately burning the place. But the houses being all of stone, and remarkably well built, they could not consume above one-third of it.

At. last the Spaniards agreed to give 25,000 ducats, value five shillings and sixpence each, that the portion of the city remaining might be 'spared. He carried off a vast quantity of rich apparel, linen, woollen, and silk stuffs, with wine, oil, vinegar, wheat, and store of china, but very little plate, and, save the ransom, no money of consequence, as the Spaniards had only copper, for want of hands to work the mines of silver and gold.

He next appeared off Carthagena, in New Andalusia, as it was then named. The harbour had two entrances, the chief of which lay half a league east-Ward from the city, and the other nearer, named La Bocachico. Both of these have ever been dangerous, on account of the many shallows at the entrance, causing the most careful steerage to be necessary. But though the city was fortified by many "sconces," or batteries, Sir Francis Drake sailed boldly in with his pinnaces, and took it by storm on the land side. He also captured two forts, one of which secured the mouth of the smaller entrance together with a boom. He took and plundered a great-Franciscan abbey that stood thereby, surrounded with strong walls. Here many of the English perished by wounds from poisoned arrows, and poisoned spikes which were stuck in the earth. He completely pillaged Carthagena, set it on fire, and would have destroyed it completely, had it not been ransomed by the neighbouring colonies for the sum of 120,000 ducats.

San Antonio and Santa Elena, on the coast 61 Florida, shared the fate of Carthagena; and soon after he appeared off San Augustine - a little town with a castle, in the province of Sagasta, near the river May, upon a pleasant hill covered with fine trees. Fort St. John defended the town, which was almost square, with four streets, composed entirely of wooden houses.

Fort St. John was octagonal, with a round tower at each corner. Drake instantly attacked it, upon which the garrison fled, abandoning £2,000 in a treasure-ship, and fourteen pieces of brass cannon, all of which were sent off to the fleet, which, after pillaging and burning the town, bore along the coast of Virginia, where Sir Francis found the small remains of the colony which Sir Walter Raleigh had planted there, and which had gone to extreme decay. The poor planters implored Drake to take them back with him to England, to which he returned with so much riches that privateering became greatly encouraged; and he brought such accounts of the weakness and cowardice of the Spaniards, that the spirit of the nation became inflamed for further enterprise. Even the great mortality which the climate had produced in his fleet - which lost 700 men - the result also of excess and meagre medical arrangements - was but a slender restraint on the avidity and sanguine hopes of young adventurers. Ralph Lane, one of the Virginian colonists who came home with Drake, is said by Camden to have been the first man who brought the tobacco-leaf to England. The fleet came to anchor in- Portsmouth Harbour on the 28th of July, 1586.

Drake brought back with him to England plunder to the value of £60,000 sterling, with 240 brass and iron cannon; and the fame of this induced a gentleman of Devonshire, named Thomas Cavendish, who had dissipated a good estate by living at Court, to seek his fortune, sword in hand, among the Spaniards. He fitted out three ships at Plymouth, one of 120 tons, another of 60 tons, and a third of 40 tons, and with these small vessels he had the hardihood to sail for the southern seas, where he committed terrible depredations. He took no less than nineteen Spanish vessels, richly laden; and returning by the Cape of Good Hope, he came to London, where he sailed up the Thames in a kind of picturesque triumph. His mariners and soldiers were all clothed in silk of the most brilliant colours his sails were of damask, his topsail was glittering cloth of gold, and the prizes were the richest that had as yet been brought to England.

But now Elizabeth, on hearing that Philip of Spain, though he seemed to dissemble, or to ignore the daily insults and injuries sustained by his flag from the English, was equipping a great navy to attack her, ordered Sir Francis Drake once more to prepare for sea.

These equipments ultimately developed themselves as the Great Armada; but the arrangements were so vast that Sir Francis Drake says in one of his letters, quoted by Strype, that the Spaniards had provisions of bread and wine alone sufficient to maintain 40,000 men for a whole year. And that these preparations were aimed against England was discovered by Walsingham in a very singular manner. On learning that Philip had dispatched an express to Rome with a secret letter, written by his own hand, to the Pope, Sixtus V., "acquainting him with the true design in hand, and asking his blessing upon it;" Walsingham, by means of a Venetian priest, retained by him as a spy upon the Vatican, got a transcription of the original, which was abstracted from the Pope's cabinet by a gentleman

Drake attacking the Spanish treasure ships.

of the bedchamber, who (Welwood asserts in his memoirs) stole the keys from the pocket of the pontiff while he slept. Bishop Burnet observes that Walsingham's chief spies were priests, and he used to say "an active but vicious priest was the best spy in the world."

Drake sailed from the Thames, Strype says, with forty galleys, for the coast of Spain. Four of these were the largest ships of the queen; the remainder were furnished and equipped for him by the merchants of London, in hope of making profit out of the plunder. His chief ships were the *Bonaventure*; the *Lion* commanded by William Borough, Comptroller of the Navy; the *Dreadnought*, Captain Fenner: and the *Rainbow*, Captain Bellingham.

After anchoring in Plymouth Sound, he learned from two Dutch vessels which he hailed, that a Spanish fleet, richly laden, was lying at Cadiz, ready to sail for Lisbon, the rendezvous of the intended Armada. He bore boldly for that harbour. Six galleys which endeavoured to make head against him he compelled to run for shelter under cover of a fire from the forts. In spite of the latter, he plundered and sank or burned more than 100 vessels laden with provisions, arms, and ammunition. Among them were two stately galleons, one belonging to the Marquis of Santa Cruz, the other to the Venetians of Ragusa, mounting many brass cannon. Running thence along the coast to Cape St. Vincent, he stormed the castle on that promontory, and other fortresses, and pillaged the towns in succession, till he came to the mouth of the Tagus, when he in vain endeavoured to lure out the Marquis of Santa Cruz to fight him, by plundering and burning all the ships he found there.

Sailing thence to the Azores, he met on the way, near the isle of St. Michael, a mighty carack, called the *San Philipo*, returning from the East Indies, and captured her with ease; and the papers that were found on board of her so fully illustrated to the English the value of Indian merchandise, and the mode of trading in the Eastern Hemisphere, that "they afterwards," says Camden, "set up a gainful trade and traffic, establishing a company of East India merchants."

The loss of the provisions and stores which Drake destroyed at Cadiz, in what he jocularly termed "singeing the King of Spain's beard," compelled Philip to defer his darling project of invading England for another year, and gave that country time to prepare; while, by the success of the expeditions of Drake, her seamen were fast learning to despise the great and unwieldy ships of the Spaniards, who ere the year closed had fresh source for disgust, when Rear-Admiral Sir John Hawkins, when lying with a fleet of Her Majesty's ships in the Catwater, fired a shot into the Spanish admiral, who came into Plymouth with the fleet that was to escort Anne of Austria, for not striking his flag, "and paying the usual honours to Her Majesty's colours, which, after much altercation, he compelled him to do "("Lives of the Admirals "). And now came the year 1588, when Philip II hoped to have a sure and terrible vengeance for all the past.

- C H A P T E R I I -
THE SPANISH ARMADA, 1588

UNDOUBTEDLY THE greatest event of Elizabeth's reign was the defeat of the Invincible Armada - the mighty fleet destined by Philip to conquer England. His grand or ostensible object was the destruction of Protestantism; but he was smarting under a consciousness of repeated insults, of territories ravaged, cities burned, and the loss of many great treasure-ships. His vanity was also wounded by Elizabeth's refusal to marry him, as her sister had done; and after the death of Mary Stuart, whose execution was deemed by all Europe an outrage on the law of nations, he did not conceal his claims to the double inheritance of the crowns of England and Scotland, which she had bequeathed to him from the scaffold at Fotheringay.

His ambassador, Mendoza, thus wrote to him: "God having been pleased to suffer this accursed nation to fall under His displeasure, not only in regard to spiritual affairs by heresy, but also in what relates to worldly affairs, by this terrible event (the death of Mary), it is plain that the Almighty has wished to give your Majesty these two crowns as your own entire possession."

John Leslie, the celebrated Bishop of Ross, and the devoted adherent of Mary, wrote in French and Latin and in English, a declaration to prove that Philip II was lawful heir to the throne of England, the King of Scotland having rendered himself incompetent to succeed, in consequence of his heresy from Rome. The Duke de Guise was of the same opinion, and consigned to the King of Spain the task of avenging Mary Stuart, and securing Catholicism in England; and having at his disposal the ships and seamen of all Spain, Portugal, and

Italy, with troops deemed then the finest in Europe, with all the treasures of the New World, he seemed to possess resources sufficient for the mighty enterprise he resolved to undertake - an enterprise which he had conceived so early as 1570, and began to execute in 1588.

The roadstead of Lisbon was to be the general muster-place of the fleet; and there, in the spring of 1588, assembled the shipping furnished by Sicily, Naples, Catalonia, Andalusia, Castile, and Biscay. These vessels were of various dimensions. There were caravels, caracks, xebecs, galleys (the general craft of the time), some with sails, some with oars; a number of galleons; and four galeases of enormous size, that towered like wooden citadels amid the lesser vessels of the fleet. Their forecastles were literally fortified, and carried several tiers of guns. This fleet had on board 21,556 troops, who were to land on the coast of England. They were carefully equipped with arms and ammunition of every kind, and had provisions sufficient for a six months'campaign in the field. The Vicar-General of the Holy Office was on board, with a hundred Jesuits and other priests, to work the re-conversion of the island; and while this vast armament was preparing at Lisbon, under the command of the Marquis de Santa Cruz, one of the most successful admirals of the age, the Duke of Parma was concentrating a vast force on the coast of Flanders to follow up the first blow, if successful. That able captain, besides his garrisons, received under his

Wrought-iron breech-loading ship gun, from the wreck of the "Mary Rose" (Tower Collection).

colours 5,000 men from Central Italy, 4,000 from Naples, 9,000 from Castile and Arragon, 3,000 from Germany, together with four squadrons of reiters; and he had 800 Englishmen under the deserter Sir William Stanley, with other forces from the Walloon country and from Franche Comte'. He felled the whole forest of Waes to build flat-bottomed boats for the conveyance of 100,000 horse and foot down the canals to Nieuport and Dunkirk for transport to the mouth of the Thames, under the escort of the mighty Armada.

All manner of machines used in sieges, and of material for building bridges, forming camps, and building fortresses, fascines, field and garrison gun-carriages, were also prepared at a vast expenditure of money and labour; and Pope Sixtus had pledged himself to advance a million of ducats the moment the expedition touched the soil of England. In a bull intended to be secret until the hour of landing, the anathema hurled against Elizabeth by Pius V and Gregory XIII, as a bastard and heretic, deposed her from the throne. Nor did the scheme end there, for it was confidently expected that the Most Catholic King, who already possessed the Netherlands, Spain, Portugal, the Indies, and nearly all Italy, on making himself master of England on one hand, and on the other of Scotland, would turn the arms of them all against Constantinople, and expel the Turks from Europe. A letter of Sir John Hawkins to Sir Francis Walsingham computes the Armada at 114 vessels; but the Spanish historians affirm it to have amounted to 132 sail, divided into squadrons. (See table on opposite page).

This number is exclusive of 2,088 galley-slaves. On board the fleet was a vast quantity of military stores for the land service, consisting of single and double cannon, culverins, and field-pieces, 7,000 muskets, 10,000 halberds, 56,000 quintals of gunpowder, and 12,000 quintals of match. Moreover, the ships were laden with horses, mules, carts, wheels, wagons, spades, and mattocks, and all things requisite for a permanent residence in England. An enormous quantity of saddles and bridles were provided. At Dunkirk 20,000 empty casks were collected, with ropes to make floating bridges; and to the conquest of England, as in the days of Harold the Saxon, there came nobles and princes from many places, crowding under the banner of Alonzo Perez de Gusman, the Duke of Medina Sidonia, who had succeeded the Marquis de Santa Cruz in the command, for which he was quite unqualified; but he had two able seconds in Juan Manez de Recaldez, of Biscay, and Miguel de Orquendo, of Guipuzcoa. Among these were the Duke of Petrana, from Spain, the Marquis de Bourgou, son of the Archduke Ferdinand of Austria, Vespasian di Gonzaga, of the house of Mantua, a great soldier, who had once been Viceroy of Spain; Giovanni di

	Ships	Tons	Guns	Sailors	Soldiers
The Portuguese Galleons, under the Generalissimo	12	7,739	389	1,242	3,086
Biscayan Squadron, under Don Juan Manez de Recaldez, Captain-General	14	5,681	302	906	2,117
Castilian Squadron, under Don Diego de Valdez	16	8,054	477	1,793	2,624
Andalusian Squadron, under Don Pedro de Valdez	11	8,692	315	776	2,359
Guipuzcoan Squadron	14	7,192	296	608	2,120
Levant Squadron, under Don Martin Vertondonna	10	8,632	319	844	2,793
Squadron of Hulks, under Don Juan Lopez de Medina	23	10,860	446	950	4,170
Squadron of Xebecs, &c., under Don Antonio Mendoza	24	2,090	204	746	1,103
Galeases of Naples, under Don Hugo de Monendo	4	-	200	477	744
Galleys of Portugal, under Don Diego de Medina	4	-	200	424	440
Total	132	58,940	3,148	8,766	21,556

The squadrons on the Armada according to Spanish historians.

Medici, the Bastard of Florence; Amadeo of Savoy, and many others.

Meanwhile the Queen of England and her people were not idle in preparing to resist this mighty armament, the fame of which filled all Europe. Elizabeth summoned her most- able councillors, some of whom, like Raleigh, Grey, Bingham, Norris, and Grenville, had been bred to arms, and possessed military talents of a very high order.

It was resolved to equip a fleet adequate to the great emergency, and to raise all the land forces possible; and for this purpose circular letters were addressed to the lords-lieutenants of the different counties, and the returns showed that there could be raised for the defence of England 132,689 men, of whom 14,000 were cavalry. These levies were exclusive of the city of London, which offered the queen 10,000 men and 30 ships; and, as Stow records, "The merchants met every Tuesday to practise all points of war. Some of them, in 1588, had charge of men in the great camp, and were called Captains of the Artillery Garden." Their first place of meeting was in Tasel Close, now Artillery Lane, Bishopsgate.

Along the southern coast were disposed 20,000 men j under the Earl of Hunsdon, 45,000 men were collected for the special defence of the queen's person; 1,000 horse and 22,000 foot were posted at Tilbury, to protect London against the Prince of Parma; and, as Macaulay's noble ballad has it -

"From Eddystone to Berwick bounds, from Lynn to Milford Bay,

The time of slumber was as bright and busy as the day."

In Scotland, the king, who had rejected the proposals of the Spaniards to ally themselves with him, and to invade England by the borders with an army under Parma, took all the necessary measures for defence, by the erection of beacons, and the enrolment of every man above sixteen years of age, capable of bearing arms, in the kingdom; on which Elizabeth sent Sir Robert Sidney as a special ambassador to thank him, and promise assistance if the Spanish troops landed on the Scottish shores. On the 4th of August, he wrote to Elizabeth from Edinburgh, to the effect that he did not propose to aid the English as a foreign prince, but as their countryman and her "natural-born son" (Rymer).

The ships of the English navy at this time amounted only to thirty-six; but the largest and most serviceable of the merchant vessels were collected from various ports to form a fleet, to man which there came forward 17,472 mariners. The number of ships was 191; their total tonnage was only 31,985; but there was one, the *Triumph*, of 1,100 tons, one of 1,000, one of 900, others smaller, and twenty of only 200 tons. Assistance was given by the Dutch, who sent, as Stow has it, "threescore sail, brave ships of war, fierce, and full of spleen, not so much for England's aid as in just occasion for their own defence."

The command of the fleet was given to Lord Howard of Effingham, High Admiral of England, and his vice-admirals were Sir Francis Drake, Sir John Hawkins, and Sir Martin Frobisher, men whose names, even after the lapse of nearly three centuries, are still their country's pride.

On the 12th of July the Armada put finally to sea; the orders of Philip to the Duke de Medina Sidonia being that "he should, on entering the Channel, keep near the French coast, and if attacked by the English ships, avoid an action, and steer on Calais Roads, where the Prince of Parma's squadron was to job him." As these many vessels spread their canvas to the breeze, the grandeur of the spectacle excited the most flattering anticipations of success, and thousands of hearts beat high with the hope of conquest and visions of coming glory.

But the duke having been informed that the English fleet were lying "off their guard," in Plymouth Sound, could not resist the chance of destroying it there; and, deviating from his orders, he stood at once across to the coast of England. On the 19th of July the Armada was off the Lizard, where a Scottish privateer's-man, Captain Thomas Fleming, saw them, and hoisting every inch of canvas, ran into Plymouth to warn the English admiral. By sound of cannon and trumpet the crews were summoned on board; and though a stiff south-west wind was blowing, the, vessels worked out into the offing. Lord Howard that night got clear out to sea with only six of his ships, but between twenty and thirty more came out in the morning; and with these under easy sail, he stood along shore in view of the cliffs they had come to defend, anxiously looking out for this long expected and terrible Armada,

"On the night of that memorable 19th of July, messengers and signals were dispatched fast and far through England to warn each town and village that the enemy had come at last! In every shire and every city there was instant mustering of horse and man; in every seaport there was instant making ready for sea; and, especially along the southern coast, there was hurrying to join the Admiral of England, and to share in the honour of the first encounter with the foe "(Creasy). Among those who came thus with their ships were the Earls of Oxford, Northumberland, and Cumberland, Sir Robert and Sir Thomas Cecil, Sir Walter Raleigh, Sir Thomas Gerard, and others. "Upon the newes being sent to Court from Plymouth of their certain arrival," says Robert, Earl of Monmouth, in his "Personal Memoirs," "my Lord Cumberland and myselfe tooke post-horses and rode straight to Portsmouth, where we found a frigate that carried us to sea."

With a fleet amounting ultimately to 140 ships, when near the rock known as the Eddystone, the admiral discovered the Armada to the westward as far as Fowey, sailing in the form of a half-moon, seven miles in length. All were under full sail, yet coming slowly up the Channel. "The ships appeared like so many floating castles," says Lediard, in his old "Naval History," "and the ocean seemed to groan under the weight of their heavy burdens. The Lord High Admiral willingly suffered them to pass by him, so that he might chase them in the rear, with all the advantage of the wind;" in other words, he got the weather-gage of the Duke of Medina Sidonia.

The two fleets were sailing thus on the morning of Sunday, the 21st July, when, six miles westward of the Eddystone, Lord Howard, at nine o'clock, sent forward a pinnace named the *Defiance*, "to denounce war," by a discharge of all her guns - a demonstration which he immediately seconded by the fire of his own ship, the *Ark Royal*, which opened a furious cannonade on the ship of Don Alphonso de Leva, which from its size he

Sir Francis Drake.

supposed to be that of the Spanish admiral. Shortening sail, he poured a terrible fire into her, and would have destroyed her had she not been rescued by several other vessels closing in.

Now Drake, Hawkins, and Frobisher vigorously engaged the enemy's sternmost ship, under the Captain-General, Don Juan, the Marquis de Recaldez, who was on board one of the Portuguese galleons, and did all that a brave man could do to keep his squadron together; but, in spite of all his efforts, so sternly was he attacked, that they were given among the main body of the fleet, while his own vessel was so battered in the hull by shot that she became quite unserviceable.

The Spanish fleet being somewhat scattered now, the Duke of Medina Sidonia signalled for the ships to close, and, hoisting more sail, sought to hold on his course towards Calais; and now the battle took the form of a running fight.

In this movement a great galleon, commanded by Don Pedro Valdez, being seriously battered in her hull and wrecked aloft, fell foul of another ship, and was so disabled that she was left astern by the rest, just as night was coming on, and the sea running high; and the English admiral, supposing that she had neither soldiers nor sailors on board, passed her in the pursuit. On the morning of the 22nd, she was seen by Sir Francis Drake, who sent a pinnace with orders for her to surrender; but Don Pedro Valdez replied, "I have 450 men on board, and stand too much upon my honour to yield."

He then propounded certain conditions; to which the response of the vice-admiral was that "he might yield or not, as he chose, but he should soon find that Drake was no coward."

Don Pedro, on learning that his immediate opponent was Drake, whose name was a terror to the Spaniards, yielded at once, and his ship was sent into Plymouth. Prior to this, Drake divided among his own crew 55,000 golden ducats which he found on board of her.

On the same night that Don Pedro was abandoned, the Spaniards had another mishap. A great ship, of Biscay, commanded by Don Miguel de Orquendo, was maliciously set on fire by a Dutch gunner, whom he had ill used; but other ships closed in, and the crews extinguished the flames, yet not until her upper deck was blown off. "Drake had been ordered to carry lights that night," records Lediard; "but being in full chase of five German hulks, or merchant ships, which he supposed to be the enemy's, happened to neglect it. This was the cause that most of the fleet lay by (to?) all night, because they could not see the lights."

That night the Spanish fleet bore on by the Start, and next morning they were seen far to the leeward; and Sir Francis Drake, with his ships, did not rejoin the admiral until evening, as he had pursued the enemy within "culverin-shot" till daybreak.

The whole of this day was spent by the duke in repairing damages, and putting his fleet in order. He commanded Don Alphonso de Leva to bring the first and last squadrons together; assigning to each ship its station in battle, according to a plan agreed upon in Spain, and any deviation from which involved the penalty of death. Orquendo's great ship had her crew and valuables taken out of her, and was cast adrift. She was found by Captain John Hawkins, with "fifty poor wretches" on board, the stench of whose half-burned bodies was horrible. A prize-crew took her into Weymouth,

After a calm night - the wind being northerly - on the following morning the Spaniards tacked, and bore down upon the English; who also tacked, and stood westward. After several attempts to gain the weather-gage, another battle ensued, which was marked only by confusion and variety of success. The English ships, being better handled and lighter in draught than the unwieldy argosies of the Spaniards, stood quickly off or on, as their captains saw fit, The firing was now ringing over the Channel for many miles; and while, in one quarter, some ships of London which were completely surrounded by the Spaniards were gallantly rescued, in another, the latter, with equal bravery, saved from capture their Admiral Recaldez." The great guns on both sides rattled like so many peals of thunder; but the shot from the high-built Spanish ships flew for the most part over the heads of the English, without doing much execution."

A Mr. Cock, who was gallantly fighting a little volunteer ship of his own, named the *Delight*, was the only Englishman of note killed. Some officers advised Lord Howard to grapple and board; but knowing that the Spaniards had 20,000 soldiers on board, he wisely declined to do so, as loss on his side would peril

Blade of the sword of Sir Francis Drake
(Sir Sibbald Scott's "British Army").

the safety of all England. The Spaniards at first bore down under a press of sail, as if they meant to board the English; but seeing that the *Ark*, the *Nonpareil*, the *Elizabeth Jonas*, the *Victory*, and others, were prepared to meet them, they were content to drop astern of the second-named ship.

In the meantime, the *Triumph*, *Merchant-Royal*, *Centurion*, *Margaret*, *John*, *Mary Rose*, and *Golden Lion*, being far to leeward, and separated from the rest of the fleet, were borne down upon by the great gal-eases of Naples, and a fierce conflict ensued for an hour and a half, till the Neapolitans sheered off, when a change of wind to the south west enabled a squadron of English ships to attack the western flank of the Spanish fleet with such fury that they were all compelled to give way; and so, till the sun began to set, the desultory and running fight went on. Wherever the firing was hottest, Lord Howard's ship was seen. In this day's strife a great ship of Venice and many smaller were taken; and the *Mayflower*, a merchantman of London, behaved bravely, "like a man-of-war."

On the 24th of July there was a cessation of hostilities on both sides, and Lord Howard, being short of ammunition, sent the pinnaces inshore for a supply of powder and ball, as both had failed in the fleet. Sir Walter Raleigh, in recording this great mistake, says "that many of our great guns stood but as ciphers and scarecrows, not unlike to the Easterling hulks, who were wont to paint great red port-holes in their broadsides, where they carried no ordnance at all."

On the 25th, the *St. Anne*, a great Portuguese galleon, was taken near the Isle of Wight by Captain John Hawkins, under the fire of the Spaniards, who attempted to rescue her. On this clay, the further to encourage his gallant captains, the Lord Admiral knighted the Lords Howard and Sheffield, Roger Townsend, John Hawkins, Martin Frobisher, and others; and it was resolved not to assail the enemy any more until they came into the narrower part of the Channel, between Dover and Calais, before which last-named place the Armada came to anchor on the 27th of July, and the Duke of Medina Sidonia in vain dispatched a second urgent message to the Duke of Parma for aid.

On the 28th the Lord Admiral resorted to a means of destruction hitherto totally unknown in naval warfare - fire-ships. Selecting eight of the worst craft in his fleet, he bestowed on them plenty of pitch, tar, resin, brimstone, and everything that was inflammable. Their cannon he had loaded with bullets, chains, iron bars, and other missiles of destruction. Thus equipped, with all their canvas set, he sent them before the wind and with the tide, about two hours before midnight, under the command of two captains named Prowse and Young, right into the heart of the Spanish fleet. On coming within a certain distance, they lashed the helms, set fire to the trains, dropped into their boats, and withdrew.

Their approach was no sooner discovered by the Spaniards, as they came with their hulls, masts, and rigging all sheeted with fire, than the utmost consternation ensued. "Many of them had been at the siege of Antwerp, and had seen the destructive machines made use of there. Suspecting, therefore, that these were big with such-like engines, they set up a most hideous clamour of 'Cut your cables ! Get up your anchors !'and immediately, in a panic, put to sea."

All was now confusion and precipitation, and another large galleon, having had her rudder unshipped, was tossed about till she was stranded on the sands of Calais, where she was taken by Sir Amyas Preston, in the admiral's long-boat, accompanied by other boats manned by 100 seamen. Her flag was not hauled down without a bloody scuffle, in which her captain, Don Hugo de Moncada, was shot through the head, and 400 of her soldiers and rowers drowned or put to the sword. After 303 galley-slaves and 50,000 ducats had been taken out of her, she was abandoned as a wreck to Gordon, the Governor of Calais.

After the terror, flight, and miserable disasters by which many of their ships were driven into the North Sea, and others on the Flemish coast, the Spaniards, ranging themselves in the best order they could, approached Gravelines; but, as the English had got the weather-gage, they could obtain supplies neither there nor at Dunkirk. In the meantime, Sir Francis Drake, in the *Revenge*, Sir John Hawkins, in the *Victory*, Captain Fenner, in the *Nonpareil*, Sir George Beeston, in the *Dreadnought*, Sir Robert Southwell, in the *Elizabeth Jonas*, and other brave officers, kept pouring in their shot upon them continually, "and tore many of their ships so dreadfully that the water entered on all sides; and some, flying for relief towards Ostend, were shot through and through again by the Zealanders." In this day's action, a great galleon was so mauled by the *Bonaventure*, *Rainbow*, and *Vanguard*, that she sank, like a stone, in the night. Then a great galleon of Biscay, with two other vessels, was sunk.

The galleon *St. Matthew*, under Don Diego de Pimentelli, coming to the aid of Don Francisco de Toledo (colonel of thirty-two companies), in the *St. Philip*, which had been terribly cut up by the ships of Lord Henry Seymour and Sir William Winter, was taken by the Dutch; while the *St. Philip*, after being pursued as far as Ostend, was captured by some ships of Flushing. The Spaniards were now fighting simply to escape.

On the 31st of July the wind was blowing hard in the morning, from the north-west, and on the Spaniards making a last desperate attempt to recover the Channel again, were driven towards Zealand; upon which the English, who had followed them so closely for so many days, gave over the chase, supposing the Great Armada to be utterly ruined, and in danger of running aground upon the shoals and shallows of that flat and sandy coast.

The Duke of Medina Sidonia now held a Council of War, at which it was unanimously resolved, as it was impossible to repass the English Channel; as they were in want of many things, especially cannon-shot; as their ships were miserably battered and torn; as their anchors had been slipped in Calais Roads; as provisions were short, and water was spent; as many had been slain, and many were sick and wounded; and as there was no hope now of their being joined by the Duke of Parma, whose armament was blockaded by the Hollanders, they should return to Spain north-about by the coast of Scotland.

To save water, all the cavalry horses and baggage mules were flung overboard, and all sail was made for the North Sea. Leaving a squadron, under Lord Henry Seymour, to assist the Dutch in blocking up the Prince of Parma, and sending another, under Sir William Winter, to guard the coast, the Lord Admiral with the main body of his victorious fleet pursued the flying foe as far as the Firth of Forth. He confidently believed it was the duke's design to put in there, and he had taken measures for his utter destruction; but finding that the Spaniards bore on their course to the north, he relinquished the pursuit.

Most miserable was the future fate of the Armada. Of the duke's vessels, many were cast away among the Scottish isles, and seventeen, with 5,394 men on board, on the coast of Ireland; among others, a stately galleon and two Venetian ships of great burden. All who were shipwrecked in Ireland were put to the sword, or perished by the hands of the common executioner; the Lord-Deputy, by whose barbarous orders this was done, excusing himself on pretence that they might join the rebels. Thirty-eight ships, that were driven by a strong west wind into the Channel, were there taken by the English, and others by the Rochellers, in France.

The chief treasure-ship, it was long alleged, was plundered and blown up by Macleod of Dunvegan, in the west of Scotland;

and towards the close of the last century a frigate was sent by the Spanish Government to investigate the story and the locality. Whether the crew found any treasure in the bay is unknown; but, from the circumstance of their mutinying and becoming pirates, it was currently supposed they had done so. A cannon from this or one of the other wrecks of the Armada is now in the castle of Inverary. Macleod is said to have used her artillery and soldiers successfully in the furtherance of a feud with one of his neighbours.

In the treatment of those unfortunate castaways, Scotland, though sternly Presbyterian, was very unlike Catholic Ireland. There was one incident occurred at this period which, though it had little to do with the great events we have narrated, has been deemed worthy of a place-in history, inasmuch as it shows that the detestation of Catholicism, rendered more keen by the recent warlike attempt to subvert the Protestant institutions of both kingdoms, did not in any degree repress the promptings of humanity towards Catholic people in distress.

Early one morning, many days before the fate of the Armada was known in Scotland, one of the Spanish ships, having on board 700 men, was thrown ashore by a tempest near the little seaport of Anstruther, on the coast of Fife; but so far were the inhabitants from taking this opportunity of imprisoning or otherwise punishing their enemies, who were now completely at their mercy, that they supplied the Spanish soldiers and seamen with clothing, food, and shelter, while the commander (who was an admiral) and his officers were kept by a gentleman at his house until they obtained the king's permission to depart home. Thus far Melvil tells us in his Diary; and Lediard adds that they were sent by James VI. to the Duke of Parma, in the Netherlands; a third authority has it, after a year's detention in Scotland- For three successive Sundays the Scots celebrated the victory of the English.

Of all the ships that sailed from Lisbon, only fifty-three returned to Spain; of the four galeases of Naples, but one; of the four galleons of Portugal, but one; of the ninety-one great hulks from many provinces, there returned only thirty, fifty-eight being lost. In short, Philip lost in this expedition eighty-one ships, 3,500 soldiers, above 2,000 prisoners in England and in the Low Countries; and, to conclude, there was no noble or honourable family in all the Spanish peninsula but had to mourn for a son, a brother, or a dear kinsmar, who had found his grave in the Channel, on the shores of Ireland, or amid the bleak rocky isles of Western Scotland. Distressed, tossed, and wasted by storms and miseries, the remnant came home about the end of September, only to encounter sorrow, shame, and dishonour.

Camden says that Philip received the news of the ill-success of his fleet with heroic patience; and that when he heard of its total defeat, he thanked God it was no worse. But, according to Anthony Coppley, an English fugitive, who was present, Philip was at mass when the tidings came, and at its conclusion "he swore that he would waste and consume his crown, even to the value of a candlestick (pointing to one that stood upon the altar) but either he would utterly ruin Her Majesty and England or else himself, and let Spain become tributary to her."

The Duke of Medina Sidonia was forbidden to appear at Court. His title was taken from a small city in Eastern Andalusia, which was made, in 1445, a duchy for the powerful family of Gusman, of which there were three other dukes and two marquises. The Spanish priests, who had so frequently blessed the Armada and foretold its success, were puzzled for a time to account discovered that all the calamities of Spain were caused by their permitting the infidel Moors to linger so long in Granada.

Meantime, England resounded with acclamation and rejoicing. Eleven standards taken from the enemy were hung

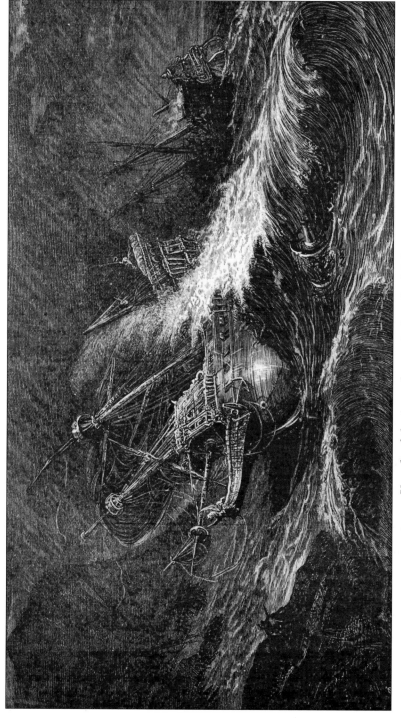

Vessels of the Armada wrecked on the Irish coast.

in St. Paul's Cathedral, whither Elizabeth went in procession from her palace at Whitehall to a public thanksgiving, on the 24th of November. She proceeded through the then quaint and gable-ended streets of Old London, in a triumphal chariot with four pillars; two supporting an imperial crown, the other two the lion of England and the dragon of Wales, with the royal arms between them.

It is from the portrait of Elizabeth taken in the dress she wore on this great occasion, that we are so familiar with the extravagant style of costume she adopted. It was engraved by Crispin de Passe, from a drawing by Isaac Oliver. She prayed audibly on her knees at the west door of St. Paul's.

Several medals were struck in England in honour of this victory. One, in honour of the queen, represented the fire-ships and fleet in hurry and confusion, with the inscription, "*Dux Fcemina Facti*." Another was struck in honour of the English navy. "It was, ''says Sir William Monson, a brave and pious old English seaman, and one of Elizabeth's most able commanders, "the will of Him that directs all men and their actions, that the fleets should meet and the enemy be beaten as they were; that they should be put from their anchorage in Calais Roads while the Prince of Parma was beleaguered at sea, and their navy driven about Scotland and Ireland with great hazard and loss, which showeth how God did marvellously defend us against their dangerous designs. By this, too, we may learn how weak and feeble are the schemes of men in respect of the Creator of man; and how impartially He dealt between the two nations, sometimes giving to the one, sometimes to the other, the advantage, yet so that He alone super-eminently ordered the battle."

THE GROYNE, 1589

T HE TOTAL defeat of the Armada had inspired the nation with an enthusiastic passion for enterprises against the Spaniards by land and sea, and nothing now seemed impossible to the English sailor or soldier. It happened in 1589, that is to say in the year subsequent to the Armada, that Don Antonio, Prior of Crato, and Knight of Malta, a natural son of one of the royal family of Portugal (the throne of which Philip I. of Spain had seized in right of his wife, Donna Maria, daughter of John III), trusting to the aversion of his countrymen to the Castilians, who tyrannised over them and treated them with contempt, had advanced a claim to the crown; and visiting first France and then England, found both Henry and Elizabeth willing to favour his pretensions, the further to humble Philip II.

A scheme was formed by the people, rather than the Government, of England, to conquer or wrest the kingdom of Portugal from Spain for Don Antonio; and the leaders of this romantic enterprise were Sir Francis Drake and Sir John Norris.

Twenty thousand men volunteered to serve on this expedition, and of these 4,000 were seamen. Resolving to act with prudence and economy, the queen gave them only six ships of war and 6,000 men. The following are the names of the ships and the commanders, as given by Sir William Monson:- *Revenge*, Sir Francis Drake; *Dreadnought*, Captain Thomas Fenner; *Aid*, Captain William Fenner; *Nonpareil*, Captain William Sackville; *Foresight*, Captain Sir William Winter; *Swiftsure*, Captain Sir William Goring.

The leaders of the land forces under Norris were - his kinsmen, Sir Edward and Sir Henry Norris, Sir Roger Williams, and Captain Williams (or Wilson), sergeant-major.

On the 18th of April, 1589, they sailed from Plymouth, having with them the Prior of Crato, whom they styled King of Portugal. The Dutch added some ships to the expedition, and these, with the queen's and others hired by the leaders, made up altogether eighty sail, according to one authority - 146 according to another - but the circumstance of Robert d'Evereaux, the Earl of Essex, K.G., joining them at sea, with certain ships which he had also hired, makes some confusion as to the exact number. With- the earl came his brother, Walter, Sir Roger Williams, Sir Philip Butler, and Sir Edward Wingfield.

A few days later saw them all off the bay of the Groyne, and menacing the Galician town of Betanzos, which is situated on the declivity of a hill washed on the east and west by the river Mandes, and four leagues south-west of La Corunna.

It is supposed that had they sailed direct to Portugal, the good-will of the people might have ensured them success; but hearing of preparations that were making at the Groyne for another invasion of England, they were induced to go thither and destroy this new armament of Spain.

This expedition was full of the elements of weakness. A number of wild spirits were collected together without discipline, and crowded in small ships, without surgeons, or carriage for sick or wounded men in case of casualties, and without sufficient provisions. Hence, we are told, in the Appendix to the "Spanish Invasion," there was much quarrelling and much drunkenness. In many of its features the enterprise somewhat resembled the British auxiliary Spanish Legion, under General Evans, in more recent times, which was partly countenanced and partly repudiated by the Whig Government, with trickery and policy.

The first landing was effected in a bay more than an English mile distant from the Groyne, by boats and pinnaces; this was accomplished without opposition, as no such invasion was expected. The force, whose strength is not stated, consisting of pikemen and musketeers, with some small pieces of artillery, advanced at once against Betanzos, within half a mile of which they encountered some Spanish troops sent forward by Don Juan de Luna, the governor. These they charged, routed, and drove within the gates. For that night they occupied the villages, mills, and other buildings around the town of Betanzos, while the Spanish fleet cannonaded them from the roadstead, filling the unfortunate Spaniards with alarm and perplexity, as many shot fell among them.

Next morning, Sir John Norris having landed some more artillery, the first shot he fired had the effect of sending the shipping out of the roadstead; and even a great galleon that lay amid them, a remnant of the last year's Armada, ceased to fire on them, though commanded by Don Juan Manez de Recaldez, Vice-Admiral of Spain. The assault of the lower town was now resolved on, and for that purpose, 200 men were landed in boats and pinnaces, the guns of which played upon it as they approached; while on the land side 500 men were to enter at low water, if the way proved passable, and 300 were to storm the walls by escalade at another point.

A few men were wounded as the boats came in shore, but in a few minutes the lower town of Betanzos was entered at three points; all who resisted were put to the sword. Thus 500 were slain in the streets. Abandoning their goods, the inhabitants fled to the upper town, to the rocks, or hid themselves in cellars and *bodegas*. A few surrendered; among others, the governor, Don Juan de Luna, and a commissary, from whom they learned that 500 of the soldiers in garrison had been in the Armada, and that there were vast stores for the new-projected expedition to England. These were all destroyed; and the soldiers, finding the cellars full of wine, indulged themselves in such excessive drinking - using even their helmets as goblets - that many of them fell sick and died.

The Spaniards seem to have acted with much pusillanimity. They now set fire to the great galleon, and such was her size that she was two days and a night in burning. Before firing her, they so overloaded her cannon that thirty-four of them burst, with a succession of mighty crashes, sending showers of burning brands over all then-other shipping, which they abandoned to the foe, who now attacked the other, or upper town, which was steeply situated, and very difficult of access. The walls were undermined, the mines sprung, and two breaches made, one of them partially in a large tower.

The stormers went bravely in with sword and pike, but the shattered tower gave way in the very midst of them, and buried about thirty under masses of masonry. The dust, the noise, and the suddenness of the catastrophe "so amazed the rest that they forsook their commanders," and, in retiring through a narrow lane, great numbers of them were shot down by the garrison.

A breach made by the cannon, "though it was well assaulted by our men," says the old folio account, "who came to push of pike at the top, and were ready to enter, yet the loose earth slipping outwards, by reason of their weight, half the wall remained entire, and so nothing was done, because our culverin and demi-culverin - we had but three pieces - were not sufficient to batter a defensible rampart."

A cloister, however, was stormed ere they fell back; and during these operations a colonel, named Huntley, with one detachment, and Captain Anthony Sampson with another, ravaged all the adjacent country, and brought into camp many cattle and sheep. On the day after the assault failed, Sir John Norris learned from a prisoner that the Conde de Andrada, at the head of 8,000 Spaniards, was advancing from Puente de Burgos to the relief of Betanzos, after forming a junction with a much larger force, under the Conde de Altamira.

On the 6th of May he marched to meet Andrada with

nine English regiments (for that military term was now fully determined and understood), leaving five with Sir Francis Drake to guard the artillery and cover the cloister. Norris moved in three columns, and a march of six miles brought him to Puente de Burgos, where he found the conde's troops under arms to receive him.

They were charged by the first column, under Captain Middleton, who was so well supported by the second, under Captain Wingfield, that they were "beaten from place to place," till they retired in confusion over a stone bridge that crossed a creek of the sea, and into their camp, which lay beyond it, and was strongly entrenched; and as they retired they left a guard at the bridge, which was heavily barricaded with barrels. But, on seeing Sir Edward Norris, at the head of his pikemen, with Colonel Sidney, and Captains Hinder, Fulford, and Barton, coming resolutely on, the barricade was abandoned, and the bridge crossed. The entrenched camp was then entered, sword in hand, Sir Edward leading the way, till he was severely wounded by a rapier. After a very short conflict, the Spaniards were routed, driven out, and put to flight.

Their royal standard, with the arms of Castile and Leon upon it, was taken, and for three miles bodies of the fugitives were pursued by the victorious English, who slew vast numbers of them among hedges and vineyards. "They put 200 to death in a cloister: and all this with the loss of only one captain and one man killed, and a few wounded."

The country was then ravaged, and for more than three miles in extent was all red flame and dusky smoke. On returning, they reshipped their artillery, with all that was found in the Groyne, set fire to the lower town and the monastery, embarked the troops on the 8th, and sailed, leaving the shore black with smoking ruins, and the bay strewed with the burned wrecks of those ships which were to have been another Armada.

This landing at the Groyne was quite a deviation from the original plan; but now, after sailing along the coast, they arrived, on the 16th, at Peniche, a fortified town of Portugal, in the province of Estra-madura. Its position is still a strong one; the fortress there had been recently erected by Philip II., and the harbour, though small, afforded the safest anchorage.

Sir John Norris now landed with the infantry, and the castle was surrendered without a shot being fired, to the Prior of Crato, as Don Antonio, King of Portugal, at whose earnest persuasion an instant march to Lisbon was resolved on. Prior to the surrender of the castle, five companies of Spaniards made a sally from the town, but were charged and routed by two of English, under the Earl of Essex. After taking from the castle 100 pikes and muskets, and twenty barrels of powder, the daring march for Lisbon began, under Sir John Norris; while Sir Francis Drake was to take up the fleet by the river Tagus, but failed to do so. The first night's halt was at Lorinha; and a twelve miles' farther march brought them next day to the now famous ground of Torres Vedras, the strong castle of which they captured. This edifice was formerly the dower-house of the Queens of Portugal.

The third day's march saw some encounters with cavalry, a few Englishmen having been mounted to serve as such, under Captain Yorke. The latter, at the head of only forty of these new troopers, charged and broke through 200 Spanish horse in half-mail; and one of his corporals, with only eight, routed nearly forty more. That night, the regiment called "General Drake's" when halted at a hill near Lores, was set upon by treachery. A body of Spanish troops advanced and as they shouted "Viva el Rey Don Antonio!" were permitted to pass the guards, whom they instantly massacred but were speedily driven off by the main body. The 25th of May brought them to St. Katherine, one of the suburbs of Lisbon, the streets of which were scoured by Captain

Wingfield, at the head of a party of musketeers, who ''met none but old folks and beggars, crying up the new king.''That night the guards were properly posted, and the main body remained under arms all night, in a field near Alcantara, surrounded by groves of orange and lemon trees. There, weary with their long march and the weight of their arms, and wasted by lack of food, the inevitable complaint of all Peninsulai soldiering, many fell asleep, and while in this state a sortie was made upon them by the Spanish garrison in Lisbon. Colonel Bret and two captains, who endeavoured to make head against them, were slain, with many mere; but ere day broke they were repulsed by the Earl of Essex, who pursued them with sword and pike to the gates of the city, and even into the houses, where many of them were followed and killed by the English; and for every one of the latter who fell there perished more than three Spaniards.

During the march of Norris, Drake had been sailing by the Tagus, and had captured the town of Cascaes, on a promontory at the mouth of the river. The people fled thence into the high

Lisbon, from the sea.

43

rocky mountains of Cintra; but by a messenger he prevailed upon them to return and accept the Prior of Crato as their king.

General Norris now held a Council of War, as the position of his little force was very critical; and the question was whether he should await those Portuguese whom Don Antonio had asserted would flock to his standard, or begin a retreat at once. The opinions of his officers were so various that Norris had to act for himself; and after staying two nights in Lisbon, on finding that, of all his promised cavalry, Antonio could not muster a troop of horse, and, of all his infantry, barely two companies, though he had assured him "that upon his first landing there should be a revolt of all his subjects,"the English leader proposed to retire.

In the castle of Lisbon, then a strong edifice on the highest of the seven hills on which Lisbon stands, there was a garrison too numerous for him to attack with success, especially as he had very light artillery, so the" retreat began in the night. "Had we marched through his country as enemies," says the old narrator before quoted, "our army had been well supplied with all sorts of provisions; or had we plundered the suburbs of Lisbon, we had made ourselves the richest army that ever came out of England: for, besides the wealth of private dwellings, there were many great warehouses by the waterside full of all sorts of rich merchandise, but we were restrained from both of these." Don Antonio insisted on his subjects, as he called them, being spared, so the English gained little by their landing, and lost much. As they marched along the banks of the Tagus, in sight of the bare, sharp granite summits of Cintra, they were followed by the *adelantado* with the Spanish galleys, whose gunners fired on every opportunity, while their rear was galled by Spanish cavalry, who cut off those sick and wounded who fell in hundreds by the wayside, and for whom there were no means of conveyance.

At last they reached the castle of Cascaes, where a friar

informed them that a Spanish force was at hand, and had come as far as San Julian, a strong fort seven miles from Lisbon. This news was welcomed by the leaders, who were highly exasperated by the turn their affairs had taken, and promised the friar 100 crowns if his news proved true. The further to provoke an issue, the Earl of Essex sent a cartel to the Spanish general, offering to fight him singly, with ten men a side, or any equal number he chose.; and thereupon he marched next day to where the Spaniards had encamped, but found that they had made a precipitate retreat to Lisbon, and had, moreover, threatened to hang the English trumpeter who had brought the gallant earl's message.

After six cannon-shots had been discharged at Cascaes, the governor capitulated, and was permitted to march off with baggage and arms, but his cannon were taken. In fact, since the terrible issue of the Armada, the spirit of the Spaniards seemed to have fled; but Admiral Drake now rather lawlessly seized sixty large ships that belonged to the free Hans Cities, and were laden with goods for Lisbon, on the allegation that their cargoes were to have equipped the new Armada against England. On board of these he put troops, and the horses Norris had seized; and now the whole expedition put to sea, repulsing an attack made upon it by twenty great galleys of the enemy.

Still loth to leave Spain, they landed at Vigo, in Galicia, and burned the city, and ravaged all the adjacent country for eight miles inland. In the capture of Vigo, the timidity of the Spaniards was painfully apparent. Though every street in the city was strongly and peculiarly barricaded, on the appearance of 2,000 English, under Drake and Captain Wingfield, the whole garrison, save one man, fled to Bayonne ! After this Admiral Drake put to sea with twenty of the best ships, in hopes to overhaul the Spanish Indian fleet, while Sir John Norris and the Earl of Essex returned to England with the rest of this expedition, which proved a great source of mortification to the Spaniards, and raised still higher the warlike glory of the English; but it cost the lives of half of those who sailed, by sickness, famine, fatigue, and the sword. Of 1,100 gentlemen who embarked to serve as volunteers, only 350 survived when the fleet returned in the beginning of July; but Camden says they brought home 150 pieces of cannon and a great booty.

After enumerating the many causes which led to the failure of the expedition, Sir William Morison adds, in his "Reflections "upon it, that the want of field-pieces "was the loss of Lisbon; for its strength consisting in the castle, and we having only an army to countenance us, but no means for battery, we were the loss of the victory to ourselves; for it is apparent, by intelligence we received, that if we had presented them with battery they were resolved to parley, and so, by consequence, to yield, and this was the main and chief reason of the Portuguese not joining with us. There is one reason to be alleged on the Portuguese behalf, and their love and favour to our proceedings; for though they showed not themselves forward upon the occasion aforesaid in aiding us, yet they opposed not themselves as enemies against us. For had they pursued.us in our retreat from Lisbon to Cascaes, our men, being weak, sickly, without powder, shot, and other arms, they had put us to a greater loss and disgrace than we had on't. And if ever England have occasion to set up a competitor in Portugal, our good treatment of the people of that country has gained us great reputation amongst them; for the general most wisely forbade the rifling of houses in the country and suburbs of Lisbon, and commanded royal payment for everything they took, without compulsion or rigorous usage. This made those that were indifferently affected before now ready upon the like occasion to assist us."

In 1590, Elizabeth allowed the sum £8,970 yearly for the repair of the Royal Navy.

SEA-FIGHTS OFF FLORES AND CAPE CORRIENTES, 1591

W E HAVE now to record one of the most brave and desperate naval engagements that had as yet occurred in the sea-service of England.

In 1591, Elizabeth employed her naval power against Philip II by endeavouring to intercept his West Indian treasures, as the chief source of that greatness which made him so formidable to his neighbours. With this view she fitted out a squadron to intercept the home-returning Plate fleet.

The command of this squadron was given to the Vice-Admiral of England, Lord Thomas Howard, K.G., who was restored in blood (though his father had been attainted and beheaded in 1572), and summoned to Parliament as Lord Howard de Walden.

His second in command was Sir Richard Grenville, who in 1585 had sailed from Plymouth with seven ships to Roanoke, where he left 108 men to form an English settlement. On this expedition there sailed the *Defiance*, Lord Howard; the *Revenge*, Sir R. Grenville; the *Nonpareil*, Sir Edward Donnie; the *Bonaventure*, Captain Cross; the *Lion*, Captain Fenner; the *Crane*, Captain Duffield; and the *Foresight*, Captain Thomas Vavasour, of Haslewood, in Yorkshire. The latter was a gentleman who had particularly distinguished himself in raising forces and equipping vessels to defend England and its queen against the Armada. To requite his zeal, and to show her regard for one of her maids of honour, who was a Vavasour, and her acknowledged kinswoman, Queen Elizabeth, who through her grandfather, Sir Thomas Bulleyn, was descended from Maude Vavasour, would never permit the chapel at Haslewood to be molested, and to this day, adds Sir Bernard Burke, it has continued a place for Catholic worship.

Howard sailed to the Azores, as being the most likely quarter to find the Plate fleet, as many vessels which lose their longitude, or require refreshments, bear up for Flores, a small island of the group, so named by the Portuguese from the multitude of flowers which covered it. The isle is thirty miles long by nine broad, and had two small towns, named Santa Cruz and Lagena.

In that solitary place Howard's squadron lingered for six months, the King of Spain having given orders that the fleet was to be as late as possible in sailing from the West Indies, thinking by this delay to weary the English, of whose departure he had heard, and compel them to return home. In the meantime, Don Alphonso Bassano, who was sent from Spain with fifty-three ships to convoy the fleet home, came so suddenly upon the little English squadron that the admiral had much difficulty in getting to sea, with more than half his men sick and unserviceable.

The first intelligence Lord Howard had of the Spaniards was by the *Moonshine*, which the Earl of Cumberland had dispatched from the Spanish coast, near which he was cruising, to report "that a great armada was getting ready at the Groyne to be sent against Her Majesty's ships waiting to surprise the "West Indian fleet." Hakluyt says that Captain Middleton, commander of the *Moonshine*, which was a swift sailer, kept company with this fleet from the Groyne, long enough to discover the strength of it; and then, outsailing it, brought the startling intelligence. It was in the afternoon of the 31st of August, 1591, that he boarded the admiral's ship off Flores and delivered his message; but he had scarcely done so, when the whole Spanish fleet appeared on the horizon !

And now ensued a most unequal battle, in which the first ship of war ever taken by the Spaniards was lost. The squadron gained the offing, all save the vice-admiral's ship, the *Revenge*, which was hemmed in between the isle of Flores and the fleet. There are two reasons assigned for this circumstance: one is, that Sir Richard Grenville lingered too long for his men, who were straggling on shore; another, that he was courageously obstinate, and would not make his escape by flight, or, as Camden has it, would not let the pilot steer the *Revenge* so that she should seem to turn her stern upon the enemy.

Though he had ninety sick men on board, he cleared away for battle, and strove to break through the Spaniards, on board of whose, fifty-three ships there were no less than 10,000 soldiers. In the annals of war, perhaps there is not a more unequal conflict. At three in the afternoon a close battle began. Many times - fifteen it is stated - the Spaniards boarded him, but they were always repulsed, and killed, or flung into the sea. At one and the same time he was laid aboard by the *St. Philip*, a seventy-eight-gun ship, of 1,500 tons, and four more of the largest in the Spanish fleet, crowded with soldiers, who by a cross fire of muskets and arquebuses, below and aloft, swept his deck. In some were 200, in others 500, and in some 800 troops, besides armed mariners. He had never less than two large galleons alongside, and these were relieved from time to time by fresh ships. The sun set, and darkness came on, but under the clear starry sky of the Azores, the unequal fight was maintained, with all the fury that religious rancour and national hate could inspire, with much of contemptuous triumph in the hearts of the English, and to the two former emotions was added a longing for vengeance in those of the Spaniards. In the beginning of the fight, the *George Noble*, of London, having received some large shot through her, fell under the lee of the *Revenge*, and her captain asked Sir Richard if he could in any way serve him, but as she was only a small victualling ship, Grenville bid him shift for himself and leave the *Revenge* to her fate.

Between three in the afternoon and daylight next morning did the single English ship maintain a close fight with fifteen of the largest vessels in Bassano's fleet, and, by the well-directed fire of her guns, sank four of them. Among these were their greatest galleon and the admiral of the hulks. Early in the action Sir Richard Grenville had received a wound, but he never left the upper deck till eleven at night, when he was again wounded in the body by a musket-ball, and then went below to have it dressed. He received another shot in the head while under the hands of the surgeon, who was killed by his side. He returned on deck, faint and weak, but high in spirit as ever, and still the fight went on. By daybreak his crew began to want powder, and soon the last barrel was expended. By repulsing such a succession of boarding parties, their pikes and swords were broken and otherwise destroyed; forty of the crew were killed out of one hundred and three, their original number, and all the rest were more or less wounded; the masts had been shot away, the whole rigging cut to pieces, and the ship had become an unmanageable hulk.

On finding her in this crippled condition when day dawned, Sir Richard proposed to the ship's company "to trust to the mercy of God, not to that of the Spaniards, and to destroy the ship with themselves - to die, rather than to yield to the enemy!"

To this desperate resolution the master-gunner and a few seamen consented, but the rest opposed it; so Grenville was compelled to surrender himself as a prisoner of war, and, after a fifteen hours'engagement, was carried on board the ship of Don Alphonso Bassano. By this time the *Revenge* had six feet of water in her hold, three shot-holes under water, and all her bulwarks beaten away. "She had been engaged not only with the fifteen ships that boarded her, but in reality with the whole Spanish fleet of fifty-three ships; she had received, upon a computation, 800 cannon-shot, and the fire of nearly 10,000 soldiers and seamen."

In this sharp and unequal action, the Spaniards lost four ships, more than 1,000 men, and several officers of distinction. Lord Howard would seem to have but indifferently seconded the desperate valour of Grenville. We are told that though his force was so small, he would have continued the engagement with the enemy, notwithstanding their vast superiority, had he not been dissuaded by his officers from an undertaking so rash. However, they fought bravely as long as they had the weather-gage, and did all that could be expected of them, till darkness came on, when the squadron bore off and left Grenville to his fate. Notwithstanding what has been said in excuse of these officers, says an old naval historian, it is more than probable that if they had behaved with the same vigour and resolution as Grenville and his ship's company did, "they might have given a good account of the Spanish fleet. At least the history of this reign furnishes us with more than one such example. It will be said they had on their side Necessity and Desperation, two violent spurs to urge them on; but every commander in the fleet might have made that his own case."

The very next day after this unfortunate action the Plate fleet, of fourteen sail, for which the English had waited so long, hove in sight of Don Alphonso's. Thus, had Howard stayed but one day longer, or had the fleet from the Groyne been one day or two later, the Indian squadron might have fallen into the hands of the English, with many millions of treasure, which the sea afterwards swallowed.

On the second day after the action, Grenville, whose valour was highly praised by the Spaniards, died of his wounds on board the ship of Bassano. His last words were: -

"Here die I, Richard Grenville, with a joyful and quiet mind; for that I have ended my life as a true Englishman ought to, fighting for his country, queen, religion, and honour; my soul willingly departing from this body, leaving behind the lasting fame of having behaved as every valiant soldier (sic) is, in his duty, bound to do."

Five days afterwards, the *Revenge*, having been refitted, perished off the isle of St. Michael, "making good her name," as she had 200 Spaniards on board; and the fourteen ships of the Plate fleet went down with her. On his homeward voyage, Lord Howard made some amends for his loss at the Azores by the capture of several rich Spanish ships. Among others, he took one bound for the West Indies, in which, besides much booty, were found 22,000 Indulgences for the Spaniards in America - documents on which the English sailors set but small value. We read that about the same time Thomas White, a Londoner, in another Spanish capture, found no less than 2,000,000 of similar papers. These had cost the King of Spain 300,000 florins; but he could have sold them for 5,000,000 in the Indies. Before Bassano attacked Lord Howard's squadron at Flores, the latter had taken at least twenty ships coming from St. Domingo, India, and Brazil. Among these were two literally laden with gold and silver, and all were sent to England. Lord Howard, says Sir William Monson, kept the sea so long as his provisions lasted, and by his prizes nearly defrayed the whole expense of the expedition.

Sir Richard Grenville was probably one of the Grenvilles of Wootton-under-Barnwood, in Buckinghamshire, where an honourable family of that name had existed from the time of Henry I.

Lord Thomas Howard for his services was afterwards created Earl of Suffolk, and installed a Knight of the Garter. The original plate of his installation still remains in the ninth stall at St. George's Chapel, Windsor. He was subsequently engaged with Lord Monteagle in the discovery of the Gunpowder Treason; became Lord High Treasurer of England; and died at a green old age, in 1626.

The next most memorable or interesting sea-fight of this year is one that occurred on the 13th of June, 1591, off Cape Corrientes, a bold and cliffy promontory on the coast of Cuba, between the Spaniards and four English ships, one of which was a small barque belonging to Sir George Carey. The latter, who was Marshal of Her Majesty's Household, Captain of the Isle of Wight, and was afterwards Lord Hunsdon, Lord Chamberlain, and Captain of the Honourable Band of Gentlemen Pensioners, would seem to have been cruising among the West Indian Isles, but whether on the queen's service or for his own personal profit is not very clear from Hakluyt.

It would appear that when off Corrientes, about five in the morning of the 13th of June, he discovered six Spanish ships, four of which were armados, then a general name for armed craft, viz., the admiral and vice-admiral, of 700 tons each, other two of 600, and two of 100 tons each. Believing them to be the Carthagena squadron, Sir George "bore up to them with joy,"and with his own ship, the *Swallow*, and the *Hopewell*, came to leeward of the Spanish admiral, while the barque, which was named the *Content*, bore down upon the vice-admiral, "and ranging along by her broadside, a-weather of her, gave her a

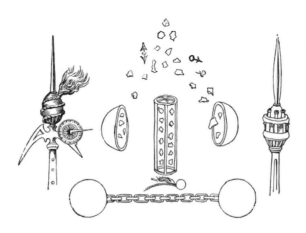

Chain-shot and firework weapons (end of the sixteenth century).

volley of their great guns and small-arms, and then coming up with another smaller ship, ahead of the former, hailed her in such a manner that she sheered off."

While engaging the latter ship, the crew of the *Content* saw with alarm clouds of smoke rising from the ship of Sir George Carey, and the *Swallow* (330 tons and 160 men) and *Hopewell* steering wide of him, with all the sail they could make. The *Content* bore towards him, to yield assistance if required; but in this movement fell to leeward of the two small vessels, who designed now to close in and board her; and then a three hours'engagement ensued between them. The *Content* had no great guns, but only one minion, or 4-pounder; one falcon, or 2-pounder; one saker, or 5-pounder; and two porte-bases. Her commander was Captain Nicholas Lisle; her crew consisted of only a lieutenant, master, master's mate, and twenty men.

This little barque, so slenderly manned and lightly armed, maintained a three hours'fight with the other two ships, who alternately drove her northward, no assistance being rendered her by either the *Hopewell* or *Swallow*. Meanwhile, Sir George Carey, after fighting for a time with the Spanish vice-admiral and another great ship, hoisted his top-gallant sails and all the other canvas he could spread, and stood off to sea. The *Hopewell* and *Swallow* had also failed to succour him, and were now standing off eastward, close-hauled.

The little craft, the *Content*, abandoned thus, had now the whole Spanish squadron to encounter. Three, however, only attacked, the two great ships and a smaller one, "they having a loom gale." The English now shipped their sweeps to row inshore, in hope of being able to anchor in shallow water, where the Spaniards dared not follow, and where they might be beyond range of their cannon.

On seeing this, the Spanish admiral double-manned one of his smaller vessels, and sent a boat ahead to tow her, in hope by their small-arms to shoot some of the English when at the oars or sweeps; but by the time the *Content* was within range of musket or arquebuse, a gale of wind had sprung up off shore, and the Spaniards being to leeward, the *Content* trimmed her canvas and stood due east. The small Spanish vessel had now crept within falcon-shot, while one of the great ships lay to the westward, so that Captain Nicholson, in his pigmy man-of-war, had no hope of escape in that direction.

Thinking he might avoid them by standing westward, he altered his course, but now the other great ship got under his lee, and the smaller one on his weather quarter, "purposing to make them pay room with the great ship, by force of her small and great shot."

By some skilful tacking and manoeuvring, they continued to make the 700-ton ship "spring her loof," or bring her head closer to the wind; and a fortunate shot from their saker pierced her between wind and water, so that her crew were compelled to careen her over, and summon assistance from the other ships.

The captain of the *Content* being now free in one quarter by the aid of the wind and the skill of his little crew, saw two sail more in the offing, which were hailed with cheers, as they were supposed to be the *Hopewell* and *Swallow*, long since out of sight, returning to their assistance. But they were painfully undeceived when they proved to be two more of the enemy's galleys; and, abandoned and surrounded thus, something like the sullen courage of despair rather than that which is gathered from hope, filled the hearts of those twenty-three unfortunate Englishmen, fighting for their lives, rather than liberty, as quarter was seldom asked or given by the Spaniards in these waters.

One of the strange galleys bore down on their lee when the evening sun was setting beyond Cape Corrientes, and fired six cannon-shot at them; closing in upon their starboard quarter, she next gave them the fire of five brass guns from her bow, but without doing damage, and then endeavoured to board; but the English fired so briskly with their small-arms that the Spaniards abandoned the attempt. They next tried it by the stern, but Nicholson threw a fire-ball among them, so the galley sheered off.

While still endeavouring to beat to seaward and escape, they saw the two galleys and a frigate bearing down upon them. Believing themselves lost now, they swore to fight it out to the last man, and, by shouts and derisive cheers, dared the Spaniards to board them.

One shot more was fired, but no closer attempt was made; and thus the swift little vessel continued a running fight with the ships and galleys from seven in the morning till eleven at night. In all that time only two men were wounded in the *Content*, and not a man killed. About two next morning they had a gale from the east-north-east, which proved the means of their escape. When day broke the Spanish squadron was far to leeward; and though they continued the chase till ten o'clock, the gallant little vessel escaped by her swift sailing beyond all pursuit.

In this flying skirmish she was engaged "for fifteen or sixteen hours with three Spanish armados, of 600 tons or 700 tons each, not being above musket-shot from any of them; and before the sun set there had come up two of the king's galleys to the fight. The armados fired continually at her with their great guns, not less than 500 times; and her sides, hull, and masts were literally sowed with musket-balls. Her sheets, tops, and shrouds were almost cut asunder with their great and small shot. Through her mainsail she had nineteen great shot; through her maintopsail four, through her foretopsail five, and through her mainmast one."

If all this be true, we cannot wonder at the sailors of Elizabeth, and those of later times, having a hearty contempt for the gunnery and seamanship of the Spaniards.

CHAPTER V

LAST EXPEDITION AND DEATH OF ADMIRALS DRAKE AND HAWKINS, 1595

I N ENGLAND the rumour was universally gaining ground that Philip of Spain had designs of invading that country with a fleet more formidable even than the Great Armada of 1588. Hence the queen ordered two squadrons to be fitted out - one to cruise in the English seas, and another for service in America or the West Indies; while the King of Scotland, now in alliance with her, levied, in conjunction with England, troops against the Spaniards.

The foreign squadron consisted of twenty-six ships; but Sir William Monson only gives the names of the following: - *Defiance*, 500 tons, Sir Francis Drake, Commander; *Garland*, 700 tons, Sir John Hawkins; *Hope*, 600 tons, Captain Gilbert York; *Bonaventurc*, 600 tons, Captain Troughton; *Foresight*, 300 tons, Captain Winter; *Adventure*, 250 tons, Captain Thomas Drake.

The land forces were commanded by Sir Thomas Baskerville. Sir Nicholas Clifford was lieutenant-general; Captain Arnold Baskerville was sergeant-major; and there were Captain Nicholas Baskerville and eight other captains over the troops.

This West Indian expedition was specially urged upon the queen by the two admirals, Drake and Hawkins, who promised "to engage very deeply in the adventure, both with their substance and persons; and such was the opinion every one had conceived of these two valiant commanders, that great were the expectations of the success of this voyage."

Notwithstanding all the preparations for defence of the coast, and for the annoyance of the foe elsewhere, in the month of

July, 1595, a body of Spaniards suddenly landed in Cornwall, under the command of Don Diego Brojen, and burned Penzance, the church of St. Paul, which stood in the fields, and the fisher villages of Newlyn and Mousehole, and all without resistance. According to Carew, the inhabitants were infatuated by an old prediction in the Cornish language, to the effect that a period would arrive when

"Strangers would land
    On the rocks of Merlin,
To burn Paul's Church,
    Penzance, and Newlyn;"

but when the prophecy had been fulfilled, they found courage to assemble on the beach, and thus intimidate the Spaniards, who re-embarked, spread their sails to the breeze, and left the coast.

In the subsequent month the fleet of twenty-six sail, under Drake and Hawkins, left Plymouth Sound, but whether direct for San Juan de Porto Rico, where the queen was informed that vast treasures were collected for the King of Spain, or for Nombre

Spanish attack on Penzance.

de Dios, and thence to march to Panama, is uncertain now, for. after putting to sea the admirals would seem to have altered their plans. On the 31st of August they last saw the Lizard, and on the 27th of September were off Canaria Grande, the chief isle of the Canaries. They made a fruitless attempt to possess themselves of it. Hawkins was averse to landing at all, deeming it a loss of time to do so, and risking the chance of greater success elsewhere; but Drake and Baskerville, especially the latter, undertook to reduce the whole island in four days with the pikemen and musketeers. To their importunities, added to those of the seamen, who were already short of provisions, he was obliged to submit; but the attempt proved a failure. Afterwards they sailed for Dominica, one of the Antilles group; the right of occupancy there being claimed by England, France, and Spain, so that it remained a neutral island till 1759, when it was finally taken by Great Britain. The expedition arrived there on the 29th of October, and as the admirals stayed too long, building pinnaces and trafficking with the natives for tobacco, tidings of their coming spread from isle to isle, and the Spaniards everywhere prepared for defence.

On the very day of their arrival at Dominica, five Spanish ships which had been sent out to watch their motions, and convey the Plate fleet home from Porto Rico, captured a little English vessel, called the *Francis*, which had strayed from the fleet. By cruel and barbarous tortures, the Spanish officers wrung from her master and mariners a confession that the English had designs on Porto Rico; for which place they at once bore up, to give intelligence of an expected attack. The result was that the treasures of gold and silver were immediately buried, and small vessels were dispatched to all the isles and sea-coasts to give the Spanish colonists timely notice; so that when the admirals arrived off San Tuan de Porto Rico, on the 12th of November, it was so secured that they had little hope of success.

As soon as they came to anchor in the harbour - the same harbour where, in the subsequent year, the Earl of Cumberland was so nearly drowned by the weight of his armour - the enemy's batteries opened on them. On the Moro Fort alone were forty pieces of cannon. The fire was sharp and heavy; and that evening Sir Nicholas Clifford and Captains Browne and Strafford were all mortally wounded as they sat at supper with Admiral Drake, whose stool was knocked from under him by the same shot, just as he was in the act of drinking a can of beer.

The resistance of the Spaniards was desperate and protracted; and during the contest Sir John Hawkins died, it was alleged, of mortification and grief, consequent on some quarrels between him and the other commanders, according to one writer. Another states that he was extremely ill, and upon receiving intelligence that the *Francis* had been taken by the enemy, knew that the object of the expedition would be made known and frustrated, and that the bitterness of this conviction preyed upon his spirits.

The Spaniards had sunk a great ship at the mouth of the harbour, to bar the entrance; they had, moreover, formed two booms of large masts lashed firmly together thence to the forts, the guns of which protected the approach by a cross fire. Within the haven were five Spanish ships, anchored broadside-on, all ballasted with sand, mounted with great guns, and well manned by cannoniers and musketeers.

Undeterred by all these preparations, on the evening of the 13th, Sir Thomas Baskerville, with twenty-five boats and pinnaces full of pikemen and musketeers, clad in half-mail, or brigandines, pulled boldly into the roadstead, between the forts or castles, whence the Spaniards fired 185 cannon-shot upon them; and the circumstance of the shots being so minutely reckoned illustrates how slow the process of gunnery was still in war. His men were under a heavy fire of small-arms, too; nevertheless, he boarded sword in hand the five ships in succession (one was of

400 tons, the rest of 200), and set them all in flames. Moreover, "he did great damage to the admiral and vice-admiral. The ships had each twenty brass guns and 100 barrels of gunpowder on board. Their loading, which consisted chiefly of silk, oil, and wine, had been already secured, as likewise the treasure, which one of the prisoners confessed to be three millions of ducats, or five-and-thirty tons of silver."

The fight on both sides was obstinate and bloody; but after various assaults, which were repulsed, with great loss on the part of the English, but still greater on that of the Spaniards, of whom many were killed, burned, drowned, or taken prisoners, Baskerville and his squadron of boats drew off to the fleet. Sir Francis Drake now concluded that further attempts in that quarter would be futile, and sailed for the coast of Terra Firma.

On the 1st of December his fleet was off the town of La Hacha, in New Granada, a small place at the mouth of a river of the same name, which he burned and destroyed, though the inhabitants offered to purchase its ransom for 34,000 ducats.

He afterwards set fire to La Rancheria, where he took many negro slaves and other prisoners, with a vast quantity of pillage, including a great store of pearls." Advancing towards the Sierra de Santa Marta, he burned all the villages in the province, and also the town of that name. The next place he took was La Nombre de Dios, a place so named by Don Diego Niquero. Last says that at this time it had high wooden houses, "broad streets, and a fair church; that it lay from east to west, in the middle of a great wood." After a short resistance from the forts that defended the harbour, he laid the town in ashes, and destroyed all the shipping, which Hakluyt states consisted of frigates, barks, and galiots. He found no money in the town, but in a watch-tower near it, on the summit of a hill, he discovered "twenty sows of silver, two bars of gold, some pearls, money coined, and other pillage."

From this place a "body of 750 pikemen and musketeers, under Sir Thomas Baskerville, began their march towards Panama. He proceeded in that direction for several days, and on some of their marches they were sorely galled by sudden volleys of musketry from concealed parties in narrow defiles and dense forests; and finding, besides, their progress through a pass completely obstructed by the erection of a new fort, which they were too weak in number to storm, they began a retreat to their fleet, on board of which they arrived on the 2nd of January, 1596, many of them wounded, and all half-starved, and harassed with fatigue, and by the weight of their arms and iron accoutrements, after having marched half way to the Southern Sea.

Sir Francis Drake now proposed to make his way to Escudo de Veraguas, a small low island near the coast of New Granada, and thence to Porto-Bello. But before he could achieve this, he was seized with a bloody flux, a distemper which was greatly aggravated by a sense of bad success in the whole details of his voyage; so this great admiral, the Nelson of the Elizabethan age, died on the 28th of January, to the great sorrow of the seamen and soldiers.

"Sir Francis Drake," says Sir William Monson, "was wont to rule Fortune; but now finding his error, and the difference between the present strength of the Indies and what it was when he first knew them, grew melancholy upon this disappointment, and suddenly, and I hope naturally, died at Puerto-Bello," a mistake for Nombre de Dios. By the latter phrase, he would seem to insinuate a suspicion of suicide. He had no other funeral, than that which falls to the lot of those who die at sea., save that his remains were cased in a heavy coffin of lead, and then cast overboard, "with volleys of shot and firing of cannon in all the ships of the fleet; so he happened to find his grave near the place whence he had borrowed so large a reputation by his

Drake's funeral.

fortunate successes." He left a widow, Elizabeth, only daughter and heiress of George Sydenham, of Combe Sydenham, Devonshire. He bequeathed all his lands to his nephew, Captain Thomas Drake, except a single manor, which he left to his old shipmate, Captain Jonas Bodenham.

Both admirals now being dead, the command of the fleet devolved upon Sir Thomas Baskerville, who, in unison with the other officers, deemed a return to England their most prudent course. Proceeding on their homeward voyage, near Isla de Pinos (or Isle of Pines), off the southern coast of Cuba, from which it is separated by a channel sixteen leagues long and six leagues wide, they suddenly encountered the Spanish fleet of twenty sail, which had been sent out from Carthagena to intercept them, and had been hovering there for some time for that purpose.

Sir Thomas Baskerville, in the *Defiance*, and Captain Troughton, in the *Garland*, led the van in the engagement that ensued. It lasted two hours, and in the end the Spaniards, finding that one of their largest ships had been set on fire and burned to the water's edge, that several of the rest were severely wounded in their hulls and tattered in their sails arid rigging, sheered off, and the English fleet continued its voyage home. It arrived in England in the month of May, after having been out eight months, with but very little booty; and the destruction of a few towns and ships was deemed but a poor recompense for the loss of two of the greatest naval commanders in Europe. Moreover, this year proved fatal to the service in that respect, as it saw the deaths of other excellent seamen and commanders, such as Sir Roger Williams and Sir Thomas Morgan.

"Sir Francis Drake had an insatiable thirst after honour," wrote a gentleman of those days who served under him and Hawkins, and whose letter is quoted by Lediard. "He was full of promises, and more temperate in adversity than in prosperity.

He had likewise some other imperfections, such as quickness to anger, bitterness in disgracing, and was too much pleased with flattery. Sir John Hawkins had malice with dissimulation, rudeness in behaviour, and was covetous to the last degree. But they were both alike happy in being great commanders, yet not equally successful. They both grew great and famous by the same means; that is, by their own courage and the fortune of the sea. There was comparison, however, between their merits, taken in general, for therein Sir Francis far exceeded."

- C H A P T E R   V I -

THE CAPTURE OF CADIZ, 1596

THE BAD success of the last expedition of Drake and Hawkins led the English people to think of endeavouring to cripple the power of Spain nearer home than the Indies, especially as rumours of hostile preparation in all the Spanish harbours sounded once more the alarm of an invasion; and such an enterprise, on a grander scale even than the Armada, now filled the mind of Philip, who never forgave, even in her shrivelled old age, Elizabeth's refusal to marry him.

Firm, resolute, watchful, and self-controlled, the queen, whose policy had ever been to defend her own shores rather than to invade her neighbours', yielded to the suggestions of Lord Howard of Effingham, High Admiral of England, who urged upon her the prudence as well as the glory of attacking the enemy in his own ports, and at length succeeded, in spite of the opposition of Burleigh, in wringing from Elizabeth a reluctant consent. The King of Scotland was roused by the rumours of the new Armada, and, by a proclamation issued from Holyrood on the 2nd of January, commanded the forces of his kingdom "to hold themselves in readiness to march "(Rymer).

An expedition was accordingly prepared at Plymouth to avert the coming storm, and, strangely enough, English authors vary very much as to the number of ships employed. Burchett says the fleet consisted of 146 sail; Camden numbers it at 150, including twenty Dutch vessels, under Admiral John Van Duvenwoord, of Warmond; while in others the numbers vary still more.

The troops consisted of 7,360 pikemen and musketeers, of whom fully a thousand were volunteers, who paid their own expenses, and 6,762 seamen and cannoniers, besides the Dutch. Burchett states that the whole of these forces were under the command of Robert, Earl of Essex, the rash and daring favourite of Elizabeth's old age, whom she beheaded five years afterwards, in his thirty-fourth year. He and Howard from their own purses spent vast sums on the equipment of the troops and ships; and they were assisted by a Council of War, consisting of Lord Thomas Howard, Sir Walter Raleigh, Sir Francis Vere (the hero of the Low Country wars), Sir George Carew and Sir Conyers Clifford. The admiral was to command at sea, and Essex on the coast of Spain.

The fleet was divided into four squadrons. The admiral led the first, Essex the second, Lord Howard the third, and Raleigh the fourth. The officers of the army, under Essex, were Sir Francis Vere, with the proud tide of Lord Marshal; Sir John Wingfield, Campmaster-General; Sir Conyers Clifford, Sergeant-Major (i.e., Adjutant-General); Sir George Carew, Master of the Ordnance. The colonels of foot were Robert, Earl of Sussex, Sir Christopher Blount, Sir Thomas Gerrard, and Sir Richard Wingfield. The captain of the volunteers was Sir Edward Wingfield; and Andrew Ashley was Secretary at War, to keep a register of the councils: and in these details we see the gradual development of that internal order and discipline which reached such perfection in more modern times.

The queen's ships numbered only fourteen, and were as follow: - The *Ark Royal*, 800 tons, Captain Sir Amyas Preston, with the High Admiral on board; *Repulse*, 700 tons, Captain Sir William Monson, with the Earl of Essex on board; *Mary Honora*, 800 tons, Captain the Lord Thomas Howard; *Warspite*, 600 tons, Captain Sir Walter Raleigh; *Lion*, 500 tons, Captain Sir Robert Southwell; *Rainbow*, 500 tons, Captain Sir Francis Vere; *Nonpareil*, 500 tons, Captain Sir Robert Dudley; *Vanguard*, Captain Sir J. Wingfield; *Mary Rose*, 600 tons, Captain Sir George Carew; *Dreadnought*, 400 tons, Captain Sir Alexander Clifford; *Swiftsure*, 400 tons, Captain Sir Robert Cross;

Aquittance, 200 tons, Captain Sir Robert Mansfield; *Crane*, 200 tons, Captain King; *Tramontana*, captain's name not given.

The "Instructions to the Captains of Ships," &c, for this expedition are not without interest, as illustrative of the good order that was to be enforced.

First, God was to be served by the use of the common prayers twice daily; swearing, brawling, and diceing were forbidden; likewise "picking and stealing;" provisions were to be carefully issued, 'and weekly returns sent in. The ships were to be washed and cleaned daily; the fleet to close in at nightfall; the red cross half-hoisted was the signal of a council on board the two leading ships; care was to be taken that no jealousy occurred between the mariners and soldiers; the night-watch to be set by sound of drum or trumpet, at eight p.m.; guns to be fired and drums beaten in cases of fog; no man to strike 'his superior officer, under penalty of death; and no evil rumours to be raised adverse to the reputation "of any officer or gentleman."

On the 1st of June, 1596, this well-ordered array sailed from Plymouth, and ere long a breeze from the north-east brought them off the north cape of Spain. Every captain had sailed with sealed orders, which were not to be opened until they were past the scene of later days of glory - Cape St. Vincent - and this is the first record in history of English ships receiving such orders. On being opened, the general rendezvous was found to be - Cadiz !

The *Litness*, the *Truelove*, and the *Lion's Whelp*, three of the swiftest little vessels in the fleet, were now sent ahead as scouts, under Sir Richard Levison and Sir Christopher Blount, who kept pretty far from the coast; but succeeded on the 10th of June in capturing three Hamburg fly-boats, which fourteen days before had left Cadiz, where their skippers reported that all was quiet, and no attack suspected.

On the 18th they hailed an Irish ship returning from Cadiz,

whose master reported "that the Spaniards lived there in the most tranquil security. He informed them that the port was full of men-of-war, galleys, galleons, and merchantmen, richly loaded for the Indies; and that there were no forces on the island (DeLeon) except the garrison."

Flushed with the hopes of conquest and spoil," the fleet bore on, and about daybreak on the morning; of the 20th of Tune it was off Cadiz, where an alarm was speedily given. It had been previously arranged by the Council of War that a landing should be effected at San Sebastian, to the westward of the city; and there the whole fleet came to anchor in four squadrons, attended by their victuallers and other ships. Armour was buckled and matches were blown, and every soldier was prepared to land; but the wind almost blew a gale, the sea was running high, and four great galleys were lying off the shore to fire upon their boats; so no landing was made, and the day was passed in sending messages from ship to ship, chiefly borne by Sir Walter Raleigh, concerning the course to be next decided upon; and, in the end, the leaders came to the resolution of attacking the shipping, and making themselves masters of the harbour before a landing was attempted.

The city, it must be borne in mind, is situated on the extremity of a long tongue of land, projecting in a north-westerly direction from the Isle of Leon. At its end the tongue expands a little, and the whole of this expansion is occupied by the city. This isthmus is so narrow that the waves of the Atlantic on one side, and those of the bay on the other, reach the walls of the causeway which connects Cadiz with the mainland of Andalusia. Its castle, built by the Moors, was strongly fortified, and four other great bastions defended the bay, which is several miles in extent. It was considered the key of Spain, and was one of the three towns which the Emperor Charles V advised his son Philip to have ever a watchful eye upon.

A dash into the harbour being determined on, a contention arose, curiously, as to who was to lead the way. Asserting his commission, the Earl of Essex claimed the honour; to this the admiral objected, being aware that if the rash young earl failed, the expedition would be futile. Moreover the old queen, in her maudlin love for him, had strictly forbidden him "to expose himself to danger, but upon great necessity" - rather odd advice to give to a leader of those sword-in-hand days. It was ultimately arranged that next morning the ships that were the fleetest sailers and drew the lightest draught, under Lord Thomas Howard, Raleigh, Southwell, Vere, Carew, and Cross, with a few others, should dash in and perform this service, by driving from its moorings the Spanish fleet of fifty sail which lay across the bay.

With the first blink of dawn and with a favourable wind they bore inward, passing the fire of the Muele de San Felipe, and attacked the Spanish fleet. "Here did every ship strive

The English fleet before Cadiz.

to be headmost," says Sir Walter Raleigh; "but such was the narrowness of the channel that neither the admiral nor any other ship could pass one by another. There was command given that no ship should shoot but the queen's, making account that the honour would be the greater that was obtained by so few." Steering his ship in mid-channel, Sir Walter Raleigh ran the bows of the *Warspite* with a terrible crash against one Spanish galleon, and, pouring the fire of his forecastle guns upon her, drove her from her anchors. Sir Francis Vere, eager to lead the way on one element as bravely as he had ever done on the other, turned the guns and small-arms of the *Rainbow* on the galleys; but the latter being anchored under the protection of the city batteries, he was very roughly handled till Essex stood in to his relief.

Then it was that several of the Spanish ships sought to escape by creeping along shore to the bottom of the bay, to where the Isle de Leon is joined to the mainland by a bridge, which an old work states to have been 700 paces long. This is called the San Pedro Channel, an arm of the sea with a strong tide running through it. It is from 200 to 500 yards wide, is deep and muddy, and nowhere fordable even at the lowest tide. The bridge, which consists of five arches, is called the Puente de San Pedro; and the city can never be captured from the land while its inhabitants are masters of the bay. By this narrow channel many of the Spanish ships escaped, Lediard says, "by the help of a machine," which probably was a drawbridge, till the entrance was made secure by Sir John Wingfield, in the *Vanguard*.

Meanwhile, many of the great galleons and galleys kept their anchorage at the Puntals, receiving the broadsides of the English, and returning them with interest, till noon; the Earl of Essex, the high admiral, and his son, being now in the heat of the action, which gradually proved favourable to the English. The Spanish ships became so miserably shattered - in some instances masts and bulwarks being shot away, two or three port-holes beaten into one - and so many of their crews were killed or wounded, that they became no longer either tenable or defensible. So their officers set many of them on fire, and scuttled others, sinking them with such precipitation that, though some of their men endeavoured to escape to the shore by boats, by far the greater number flung themselves into the sea, where some were rescued by the English, on their calling for "quarter," but others especially the soldiers and cannoniers, who were accoutred with back, breast, and head-pieces of iron, were miserably drowned, some being sucked into the vortex of many a sinking ship.

Amid this hurly-burly, the *San Philipo*, of 1,500 tons, the Spanish admiral's ship, was blown up - one account says by a revengeful Moorish slave, who fired the powder-room; another by her own officers, rather than let her become the prize of the English - but by the explosion she destroyed three great ships that lay near her. One English ship was burned, and one Dutch, by her own powder, was blown up. ("History of Holland," London, 1705).

The Dutch by this time, under their admiral, Van Duvenwoord, had bravely attacked and carried the Puntals; while the Earl of Essex landed a body of troops at a point between that place and the city, which the ships were now assailing from the seaward. Sir Francis Vere, in his Commentaries, quaintly describes the landing thus:-

"On the right hand, in an even front, with a competent distance betwixt the boats, were ranged the two regiments first named "(Essex's corps and his own), "the other three (being those of Sir Christopher Blunt, Sir Thomas Gerrard, and Sir Conyers Clifford) on the left, so that every regiment and company of men were sorted, together with the colonels and chief officers, in nimble pinnaces, some at the head and some at the stern, to keep good order. The general himself, with his boat, in which it pleased him to have me to attend him, and some other boatsful of gentlemen adventurers and choice persons to attend his person, moved a pretty distance before the rest, when, at a signal given at a drum from his boat, the rest were to follow, according to the measure and time of the sound of the said drum, which they were to observe in the dashing of their oars; and to that end there was a great silence, as well of warlike instruments as otherwise, which order being duly followed, the troops came altogether to the shore, and were landed (i.e., by rowing to the beat of the drum), and several regiments embattled in an instant, without any encounter at all, the Spaniards, who, the day before, had showed themselves with troops of horse and foot on that part, as resolved to impeach our landing, being returned to the town."

In other words, the troops landed with flying colours, and unopposed, half a mile to the eastward of Cadiz, and half that distance from the narrow neck of land which connects one portion of the Isle de Leon with the other; while the fleet, under the Howards, was taking, burning, sinking, or driving on shore and utterly destroying, the nucleus of the new Armada of Spain; work which lasted till four in the afternoon, says Sir Walter Raleigh.

As the four regiments now landed mustered only 2,000 men, and the city was strongly fortified by walls which extended from sea to sea, it was deemed imprudent to attempt anything further than the occupation of sufficient ground whereon to bivouac; but as the column advanced inland, a bolder policy, of which Vere is confessed on all hands to have been the suggester, was adopted. Perceiving that crowds of people on foot and on horseback were passing from the island into the town by a road that skirted the opposite side of the steep promontory, he urged its immediate occupation by a body of troops. Essex instantly adopted the advice, and sent the regiments of Clifford, Blunt, and Gerrard on this service, giving them strict orders also "to break down the bridge and the engine which had secured the escape of the galleys;" and this was all promptly done, while at the same time Essex and Vere continued to advance with something less than a thousand combatants under their orders.

Among these were Lodovick, Count of Nassau (who was afterwards defeated and slain by Don Sancho de Avila); the Earl of Sussex; William Herbert, son of the Earl of Worcester; Bourke, an Irish chief; Sir Christopher St. Lawrence; Sir Robert Drury, and others, all men of rank, and possessed of considerable influence.

As they drew nearer Cadiz, the Spaniards were seen ready to meet them, arrayed in front of the ditch, "with cornets, and ensigns displayed, and thrusting out some loose horse and foot, as it were to provoke a skirmish." Essex had never conceived that a place so strong by art and nature as the city of Cadiz could be reduced in any other manner than by a protracted and vigorous siege; but somehow the aspect and conduct of the Spaniards led the ardent and energetic Sir Francis Vere to believe that the city might be won sooner than they could have hoped. If he could possibly help it, the attempt should be made without delay.

"These men now standing in battle before the ditch," said he to Essex, "will show and make the way into the town for us this night if they be well handled."

In consequence of this, the manner of "handling" them was entirely committed to him, and he lost no time in issuing his orders, and planning his mode of attack.

The approach to Cadiz in the direction pursued by the English was then, and to some extent is still, through the midst of a succession of sandy hillocks, well adapted to the purpose of concealing small bodies of troops, though inadequate to mask the movements of a large column. Vere formed his force into three divisions, the first consisting of 200 men, the second of 300, and the third of 500. Led by Sir John Wingfield, the first was ordered to assail the Spaniards briskly with pike and musket, and engage them in a desultory skirmish. The second, under Sir Matthew Morgan, was to follow in support at a moderate distance, but on no account to close to the front till the proper crisis should arrive; while the third and -last, being under the immediate guidance of Essex and Vere, acted as a reserve. Thus it will be seen that Sir Francis Vere had rightly understood the relative positions of besieged and besiegers.

When each officer had been fully instructed, Sir John Wingfield led on the first division, which, as Vere expected, was furiously assailed by the Spaniards, and fell back in apparent confusion, drawing on the pursuers till they reached the hillock where Morgan was posted. The second corps instantly charged, upon which the garrison, taken completely by surprise, fled with such precipitation that their officers were incapable of rallying them, even under the guns of the city. They plunged, tumbled, or rolled into the ditch, which, though deep and wide, was dry; they scrambled in scores up the steep face of the unscarped rampart, promptly followed by the first and second divisions; while the men of the reserve, coming on at a rush, had also flung themselves into the ditch. One party aided their comrades by scaling a portion of the main wall, while another select band of stormers, under an officer of tried courage, poured silently but swiftly along the ditch till they came to a place destitute of guards, and more than ordinarily accessible. Through this they made good their entrance, led by Lieutenant Evans, Arthur Savage, and Samuel Bagnal, "who bravely leaped from an eminence of a pike's length, to be first in the town," and boldly advancing to the scene of action, speedily cleared the rampart of its defenders. Pell-mell the assailants now rushed in, with levelled pikes and clubbed muskets; and a fierce hand-to-hand battle raged in all the streets and by-lanes of the city, until the marketplace was reached.

By this time a body of seamen had poured in, led by the Howards, Sir Walter Raleigh, Sir William Paget, Sir Robert Southwell, Sir Robert Mansel (afterwards vice-admiral under James and Charles I.), Richard Levison, and Sir Philip Wodehouse, of Kimberley; and with them came Sir Edward Hobby, carrying the colours of England. Both parties now met in the streets, when a heavy fire was maintained on them from the windows and housetops. The Casa de Ayuntimiento, or town-hall, was now stormed by Vere, at the head of 300 men; he cleared it of a body of the garrison who had taken possession of it, and the market-place was finally scoured; but there Sir John Wingfield, who had bravely performed his part in the assault, was shot through the head and slain. Savage and Bagnal, who were covered with wounds and blood, were knighted on the spot.

The storming of Cadiz.

76

Vere now compelled a more numerous force in the abbey of St. Francis to surrender and so environed a battalion in Fort San Felipe, that when summoned the gates were opened. "Thus, by his good conduct," says Vere's biographer, "was a conquest secured, the first attainment of which may be traced to his gallantry; for except the battalion which followed himself, there were not, within ten minutes after the assault, forty men in one mass throughout the entire compass of the city."

A contribution was levied upon the inhabitants, and great booty acquired; but not a single life was taken in cold blood, and no woman had to complain of suffering insult from any English seaman or soldier - a praiseworthy forbearance, rare in those days. Under a guard, all the Spanish women were sent to Santa Maria, a place of safety, in English ships; and the men, to the number of 5,000. were disarmed and expelled - a treatment of prisoners of war which is worthy of special remark.

Many of the ladies quitted Cadiz in their richest apparel, with all their jewels on; while the Earl of Essex stood in person by the water-side, to see them safely embarked. Sir Francis Vere tells us that "he got three prisoners worth 10,000 ducats; one a churchman and President of Contradutation of the Indies, the others two ancient knights." This admission shows that the old practice, by which individuals were allowed to ransom their own prisoners, was not, as yet, obsolete.

By the capture of Cadiz, the King of Spain lost in shipping, provisions, and stores, destined for a new expedition against England, more than twenty millions of ducats. Besides the merchantmen, he lost two great galleons, which were captured with above 100 brass guns in them, thirteen other men-of-war, eleven ships freighted for the Indies, and eleven for other ports; and Stow has it that 1,200 pieces of ordnance were taken or sunk in the sea. Camden gives the names of sixty English gentlemen who were knighted for bravery on this occasion. All the commanders were enriched by plunder, with the exception of the Earl of Essex, who appropriated nothing but a noble library which he found in a public building.

A difference of opinion now arose among the leaders as to what was to be done with their new conquest. Sir Francis Vere insisted on the good policy of retaining the town; and offered, if left with only 4,000 men, to defend it against all the power of Spain (see his Commentaries). But his wish was not accepted; and it was resolved in the end to retire, after demolishing the defences and burning the houses. The artillery, stores, and general plunder were put on board of the fleet, which sailed after the troops were re-embarked, and Cadiz was left reduced to a heap of cinders overlooking a wreck-strewn shore; for the Duke of Medina, the Spanish admiral, while the assault was at its height, and the town was in the act of being captured, had beached a vast number of vessels and destroyed them by fire, to prevent them becoming prizes of the English.

All on fire for further glory, Essex now proposed to steer for the Azores, and there lie in wait for the East India caracks, on their homeward voyage; but, save Lord Thomas Howard and the Dutch admiral, no officer in the fleet would consent to such a movement.

The result of the attack on Cadiz filled Philip of Spain with greater fury than ever. Disappointed in all his projects for vengeance on the English by invasion, he found himself unable to defend even the shores of Spain. To revenge the losses he had last sustained at Cadiz, and to recover in some measure his tarnished glory, he was determined to make another effort ere the year 1596 came to a close, and ordered all his ships to rendezvous in the roads of Lisbon. He hired all the foreign ships that were in Spanish ports, and embarked on board of them a large body of newly-levied troops, together with a number of Irish refugees, at the port of Ferrol, in order to effect a landing in Ireland or England. But as soon as the fleet sailed, a tempest scattered it, destroying one-half and rendering the other completely unserviceable, so that Philip had to relinquish all ideas of aggression for the time; while Elizabeth, the further to secure England against any such attempts for the future, gave orders to strengthen and fortify Sandsfort, Portland, Hurst, Southsea, Calshot, St. Andrews, and St. Maudits.

About the middle of August, the troops from Cadiz were disembarked at the Downs, near Sandwich, and were, after the fashion of the times, when standing armies were scarcely known, immediately disbanded, save the regiments which Vere had brought from the Low Countries, and these were sent back to their original stations; the remainder returned to their homes, to tell in many a secluded English village the story of the capture of Cadiz.

PORTO RICO, 1598

O NE OF the most remarkable occurrences of the year 1598 was the tenth and last privateering expedition of George Clifford, the famous and adventurous Earl of Cumberland, against the Spaniards. His father had been raised to an earldom in 1525, by Henry VIII, and he was the first English subject who ever built a ship so large as 800 tons burden; and this vessel he employed in many actions against Spain, particularly in the West Indian seas.

It was in his favour that the venerable Sir Henry Lee, of Ditchley - than whom, perhaps, no knight of chivalry was more thoroughly imbued by the spirit of old romance - resigned, on the 17th of November, 1590, the anniversary of the queen's accession, the office of champion and president of a society which he had formed for promoting the exercise of arms.

No European prince ever possessed such vast resources as Philip II, of Spain. In addition to his Spanish and Italian dominions, the Kingdom, of Portugal, and the States of the Netherlands, he was master of the whole East Indian commerce, and reaped the richest harvest of ores from his South American mines. But his mighty armaments against England, his intrigues with France, and his long and aggressive wars in the Low Countries, enriched those whom he sought to subdue; while the Spaniards, dazzled by the sight of the precious metals, and elated with the idea of vast wealth, neglected the agriculture of Spain; its ingots and wedges of gold were no sooner coined than called for; while the interception of his Plate fleets and the plunder of his colonies became the incessant occupation of the English sea-adventurers, until "Spanish "became a term synonymous with money or treasure.

Lord Cumberland's expedition in 1598 was the largest he had ever fitted out, and was the greatest that any English subject had as yet set upon the sea. Several of the fleet were his own vessels, equipped entirely by his private purse, and without any assistance from the queen.

Including a vessel called *The Old Frigate*, and two barges for landing troops, the armament consisted of twenty sail. The leading ship, the *Scourge of Malice*, was commanded by the earl himself as admiral; the *Merchant-Royal* was commanded by Sir Tom Berkeley, as vice-admiral and lieutenant general. "There were besides, a noble train of commanders and other gentlemen for the land service."

On the 6th of March these adventurers sailed from Plymouth, to improve their fortunes on the high seas and among the Spanish colonies; and they had not long lost sight of the white cliffs of England before they received intelligence from a passing ship of five great caracks that were speedily to set sail from Spain with more wealthy cargoes than ever before had gone to the Indies, and that they were accompanied by five-and-twenty vessels bound for Brazil. In every ship of the squadron the most active preparations were made for meeting and attacking them, but made in vain; for the Spaniards had no sooner heard that Lord Cumberland was on the sea, than caravels of advice ran along the coast to prevent all ships of importance leaving their harbours. So the earl, who does not seem to have been particular as to what flag a ship carried, had to console himself by taking a Hamburger laden with corn, copper, and powder, and a French vessel laden with salt.

Finding that it was in vain to wait for the caracks or the Brazilian ships, the earl bore on with his whole fleet for the South Cape, capturing on the way "two Flemmings "laden with corn. In a few days he was off the Canary Isles, and effected a landing on Lanzerota, which is thirty-six miles long by fifteen broad, and contains several volcanoes. He anchored his whole fleet in the roadstead, which lies on the south-east of the island. In this solitary part of the world, a wealthy Spanish marquis had built for himself a strong castle of stone, defended by ramparts and brass cannon, flanked, and situated in a good position. In this place he had 200 guards and servants. This retinue enabled him to tyrannise like a petty king over all the inhabitants of the isle and of the adjacent one, of Fuerteventura, from which it is separated by the channel De Bocagna.

Sir John Berkeley advanced against this stronghold at the head of 600 pikemen and musketeers; and though twenty men might have held the keep against them, as the entrance was in the upper story, by ladders which were drawn in, the little garrison abandoned it, "and ran like bucks, leaving it a prey to the English, so terrible was the very name of the English to them at that time."

The arms of the natives were lances and stones. When a musketeer levelled his weapon at them, they threw themselves flat on the ground, and the moment he fired, they sprang up, hurled their missiles, and fled. The town, consisting of a hundred houses, roofed with canes and mud hardened in the sun, was pillaged of all that was worth taking; and also "an old tattered church," which had an altar at one end, but was without chancel or vestry. Sailing thence on the 21st of April, on the 23rd of May the fleet was off Dominica and the Virgin Isles, where the earl remained a month. Helanded mustered all his men, and announced to them that his next desire was to capture San Juan de Porto Rico, the attempt in which Drake had failed so recently, and the intelligence was greeted by reiterated cheers.

On the 6th of June he was off this island, which is the most eastern of the Great Antilles, and his plan of attack differed from that of Drake. He landed 1,000 men at a considerable distance from the town; and, seizing a negro, "who was half frightened to death, for their guide," marched towards it. Both the earl and Sir John Berkeley were in complete armour. Their way, we are told, was by steep cliffs and rugged rocks, till they reached an arm of the sea about a musket-shot in breadth, which separated them from the town, and where they found themselves exposed to the fire of a fort.

Opposite, on a slope, rose San Juan, on an isle, or isthmus rather, about half a league long, "fairly built, neat, and strong, after the Spanish manner. It had several large streets, was bigger than Portsmouth, was more agreeable to the eye, and had a good monastery and a cathedral what diminished from the whole was the want of glass, as they had only canvas or wooden shutters in their windows" ("Atlas Geographus," London, 1717). Its port was deemed by the Spaniards as the key of South America.

Powder-flasks and spanners for officers of horse. The lower for infantry (end of sixteenth century).

Cumberland's force was without boats by which to cross the little strait, and for a time he and his other captains were much perplexed, till a communication was discovered between the city and the mainland, by means of a narrow causeway that led to a bridge which was drawn up. Beyond this bridge was a strong barricade, and higher up was the fort, whence the Spaniards swept the causeway with ordnance and small-arms. This causeway was so rough and difficult to traverse, that the English preferred to wade through the sea by the side of it. A very dark night had succeeded a hot and brilliant day, when the attack was resolved on, "and though the earl was carried away very ill, by a fall from the causeway into the sea, when the weight and encumbrance of his armour nearly drowned him," his soldiers pressed on with ardour, passed then draw-bridge in the sea, which came up to their waist-belts, and assailed the gate of the barricade with their bills and hatchets; but so stout was the resistance of the Spaniards, and so heavy their fire upon the English, who were compelled to fight in the water, that the assailants were forced to retire.

The next attack was attended with better success; and, flushed with rumours of the gold mines that were alleged to be in the rocky parts of the isle, and the precious ore found in the sand of its rivers, Cumberland's men advanced with fresh ardour. While a party of musketeers, levelling their weapons over rocks or their rests, picked off the Spanish cannoniers at their guns, another, which was composed of pikemen and musketeers, was set ashore on the other side, midway between the fort and town. Finding their retreat about to be cut off, the garrison of the former were compelled, after a sharp resistance; to abandon it, and fell back on the town; but this they soon after deserted.

El Moro, a place of great strength, together with the strong castle in the western part of the town, and a third fort between it and the Moro, all surrendered in quick succession to the adventurous earl, who then found himself in undisturbed possession of the place.

He now resolved to retain it, to increase its fortifications, and to make it a point whence fleets might cruise against the Spaniards, now deemed, as the Scots had been for centuries, the natural enemies of England. This plan met with the warm approval of his followers; and a roll was prepared of those who volunteered to remain there as the nucleus of an English colony and garrison. In furtherance of this great scheme, the earl ordered all the Spanish inhabitants to depart to other isles, notwithstanding the offers they made him of rich goods and gold and silver plate, to be permitted to remain.

But an unforeseen misfortune came, in the form of a deadly sickness that decimated his slender force. Of the 1,000 men who landed, Camden records that 700 died, exclusive of those slain by the Spaniards. This mortality so scared the survivors, who were led to expect the same fate, that all resolved to quit the island as speedily as possible. The earl wished, ere doing so, to make some profitable terms with the Spaniards for its ransom. To these proposals they pretended to listen, and several messages passed between them and the earl; but the negotiations proceeded so slowly that he began after a time to perceive that they were only seeking to delay till death had further weakened his force, and to suspect that they had some treacherous design on foot.

While these negotiations were pending, there came into the harbour of San Juan a caravel from Margarita, an island of Venezuela, in the Caribbean Sea, with passengers bound for Spain; and these were very much surprised to find the island of Porto Rico in possession of the English. In the caravel the earl found pearls to the value of a thousand ducats; and learning from her crew that the pearl-chest at Margarita was very slenderly guarded, he sent three ships of his fleet to seize it. In the rich pearl-fishery there the Spaniards employed vast numbers of negroes from Guinea; and Lait records that they forced these wretched slaves to such excessive labour, that many killed themselves in despair, while others were drowned and maimed by sharks. But great though the prize looked for at Margarita, the earl's ships were driven back by adverse winds, and he, now becoming more than ever convinced that the Spaniards of the captured island had some ulterior and, perhaps, savage ends in view, sailed from Porto Rico with less than half his fleet, in search of fortune elsewhere, leaving Sir John Berkeley with the other half of his armament, and full power to act in his absence.

The separation took place on the 14th August The earl hoped to be in time to intercept the Mexican home-fleet, or some of the East Indian caracks off the Azores, but he came there too late, luckily for himself perhaps, as but a few days before his arrival at Flores, no less than twenty-nine large Spanish men-of-war had been there. How long Sir John stayed at Porto Rico after the earl is uncertain, and what terms he made with the colonists are unknown; but after a dreadful storm, in which all their vessels nearly perished, and were severely damaged, the fleet was reunited at Flores, and eventually returned to England in the month of October.

The earl held possession of Porto Rico for only forty days, but in that time he collected and brought away a vast quantity of hides, ginger, and sugar; eighty pieces of cannon; some ammunition; the bells of the churches; and a thousand ducatoons' worth of pearls. This is the general account given of the results of the expedition; but it is supposed that, as a matter of fact, he collected a much greater quantity of plunder, in the form of ingots and gold dust.

He lost only sixty men at the storming of Porto Rico; but forty were drowned in *The Old Frigate*, in a storm off Ushant.

The character of the Earl of Cumberland, is tersely

Attack on Porto Rico.

summarised by an old naval historian, who speaks of him as "a man of admirable qualities, both in civil and military affairs. He knew as well how to fight as to govern, and had virtues capable of rendering him equally illustrious both in war and peace. He was so excellent a person that it can hardly be said what was lacking in him, and yet he had one very considerable want, viz., a steady gale of good fortune; and, considering the vast expenses he was at, in building, hiring, and furnishing ships, it is a question whether his expeditions increased his estate."- His earldom became extinct in the year 1643.

IN THE BAY OF CEZIMBRA, 1602

THE LAST but one important event in the long and stirring reign of Elizabeth was the great sea-fight in the roadstead of Cezimbra, between her ships and those of the Spaniards. A rich carack of which the former were in pursuit had taken shelter there. "The harbour," says Hume, "was guarded by a castle; there were eleven galleys stationed in it. and the militia of the country, to the number of 20,000 men, appeared in arms upon the shore; yet, notwithstanding these obstacles, and others derived from the winds and tides, the English squadron broke into the harbour, dismounted the guns of the castle, sunk, burned, or put to flight the galleys, and obliged the carack to surrender. They brought her home to England, and she was valued at a million of ducats; a sensible loss to the Spaniards, and a supply still more important to Elizabeth."

The details of this gallant sea-fight, as given by one of the commanders, and other authorities, are as follow: -

To prevent the Spaniards from invading the coast of Ireland, the queen fitted out a squadron of eight ships of war, which she placed under the- command of Monson and Levison, who, since the death of Drake and Hawkins, were deemed the most skilful officers in the English navy. These vessels were the *Repulse*, Sir Richard Levison, Admiral; the *Garland*, Sir William Monson, Vice-Admiral; the *Defiance*, Captain Gore; the *Mary Rose*, Captain *Slingsby*; the *Warspite*, Captain Sommers; the *Dreadnought*, Captain Manwaring; the *Adventure*, Captain Trevor; and an English caravel, Captain Tawkell.

The Dutch had promised to aid the queen with twelve ships of war, that together they might scour the seas and molest the

Spaniards. The new expedition was prepared in great haste, so much so, that the squadron was not fully equipped either with men, ammunition, or provisions; when, on the 19th of March, 1602, Sir Richard Levison set sail with five vessels, leaving his vice-admiral, Monson, with three, to await the arrival of the Hollanders. Ere the latter arrived, and three days after Levison's departure, Sir William received a dispatch from the queen to go to sea with all speed, as she had received tidings that the Plate fleet was off the Isle of Terceira.

Sir William put to sea, with the *Garland* and two other ships, on the 26th of March, and stood down the Channel.

The queen's intelligence had been true, as the fleet had been at Terceira, which is the central island of the group named the Azores, but had shaped its course to Spain. On the voyage they were met by Sir Richard Levison, who, though the Spaniards mustered thirty-eight sail, bravely attacked them with his five. But being without Monson's vessels, and still more the twelve Hollanders, his bravery was exerted in vain, and he was beaten off, while the Plate fleet stood on its homeward course. Levison was naturally exasperated with the Hollanders for their delay, by which so much treasure escaped him. He now steered towards the Rock of Lisbon, which had been previously appointed by him as the place where he and Monson were to rendezvous; but Sir William having spent fourteen days cruising off the coast of Portugal, and seeing nothing of him, stood around the South Cape, "where he was likewise frustrated of a most pleasing expectation."

He came in sight of some ships, which showed the Scottish and French colours. These were merchantmen from San Lucar, where, as the Scottish skippers reported, there were five great galleons ready to sail with the next tide for India. They also told him that three days before two others had sailed, having on board Don Pedro de Valdez, the Governor of Havannah, and his retinue - the same Don Pedro who held a command in the Great Armada, and had been prisoner of war in England in 1588.

These two ships were met one night by Captain Sommers, in the *Warspite*; but, in consequence of the extreme darkness, and perhaps of their own strength, no engagement ensued.

This news of the five galleons at San Lucar, made Sir William Monson steer in the direction where he would be most likely to meet with them; and, in a shorter time than he anticipated, he discovered five ships, which he conceived to be, from the size and number, the identical galleons he was in quest of. But he was again doomed to disappointment, for on coming within gunshot they showed their colours, and proved to be English.

Next day he captured a Spanish Indiaman; "but he had better been without her, for she brought him so far to the leeward that the same night the five galleons passed to windward "unseen, and not above eight leagues off, as he was informed by the skipper of an English pinnace.

"These misfortunes," says Lediard, "lighting upon Sir Richard first and Sir William after, might have been sufficient reasons to discourage them; but they, knowing the accidents of the sea, and that Fortune could laugh as well as weep, and having good ships under foot, their men sound and in health, did not doubt that some of the wealth which the two Indies sent yearly to Spain would yet fall to their share."

On the 1st of June, the squadron, now united, was hovering off the Rock of Lisbon, as that round promontory in which the ridge of Cintra ends is named by seamen. There they, captured two Easterlings; and while overhauling their cargoes, they descried a caravel coming round Cape Espichel, a headland twenty-one miles south-west of Lisbon. She proved to be English, and reported to Sir Richard Levison that "a large carack, of 1,600 tons, was just arrived at Cezimbra, near St. Ubes, from the East

Indies, richly laden; and that there were eleven galleys in the same harbour, three of them Portuguese, under the command of Don Frederick Spinola, to cruise against the Dutch." Her master added that he had been sent with this message by the captains of the *Nonpareil* and *Dreadnought*, who were thereabout, looking out for the admiral.

With cheers and joy this news was received. Sir Richard immediately signalled Sir William to stand on with him, and, lest the signs should not be discerned, sent the caravel with a message to bear up for the roads of Cezimbra; but before they had rounded Cape Espichel night had closed in, and nothing took place but the exchange of a few cannon-shot between the admiral and the galleys of Spinola, who is called by Rymer a Genoese.

On the 2nd of June, when day dawned, "every man looked out early for what ships of Her Majesty were in sight," and there were but five - the *Warspite* (having the admiral on board, as the *Repulse* had become leaky, and been sent to England), the *Garland*, the *Nonpareil*, the *Dreadnought*, and the *Adventure*, besides the two Easterlings, with prize-crews on board.

A council, at which all the captains were present, was held on board the *Warspite*, and it lasted the most part of the day. Some alleged that it was impracticable to cut out the carack, defended as she was by eleven galleys, and lying close under the guns of the castle of Cezimbra; but Sir William Monson urged so vigorously that the attempt should be made - an attempt which he affirmed would be crowned with brilliant success - that it was resolved to make an attack next day, in the following manner.

He and Sir Richard were to come to anchor as near the carack as they could venture; the rest to keep under sail, and ply up and down without anchoring. Sir William Monson, we are told, was glad of this opportunity of having vengeance on these same galleys, "hoping to requite the slavery they had put him to when he was a prisoner in one of them."

He now sailed a league in front of the squadron, with his colours flying in defiance of the galleys. The Marquis of Santa Cruz and Frederick Spinola, the former general of the Portuguese,. and the latter of the Spanish galleys, accepted the challenge, and came out to fight him; but we are told that, "being within shot, they were diverted (from their purpose) by one John Bedford, an Englishman, who pretended to know the force of the ship, and Sir William, who commanded her."

The town of Cezimbra lies at the bottom of a bay which affords excellent anchorage. It was then, as now, built of stone; and near it was the ancient fort or castle still named the Cavallo, strong, spacious, and then well mounted with heavy ordnance. On the summit of the hill behind it was an old priory, the situation of which, with cannon, rendered it impregnable, and able to command the town, the castle, and the roadstead. Close to the shore, and under the guns of the Cavallo, lay the rich carack, which was the object of so much warlike solicitude.

Attack on Cezimbra.

The eleven galleys had secured themselves beside a small neck of rock on the western part of the roads, anchored side by side, with the stems outward, to play upon the English as they entered; for each galley carried a very large cannon in her lofty beak, besides four other pieces in the prow below it; and they were secure from the fire of the English till the latter were under that of the castle and town. So advantageously were they placed that, as the captain of one of them confessed after his capture, their officers confidently expected with their great guns to sink the English easily. The latter saw vast quantities of tents pitched near the shore, and troops, as we have said, to the number of 20,000 men, under the Conde de Vitageria, were mustered there. Boats were seen passing all day long between the carack and the town. At first it was supposed the Spaniards were unloading her; but instead of this, they were filling her with men and ammunition.

At daybreak on the morning of the 3rd of June, the admiral fired a gun and ran his ensign to the mainmast-head; Sir William Monson responded by another, and displayed his colours at the foretop-mast-head, while the squadron stood in towards the point of attack. The vice-admiral was the sternmost ship; and each vessel as she entered the roadstead had to fight her guns on both sides at once, as they had to encounter the fire of the town, the castle, the galleys, and the carack.

The vice-admiral himself relates that, when he entered the action, he strove to luff up as near the shore as he could, when he came to anchor, plying both his broadsides the while; and by that time the fire of the leading ships had battered the galleys, torn up the benches, freeing in vast numbers the slaves, who were usually chained thereto, but who were now seen throwing themselves into the sea, and swimming towards the English ships.

The battle in the roadstead lasted till five o'clock in the

afternoon, and by that time the galleys were rowed from side to side of the harbour, making desperate efforts to avoid the fire of the ship of the vice-admiral, which he had anchored so skilfully that Sir Richard Levison "came on board him and openly, in the view and hearing of the whole ship's company, embraced him, and told him that he had won his heart for ever."

Levison's ship was less skilfully handled, for, by the negligence of her master, or some other cause, she failed to anchor at the place intended; and falling away to leeward, was ultimately carried by wind and tide, not only out of the action, but actually out of the harbour, and could not be brought in again till next day.

This circumstance enraged Sir Richard, who put himself on board the *Dreadnought*, and had anchored her near the vice-admiral, about two in the afternoon.

Three hours afterwards it was resolved to parley with the enemy, and orders were issued to all the ships to cease firing, till the English messenger returned. The man selected for the service was a merchant captain, named Sewell, who had escaped and swum off from the galleys (after having been four years a prisoner in one), as many other Christians and Turks did, when chance shots had freed them of their fetters; for by this time the galleys, on whose strength the defence had mainly rested, were some in flames, with their wretched crews on board, others were knocked to pieces, and had their benches covered by bloody corpses, and some had slipped their cables and fled.

Sewell was to intimate that the English had full possession of the roadstead; that the fort could not withstand their ordnance, nor the carack either, and that unless the latter was given up the Spaniards "were to expect all the cruelty and rigour that a conqueror could inflict upon his enemy."

After some conference, the officer commanding in the carack said that "he would send some gentlemen of quality on board with commission to treat, and desired that some of the same rank from the English might repair to him for the same purpose."

The Spanish cavaliers came on board the *Dreadnought*, where the admiral and Sir William Monson were awaiting the return of Captain Sewell; but they had immediately to return to the carack, on board of which an uproar had taken place, as one party there proposed to yield her up, and another wished to set her on fire. On learning this, Sir William Monson lowered himself into his barge, and instantly boarded her. When on deck, he was recognised by several Spanish gentlemen, who had known him when he was a prisoner of war among them.

The captain of the carrack was Don Diego Lobo, a hidalgo of noble birth. He came down into the waist, and between him and Sir William there followed a conference in the Portuguese language. He proposed to give up the cargo, provided he was permitted to retain the crew, with their arms, and the ship with her ordnance, and her colours flying. But these terms Sir William rejected, adding that he "would never permit a Spanish flag to be borne in presence of the queen's ships, unless it were disgracefully over the poop;" a reply the exact significance of which is not very clear in the present day, as it is there the colours are now shown on the jack-staff.

It was ultimately arranged to yield her up, and that the castle of Cezimbra should not fire on the English ships while they rode in the bay; and that night Sir William had the Captain Don Juan and many other Spanish gentlemen at supper in his cabin, where they had music, mirth, and pleasure.

In the beginning nearly of this engagement, the Portuguese galleys, under Santa Cruz, took to flight; the Spanish, under Spinola, fought bravely, on which in very shame the former returned to their stations; but had the English fleet possessed sufficient boats, they had all been taken or burned. One of them was named the *Leva*, in which Sir William Monson had been a prisoner in 1591, The loss of the Spaniards in the castle, carack, and galleys is unknown, but they were so full of men that it must have been considerable, while the loss of the English was most trivial - only twelve killed and wounded, chiefly on board the *Garland*. Sir William had the left wing of his doublet carried away by a,ball, from which we may infer that he did not fight in armour, The next day the squadron sailed for England, bringing with it the carack, which had wintered in the Mozambique Channel, where 600 of her crew had died of disease, and only twenty survived to see Europe; and they had suffered many calamities and misfortunes, before they unluckily came to anchor in the harbour of Cezimbra.

Carack, or *carraca*, was the name usually given by the Spaniards and Portuguese to the vessels they sent to Brazil and the Indies; they were large, round-built, and adapted, alike for; battle and burden. They were narrower above water than below, and had sometimes seven or eight decks, and were capable of carrying 2,000 tons and 2,000 men. Similar ships were used by the Knights of Rhodes and the Genoese.

The Viceroy of Portugal, Don Christoyal de Moro, was indignant and infuriated by the capture of this particular carack, under the guns of Cezim Tara, those of eleven galleys, and in the face of 20,000 troops.

He made a prisoner of Don Diego Lobo, and would have put him to death, had he not, with the aid of his sister, escaped by a window, and fled to Italy; but his patent as Governor of Malacca was confiscated, and he was reduced to penury.

Thirteen, years afterwards, in 1615, he was wandering about London, when he suddenly bethought him of Sir William Monson, who interested himself in his behalf with the Archduke and the Infanta, who restored to him his rank and property; "the poor gentleman," concludes Sir William, "being thus tossed by the waves of calamity from one country to another, and never finding likelihood of rest till now (when) Death, that masters all men, cut him short just as he was preparing his journey to Spain. And this was the end of an unfortunate and gallant young gentleman, whose deserts were worthy of a better reward, if God was pleased to afford it to him."

But Sir William Monson had not seen the last of the roads of Cezimbra. He had barely cast anchor in Plymouth Sound when he was summoned to the presence of Queen Elizabeth, who had a long conference with him, in presence of the High Admiral, her treasurer, and secretary, concerning the defence of the coast of Ireland, and certain armaments which the indefatigable Spaniards were again collecting at the Groyne; and it was resolved that he should at once sail, with what would now be called a fleet of observation, to watch that place, and not leave the coast of Spain until he saw the object of those preparations. If they proved to be simply for defence, and not invasion, he was then to join the Dutch fleet at the Rock of Lisbon. On receiving his final orders, he repaired to Plymouth, and took command of his squadron. It consisted of ten sail, as follows:- The *Swiftsure*, of 400 tons and 200 men, commanded by himself in person; *Mary Rose*, 600 tons and 250 men, Captain Trevor; *Dreadnought*, 400 tons and 200 men, Captain Cawfield; *Adventure*, 250 tons and 120 men, Captain Norris; *Answer*, 200 tons and 100 men. Captain Bredgate; *Quittance*, 200 tons and 100 men, Captain Browne; *Lion's Whelp*, 200 tons and 100 men, Captain May. With these were the *Paragon*, a merchant ship, and a small caravel.

On the 31st of August he sailed from Plymouth, and encountered much rough weather, but preferred to keep at sea rather than return. He reached the Groyne, and found the Spanish squadron had left that place, under the flag of Don Diego de Borachero, for Lisbon. He dispatched the little caravel to the Bayona Isles, a number of insular rocks at the entrance of the

Bay of Bayonne, off the Galician coast, to gather intelligence; and there she saw the Spanish fleet, consisting of twenty-four sail; and her captain learned from the crew of a boat he captured that they were on the look-out for the English.

Pursuing a ship, with the *Dreadnought*, into the roads of Cezimbra, he cannonaded the castle, and was fired on in return, and captured a caravel, but afterwards dismissed her. Sailing once more to the Rock, he could see nothing of the Dutch fleet, without a junction with which it would have been perilous, with so small a squadron, to engage the Spaniards.

On the night of the 26th September he saw a light upon the sea, and, thinking it might come from the fleet of St. Thomas or the Brazils, he gave immediate chase, and on hailing the vessels in the gloom, he suddenly found by their great size and number that he was among the armada of Don Diego, with only the *Adventure* and *Whelp* in his company, the rest of his squadron having been scattered four nights before in a storm. He compelled a Spanish prisoner to respond to the hailing of

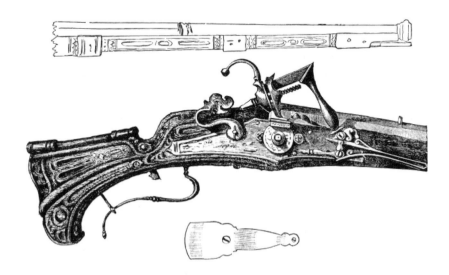

Musket of 1620, showing wheel and match combined.

his countrymen, but the wind was so high that they could not hear him.

The *Adventure* was now discovered to be an English ship; she was fired upon, and had many of her men killed and wounded; but she, with the *Dreadnought* and *Whelp*, passed right through the enemy's fleet, with their poop lanterns lighted, and when day broke they were far ahead of the Spaniards, who immediately made all sail in chase, and their leading ships soon overtook the *Whelp* and opened their guns upon her.

Then it was, as Sir William relates of himself, that, "resolving not to see even a pinnace of Her Majesty's so lost, if he could rescue her with the hazard of his life, though it was much against the persuasions of his master and company," he shortened sail and ordered the *Whelp* to lie her course, while he prepared to engage the three leading ships of the enemy.

On perceiving by this movement how reckless was the bravery of Monson, the Spanish admiral, to the astonishment of the English, fired a gun as a signal for his fleet to follow him, and sheering off, stood in shore.

Monson now bore up for the South Cape, in hope to meet the San Domingo fleet of richly-laden merchantmen, but it had escaped him by passing two days before; and on the 21st of October, descrying a great galleon of the King of Spain, he gave immediate chase to her, though she steered for shelter in shore, and at length came to anchor under the guns of the castle situated on Cape. St. Vincent, a rocky promontory, forming the most western point of Portugal and at the same time also of Europe.

His boarders were all ready with pike, and bill, and axe, but he failed to board her, "through the fear and cowardliness of the man at the helm, who bore up" when he was ready to do so; and the fight that ensued was long, sharp, and dangerous, though not a shot was exchanged till they were only the ships' length apart.

The castle, which was one of great strength, was playing upon Monson's ship, and its cannon so battered and rent her that he says "a team of oxen might have crept through her under the half-deck." He had seven men slain by one shot alone. He had others killed and many more wounded, as he had to encounter both the galleon and the fortress; and this unequal conflict he maintained in sight of a Spanish squadron, under Sirriago, that lay to the westward of the cape, and several English men-of-war that lingered to the eastward, but dared not attempt his rescue, "for fear of the castle."

He continued the battle till nightfall, and then, to elude the fleet that lay to the westward waiting to capture him, and to seek for belter fortune, he sailed for the island of Terceira; but when within fifty leagues of it he was long becalmed. Then, finding that provisions were failing him, and that one of his masts, which had been wounded, went overboard, with the first suitable breeze he bore up for England; and in this crippled condition reached Plymouth on the 20th of November, 1602, where he found that the *Dreadnought*, the *Adventure*, and *Mary Rose*, with nearly all their crews dead or sick, had preceded him.

Sir William Monson tells us that he was the general (by which he means admiral) of the last fleet of Queen Elizabeth, and adds that he had served her from the beginning of the Spanish wars; having, when a youth, been at the capture of the first Spanish prize that was brought into an English port, and which was taken with the loss of twenty-five men killed and fifty wounded. She was afterwards manned as a ship of war against the Spaniards, and named the *Commander*. She belonged to Sir George Carew, then Governor of the Isle of Wight.

At the death of Elizabeth her fleet consisted of forty-two sail, ranging from the *Triumph*, of 1,000 tons and 500 men, down to the *Penny Rose*, hoy, of 80 tons and 8 men, and the *Squint*, of 20 tons and 2 men, when in harbour.

SEA-FIGHT WITH THE TURKS OFF CAGLIARI, 1617

THE YEAR 1603 saw the peaceful accession of James VI of Scotland to the English throne. This pedantic monarch had none of those qualities that distinguished his ancestors, but the union of the crowns in his person was a great benefit to the people of. Great, Britain. Never more on British soil could there be such battles as Bannockburn or Flodden, fought by rival monarchs. Nor was there need for the future to keep watch and ward along the border-side by tower and beacon; while, as subjects of the same king, the moss-troopers of both countries had to cease their raids and predatory warfare. But civil wars were to come, and Englishmen and Scotsmen were yet, unhappily, fated to meet each other in battles that were fierce and bloody, when armies had taken the form of divisions and brigades, regiments and companies, according to the tactics of the present time.

On the 12th of April, 1606, the Union Jack - the flag that has waved in so many bloody and victorious battles by sea and shore - first made its appearance. From Rymer's "Fœdera," and the Annals of Sir James Balfour, Lord Lyon King at Arms, we learn that some differences having arisen between ships of the two countries at sea, His Majesty ordained that a *new flag* be adopted, with the crosses of St. Andrew and St George interlaced, by placing the latter fimbriated on the blue flag of Scotland as the ground thereof. This flag all ships were to carry at their main-top; but English ships were to display St. George's red cross at their stern, and the Scottish the white saltire of St. Andrew. The Union Jack, however, was not adopted by the troops of either country till their Parliamentary union, in 1707.

In Munro's account of the expedition with Mackay's regiment in Denmark, he states that in 1626 the Scots in the Danish army persisted in carrying their national flag, and refused to place the Danish cross upon it.

The arms and armour of the time of James were little more than a continuation of those of Elizabeth; but the increasing use of fire-arms, and the improvements thereon, brought mail more into disrepute, so that by the close of his reign that of the heaviest cavalry terminated at the knees. In Drayton's "Polyolbion," Henry Prince of Wales appears in armour only to the waist, with a plumed and visored basinet beside him, and steel gauntlets on his hands. The armour of Sir Horace Vere, a plain suit in the Tower, is, however, complete from head to heel, and is about the date" of 1606.

It was now begun to be found that good buff leather would, of itself, resist the cut of a sword, and was thus adopted as the dress for lightly-armed cavalry; so armour was now beginning" to terminate "in the same materials with which it began - the skins of animals, or leather" (Grose's "Military Antiquities").

To the rest for the musket or matchlock, there was added to the equipment of the musketeer in the time of James a long blade, for his defence after he had fired. This was called a Swedish feather, or "hog's bristle." It was originally a Swedish invention, and was put by the musketeer to the same use that the English archers were wont to put their pointed stakes in the days of Cressy and Agincourt.

In this reign we first read of the simple military mourning which is in use to the present day. Colonel Munro, in his "Expedition," mentions that when Captain Learmonth, of Mackay's Highlanders, died of his wounds at Hamburg, in 1627, "for his sake, and in remembrance of his worth and valour, the whole officers of the regiment did wear a black mourning ribband."

Save the expedition under Sir Robert Mansell to Algiers - an abortive affair, which covered the Government with ridicule - no warlike event of importance marked the reign of the peaceful and pedantic James I of Great Britain; though there occurred a sea-fight off the Isle of Sardinia, between one English merchant ship and no less than six Turkish men-of-war, which made much noise, in the year 1616.

Two accounts of this spirited battle were published: one by the English captain, in the following year, and dedicated to Henry Stuart, the young Prince of Wales; and the other by John Taylor, the "water poet," an author now little known, though a note to the "Dunciad" states that "he wrote fourscore books in the reigns of James and Charles I."

Towards the close of December, 1616, the ship *Dolphin*, of London, Captain Edward Nicholls, left Zante, one of the Ionian

Musketeer   *Pikeman*
(From an Undated Tract, "Exercise of the English Militia" - about 1625.)

Isles, with a full cargo for the Thames. She was a craft of 220 tons, or thereabout; her crew consisted of thirty-six men and two boys; and she was armed with nineteen pieces of cast ordnance and five "murderers," a name then given to small pieces of cannon having chambers, and made to load at the breech. They were mostly used at sea, in order to clear the decks when an enemy had boarded a vessel. Her master was "a man of great skill, courage, industry, and proved experience;" and these good qualities were soon to be put to a terrible test.

On the 1st of January, 1617, the *Dolphin* lost sight of the Fior de Levante, and on the morning of the 8th sighted the island of Sardinia. The wind being westerly, at nine in the morning she stood in shore for Cagliari, and about noon was close to two small watchtowers, from which two cannon were fired, as a signal that the guards there wished to speak with the crew. Their object, Captain Nicholls afterwards learned, was to acquaint him that Turkish war-vessels were cruising off the coast; but their intention was misunderstood, and the *Dolphin's* course was continued towards the Cabo di Paula, westward of the Gulf of Cagliari.

On the 12th of January, at four o'clock in the morning watch, they discovered, with doubt and alarm, a large ship steering towards them. She proved to be a sattie, or Turkish craft, which Captain Nicholls describes as being "much like unto an argosy, of a very great burthen and bigness," and manned by armed men. Perceiving that she was endeavouring to get between the *Dolphin* and the island of Sardinia, the master sent a seaman into the maintop "with his perspective glass," from where he saw five other vessels coming up before a south-west breeze.

"He perceived them to be Turkish men-of-war, the first of them booming by himself before the wind, with his flag in the maintop and his sails gallantly spread abroad. After him came the admiral and vice-admiral, of greater burden than the first;

after him two more - the rear-admiral, larger than ail the rest, and his companion."

Their ports were open, and it was evident they were bent on hostility and mischief; so the *Dolphin* cleared away for action. Powder and shot were served out for the guns; the crew armed themselves and stood to their quarters, while the captain harangued them in the following terms from the poop:-

"Countrymen and fellows! You see into what an exigency it has pleased God to suffer us to fall. Let us remember that we are but men, and must of necessity die, where, when, and how, is of God's appointment; but if it be His pleasure that this must be the last of our days, His will be done; and let us, for His glory, our souls' welfare, our country's honour, and the credit of ourselves, fight valiantly to the last gasp ! Let us prefer a noble death to a life of slavery; and if we die, let us die to gain a. better life !"

He then assured those who might survive that, if maimed, they should be maintained as long as they lived, and be secured from want, adding, "Be therefore resolute, and stand to it, for here there is no shrinking. We must be either free men 01 slaves. Die with me, or if you will not, by God's grace, I shall die with you!"

He brandished his sword; the crew responded by loud cheers, and the trumpets were sounded, as he was assailed in succession by the sattie and the five other Turkish ships, the size and strength of which vary in the two accounts, but are given thus by Captain Schomberg in his "Naval Chronology:"Two of 300 tons, 28 guns, and 250 men each; one of 200 tons, 24 guns, and 250 men; two of 200 tons, 22 guns, and 200 men each. In the sattie were said to be 1,500 men.

The leading Turkish ship got to windward of the *Dolphin*, one of whose crew was killed by the first shot from her; and in the fight that ensued, her heavy guns so battered and beat down the bulwarks of the *Dolphin* "that," says Nicholls, "we used our guns clear of the ports," as she was all exposed and open. But so bravely fought the crew of the little English ship, that the ordnance of the Turk was dismounted, nearly half her crew were slain, and the officers were seen beating the others with their scimitars to keep them to their duty. Moreover, the *Dolphin* had given her many dangerous shots between wind and water.

By this time she was laid aboard by the 200-ton ship, the captain of which proved to be an English renegade, named Walsingham. He fought his way over her larboard quarter at the head of a gang of ferocious desperadoes, armed with sabres ("which were called faulchions"), hatchets, and half-pikes. The conflict on the poop continued for half an hour, during which the Turks strove to tear up the "nail-board and trap-hatch j "but the well-directed fire from a murderer in the round-house abaft the mainmast swept them away and cleared that portion of the ship; while theirs was plied by cannon, musketry, and another murderer, that was planted in the trap-hatch, till her hull was shot through and through. She fell away astern, receiving a parting broadside as she passed, and lay to, that her leaks and shot-holes might be plugged; and this ended "Walsingham's part in the fight," which the Sardinians on the shore gathered in numbers to see.

And now the shattered *Dolphin* was assailed by two other Turks, of 300 tons each, one of which was commanded by another renegade, named Kelly, probably an Irishman, who carried his flag in the maintop, while the other's ensign was hoisted at the fore. Ranging close alongside, one boarded her on the starboard quarter, the other on the larboard, or, as it is now called, port side. They poured in "thick and threefold, with their scimitars, hatchets, half-pikes, and other weapons," and with loud shouts and yells of fury and defiance. They succeeded in tearing down the British flag; but the steward of the *Dolphin* shot the Turk who had it, and he was flung into the sea, while the flag remained on deck. After a conflict maintained for an hour and a half, by sweeping the deck with the murderers, and the vigorous use of their weapons, the ship was again cleared, and the Turks were compelled "to lay their ships by to stop their leaks, for they had been grievously torn and battered;" but the *Dolphin* was not yet free, for she was almost immediately assailed by "two more of Captain Kelly's ships."

But notwithstanding this overwhelming force, that the *Dolphin's* crew was lessened by death, and that nearly all who were left to fight did so covered with wounds and blood, "we shot them quite through and through," says Nicholls, "and laid him likewise by the lee, as we had done the others before." But they were boarded again by the other ship, on the starboard quarter, and summoned to yield, with promises of quarter, liberty, and half the cargo. To these offers no attention was paid; by pike and sword they were all tumbled overboard, and the ship again cleared, but ere this was achieved the *Dolphin* caught fire, balls of burning matter being tossed into her by the enemy. One of these lighted in the basin of the surgeon, as he was in the act of dressing the wounds of the master, who, though injured in both legs, had still to stand by the tiller, and steer.

The fire was extinguished, and the sorely-battered *Dolphin* crept in shore, and was about to anchor, when another ship bore down to attack her.

Her appearance so alarmed Nicholls, that he slipped or cut his cable and ran into the roadstead of Cagliari, and took shelter between the two forts whose signals he had some time before disregarded. There he remained for five days repairing damages, attending to the wounded, and burying the dead on shore; for, after all this boarding and cannonading, his loss was only seventeen killed, but all the survivors were more ox less injured.

These Turks were doubtless corsairs; as Nicholls says that three of their captains were Englishmen, who came "to rob and spoil upon the ocean, and their names were Walsingham, Kelly, and Sampson. After encountering a dreadful tempest, during which one of her wounded men died and was cast overboard, in the middle of February the *Dolphin* came safely to anchor in the Thames.

- C H A P T E R   X -

SEA-FIGHT OFF TOULON, 1744

W HEN THE alliance between France and Spain was
fully concluded at Fontainebleau, the admirals of
their combined fleets which lay in the harbour of
Toulon resolved to give battle to that of Britain.

While Admiral Thomas Matthews, who commanded the
latter - an old, distinguished, and ultimately most ill-used officer
- was at the Court of Turin on the public service, he received
tidings that a French squadron, consisting of eleven sail of the
line and ten frigates, had sailed from Brest, for the purpose of
forming a junction with the squadron under Admiral de Court
at Toulon, and thereby to favour the escape of the Spanish fleet,
which had been for some time blocked up in that port.

He immediately repaired to Villafranca; and on the 3rd of
January he joined the fleet under Vice-Admiral Lestock, in
Hyeres Bay, eleven miles eastward of Toulon. The fleet consisted
at this time of sixteen sail of the line, and four fifty-gun ships;
but a few days after he received a reinforcement, and ultimately
his force consisted of fifty-four sail, carrying 2,680 guns, and
18,805 men-All those vessels, however, did not take a part in
the subsequent action.

On the 9th the combined fleets were seen standing out of the
roadstead of Toulon, and forming in order of battle as they came.
At ten o'clock Admiral Matthews threw out the signal to weigh
anchor, and to form the line of battle ahead. The British fleet
continued plying to windward, between the mainland and the
group of sterile islets named Porquerolles, Portcros, Bagneaux,
and Titan, called of old the Isles d'Or; but the confederate fleets
not evincing any disposition to bear down, Admiral Matthews
returned to his anchorage in the Bay of Hyeres, which is

overlooked by an ancient castle and steep old town of that name on the slope of a hill.

All next day the fleets manoeuvred in sight of each other, and stood out to sea in a line abreast, without exchanging shots.

On the 11th, Admiral Matthews began to suspect that M. de Court had in view the decoying of the British fleet towards the mouth of the Straits, where there was a probability of his being joined by the expected squadron of Brest. The moment this suspicion crossed the mind of Matthews, he resolved to bring the French and Spaniards to close action at once. Irrespective of frigates and fire-ships, the van, centre, and rear divisions of the enemy consisted of 28 sail, carrying 1,832 guns, and 17,430 men.

The first was led by M. de Gabaret, the chef d'escadre; the second by De Court, in *La Terrible*, 74; the last by Don Navarro, Rear-Admiral of Spain, in the *Royal Philip*, 1T4 guns. His captain bore the Irish name of Geraldine.

Admiral Rowley led the British van, in the *Barfleur*, 90; Matthews the centre, with his flag flying on the *Namur*, 90; Admiral Lestock led the rear, in the *Neptune*, 90. But the latter officer kept two full leagues to windward, by which means twelve sail of the line, two frigates, and a fire-ship "were of no use except to intimidate."

At half-past eleven the signal to engage was hoisted on the *Namur*, which bore down upon the Spanish admiral, attended by the *Marlborough*, 90 guns, commanded by Captain James Cornwall, and by one o'clock the battle began. But while it continued, M. de Court, in his anxiety to reach the Brest squadron, made sail and lay-to by turns, so that the British could not engage his ships in proper order; and as they outsailed ours, Matthews feared they might escape him altogether if he waited for the division of Admiral Lestock, who purposely, as the sequel proved, lagged far astern, leaving the brunt of battle to be maintained by the van and centre.

In coming into action the *Marlborough*, amid the smoke, drove so far ahead that Matthews was compelled to fill his sails to prevent her coming on board of him. There was but little wind, with a heavy ground swell, which rendered the gunnery practice on both sides somewhat ineffective: yet the "London Magazine" for 1744 states that early in the engagement the masts and rigging of the flag-ship were much cut up and disabled; that Admiral Matthews "hoisted his mizzen-topsail to prevent the spars and rigging tumbling about their ears;" and that this "hindered the working of the ship (though he reeved new braces three times), so that he could not give the assistance "to Captain Cornwall that was requisite. This officer had both his legs carried away by a cannon-shot, which killed him on the spot. His nephew, a first lieutenant, was also killed j another, named Frederick Cornwall, had an arm torn off by a ball, but died an admiral in 1786. She had forty-three men killed and ninety wounded.

It is also stated that the French gunners were most expert, as they had been trained for the previous three months by daily target-practice; and that the *Marlborough's* mainmast was swept away "by the board, as if it had been a twig," while Matthews' mainmast and bowsprit were shot through and through, the former having only two shrouds left to support it."

The ships were now engaged at pistol-shot distance, but as the enemy fired chiefly at our masts and rigging, in their anxiety to escape, the admiral had only, according to one account, nine men killed and forty wounded; by another, sixty casualties in all. The flag-captain, John Russell, had an arm shot away, and afterwards died of the wound.

By four in the afternoon the towering three-decker of Don Navarro was quite disabled, and, according to the "London Magazine," bore away out of the action, under all the sail that could be set upon her.

"The fight," says Smollett, "was maintained with great vivacity by the few who engaged. The *Real* (*El Royal Philip ?*) being disabled, and lying like a wreck upon the water, Matthews sent a fire-ship (the *Anne*, galley) to destroy her; but the expedient did not take effect. The ship ordered to cover this machine did not obey the signal, so that the captain of the fire-ship was exposed to the whole guns of the enemy. Nevertheless, he continued to advance until he found the vessel sinking, and being within a few yards of the *Real*, he set fire to the fusees. The ship was immediately in flames, amid which he and his lieutenant, with twelve men, perished." He was a skilful Scottish seaman, named Mackay.

This was also the miserable fate of a Spanish launch, which had been manned by fifty seamen, to prevent the fire-ship from running on board the *Real*.

Though Admiral Lestock lingered in a manner so unaccountable, and some captains neglected orders, Admiral Matthews, in this most confused action,, was nobly supported by the *Marlborough* which, after the captain's and first lieutenant's fall, was fought by Lieutenant Neuceller with dauntless intrepidity; by the *Norfolk*, 80 guns, Captain the Honourable John Forbes, son of Earl Granard and by the *Princess Caroline*, 80 guns, Captain Osborne.

Captain (afterwards Sir Edward) Hawke, in the *Berwick*, 70 guns, observing that *El Poder*, a Spanish sixty-gun ship, commanded by Don Roderigo Euretia, maintained a heavy fire on several of our ships, which were unable to make any effectual return, gallantly bore out of the line and brought her to close action. By his first broadside he dismounted seven of *El Poder's* lower-deck guns, and killed twenty of her men; soon after he shot away all her masts close by the board, on which she struck her colours, and became the prize of the *Berwick*.

The *Norfolk* beat the *Constante*, a Spanish seventy-gun ship, commanded by Don Augustino Eturagio, completely out of the line, but was too much disabled to pursue her. The "London Magazine "says that "the *Cambridge*, of Lestock's division, now came up, and began to fire at five ships with which the *Rupert* and *Royal Oak* were engaged. Two ships, it is said, were brought into action by their lieutenants, against the consent of their captains, whom they confined," an almost incredible story; and the writer adds that Admiral Matthews, during the hottest part of the battle, "stood on the quarterdeck, or arms-chest, making use of his spy-glass, as coolly as a beau in a playhouse, even while a double-headed shot carried away the place he leaned on."

Admiral de Court, who had been engaging Rear-Admiral Rowley, on seeing the disabled condition of Don Navarro's ship, came with his squadron to assist the Spaniards; but Rowley tacked to pursue him, and just about that time - eight in the evening - Admiral Matthews hauled down the signal for battle, and darkness put an end to the conflict. By this time his flag-ship was so shattered that he repaired on board the *Russell*, 80 guns; and *El Poder*, with her prize-crew, being unable to keep up with the fleet, was retaken in the night by the French squadron.

By daylight next morning the enemy's fleet was observed to leeward, going off with all their disabled ships in tow. Admiral Matthews threw out the signal for a general chase, and then to draw into line of battle abreast. Seeing that the British fleet was fast coming up with them, the enemy cast off *El Poder*, set her on fire, and she shortly after blew up. After five in the evening the wind died away; and as there was then no prospect of coming up with the flying enemy, the fleet brought to.

On the morning of the 13th, Admiral Matthews signalled to Admiral Lestock to give chase to twenty-one sail of the enemy that were in sight to the south-westward. The vice-admiral came fast up with them; and had not Matthews signalled to recall the chase, the enemy must either have cast off their crippled ships or risked a general engagement.

The reason assigned by Admiral Matthews for this change of plan was, "that had he continued the pursuit he might have been drawn too far down the Mediterranean, and, in that case, have left the coast of Italy unprotected, and deviated from his instructions." The fleet kept the sea a few days longer and on its arrival at Port Mahon, Admiral Lestock was put under arrest and sent home to England.

Exclusive of those who perished so miserably amid the flames of the fire-ship, the total loss of the British in this unfortunate and indecisive action was 277. Captain Godfrey, of the Marines, was killed on board of the ship of Captain Cornwall, to whom a handsome monument was erected in Westminster Abbey.

A letter from the *Rupert*, says, "Upon the whole it was a confused running action; but sixteen English ships did engage; and another from the *Norfolk* says, bitterly, "Thus did fate, misconduct, and backwardness contribute to the easy escape of the enemy."

The slaughter on board the combined fleets was very great. The Spanish flag-ship had no less than 500 men killed or wounded; the *Neptune*, 200; the *Isabella*, 80 guns, Don Ignacio Dutabil, 300; and all the other ships were in the same proportion. Among the officers killed were Don Nicholas Geraldine; Don Enrique Olivarez, captain of the *Neptune*, and his first lieutenant. Two wounds were received by Admiral Navarro, who immediately on his return to port, complained so bitterly to the Spanish Ministry of the conduct of M. de Court, in not seconding him sufficiently, that the King of France superseded that officer, then in his eightieth year, in command of the fleet.

In England, Admiral Lestock became in turn the accuser of Admiral Matthews, his superior.

"Long before the engagement," says Smollett, their contemporary, "these two officers had expressed the most virulent resentment against each other. Matthews was brave, open, and undisguised; but proud, imperious, and precipitate. Lestock had signalised his courage on many occasions, and perfectly understood the whole discipline of the navy; but he was cool, cunning, and vindictive. He had been treated superciliously by Matthews, and in revenge took advantage of his errors and precipitation. To gratify this passion he betrayed the interest and the glory of his country; for it is not to be doubted but that he might have come up in time to engage, and in that case the fleets of France and Spain would in all likelihood have been destroyed: but he intrenched himself within the punctilios of discipline, and saw with pleasure his antagonist expose himself to the hazard of death, ruin, and disgrace. Matthews himself, in the sequel, sacrificed his duty to his resentment, restraining Lestock from pursuing and attacking the combined squadrons on the third day after the engagement, when they appealed disabled and in manifest disorder, and must have fallen an easy prey, had they been vigorously attacked."

Many officers were examined at the bar of the House on the subject; a court-martial sat on board the *London*, at Chatham, where several officers were cashiered, and Vice-Admiral Lestock was honourably acquitted; while Admiral Matthews was rendered incapable of ever again serving in His Majesty's navy.

"All the world knew that Lestock kept aloof, and that Mathews had rushed into the hottest of the engagement; yet the former triumphed on his trial, and the latter narrowly escaped the sentence of death for cowardice and misconduct. Such decisions," adds Smollett, himself once a naval officer, "are not to be accounted for, except from prejudice and faction."

OFF BELLE-ISLE, 1745

I N THE summer subsequent to the battle off Toulon, there ensued a very obstinate engagement between a French and British ship, which chanced to encounter each other in the latitude of 47 degrees 17 minutes north.

The former was the *Elizabeth*, a sixty-eight-gun ship, commanded by Captain d'Ean, having in convoy Prince Charles Edward Stuart; the latter was the *Lion*, a sixty-gun ship, commanded by Captain Piercy Brett, the same officer who stormed Paita in Anson's expedition. On the 22nd of June, the prince had embarked on board of a vessel named the *Doutelle*, 18 guns, at St. Nazaire, near the mouth of the Loire, to commence the memorable rising which ended at Culloden. He had with him a small retinue, known in Scotland now as "The Seven Men of Moidart," viz.: the Marquis of Tullibardine, whose younger brother, by his attainder, now enjoyed the dukedom of Athole; Sir Thomas Sheridan; Sir John Macdonald, an officer in the Spanish service; Kelly, an Episcopal clergyman; Prancis Strickland; Angus Macdonald, brother of Kinloch Moidart; and a Mr. Buchanan.

At Belle-Isle they were joined by the *Elizabeth*, on board of which the young prince had placed his warlike stores, 1,500 fusees, 1,800 French broadswords, 20 field-pieces, and other munitions; but the two vessels had barely put to sea when the *Lion* hove in sight.

Captain D'Eau immediately went on board the *Doutelle*, and requested Walsh, an Irish refugee, who commanded her, to assist him in attacking the British ship; but Walsh, influenced by natural solicitude for the prince's safety, declined. The *Elizabeth* in consequence commenced the attack alone.

Ranging alongside of each other, these two vessels, which were very nearly equal, though the *Elizabeth* had 700 men on board, began a close, obstinate, and bloody engagement, which lasted fully five hours, by which time both ships were so disabled, and their decks so encumbered by killed and wounded men, by dismounted guns, splinters, and fallen spars, that they each crept away, one towards England, and the other towards France, where the *Elizabeth* reached Brest in a sinking state. The "History of the Present Rebellion, by J. Marchant, London, 1747," states, that she had "lost her captain, 64 men killed, and 146 wounded dangerously; and that there was on board this ship £400,000 sterling, and arms for several thousand men," an exaggeration, like everything written by the Whig pamphleteers of the day.

Another large British ship had given chase to the *Doutelle*, which, however, escaped by her superior sailing, and reaching the Hebrides, landed the prince disguised as an Irish priest, on the island of Eriska, where the people received him with open arms as the son of their exiled king.

The disaster of the *Elizabeth* was, however, a great misfortune to him, as he thus lost all his arms and stores, with above 100 able officers who were to serve on the Scottish expedition. Had she reached the Highlands in safety, her guns would speedily have reduced Fort William, which was situated amidst the clans who were loyal to the House of Stuart; and such a conquest would have drawn to the field many who now remained irresolute and aloof.

- C H A P T E R   X I I -

EXPEDITION TO MORBIHAN, 1746

I N THIS year the wigs of the soldiers were abolished, and all whose hair was long were ordered to "tuck it up under their hats." All officers were to mount guard in queue wigs, or with their hair tied. Brown cloth gaiters were adopted by the privates; and in the colouring for the belts, one pound of yellow ochre was mixed with four pounds of whiting.

In the September of 1746 a secret expedition was fitted out for the coast of France.

The Government had originally intended it for the French possessions in America. A body of troops, consisting of the 1st battalion of the Royal Scots, the 15th, 28th, 30th, 39th,'and 42nd Highlanders, 200 of the artillery train, matrosses and bombardiers, was placed under the command of General the Honourable James Sinclair, son of the Master of Sinclair, who was attainted after the battle of Sheriffmuir. He was an officer who had entered the service in the reign of Queen Anne, and had served with distinction in the Scots Foot Guards, under the Duke of Marlborough. In 1734 he was colonel of the 22nd Regiment, in which the father of Laurence Sterne was then serving as a captain; and he was a general in the year of Culloden, but served with the army in the Netherlands.

The forces embarked at Portsmouth for Cape Breton, and were twice driven back by adverse winds; hence ultimately their destination was suddenly changed for a descent on the coast of France. Accordingly, the army was reinforced by the 3rd battalion of the 1st, and 2nd battalion of the Coldstream Guards, under General Fuller, making the entire strength 8,000 men.

"Early last Wednesday," says the *Westminster Journal*, "the two battalions of Guards, consisting of 2,000 men, met on Great Tower Hill, whence they marched to the King's Stairs, on Tower Wharf, where they embarked. His Royal Highness the Duke of Cumberland was present at their going aboard, and spoke to every man as he passed with the greatest freedom."

The naval portion of the armament, under the rival and enemy of Matthews, Admiral Lestock, consisted of the *Princess*, 74, Captain John Cock burn; the *Edinburgh*, 70, Captain Thomas Cotes, and fourteen other vessels, carrying in all 669 guns, with thirty transports.

On the 19th of September the squadron, with the troops on board, was close in on the coast of France, with special orders to destroy Port l'Orient, where the French East India Company fitted out their ships, and deposited the greater part of their stores and merchandise. Its trade was then very flourishing; its harbour was large and secure, easy of access, and sufficiently deep to float large ships.

That evening our fleet came to anchor in Quimperlé Bay, on the Isolle, twelve miles northward of L'Orient, and immediate preparations were made for landing; and though 2,000 infantry suddenly made their appearance, it was rapidly effected by the Guards and Highlanders, from whom the enemy, being probably militia, fled as the boats approached the shore.

The whole force, with the artillery, now disembarked, and in two columns advanced into the country. Some militia fired upon them from the woods. On entering the village of Pleumeur, they were fired on from the houses, which were soon set in flames. On the 22nd they were before L'Orient, when the governor sent a flag of truce, and proposed surrender on certain conditions. These were rejected on the 24th, by which time one mortar battery and two twelve-gun batteries were erected and armed On the 28th the French troops made several sallies, "in one of which," says Stewart of Garth, "they assumed the garb of

Highlanders, and approached close to the batteries. On being discovered, they were saluted with a volley of grape shot, which drove them back with precipitation, followed by those whose garb they had partly assumed."

The cannonading, which had done considerable damage to the town, ceased in the evening; and General Sinclair began to perceive that he bad not sufficient force to attempt its reduction by assault Smollett states that he had neither time, artillery, nor forces sufficient for such an enterprise, though the engineers predicted that they would lay the whole place in ashes in twenty-four hours; but that all his cannon were mere field-pieces, "and he was obliged to wait for two iron guns, which the sailors dragged up from the shipping. Had he given the assault on the first night, when the town was filled with terror and confusion, and destitute of regular troops, in all probability it would have been easily taken by escalade; but the reduction of it was rendered impracticable by delay."

The ramparts had been armed with cannon taken from the ships in the harbour; new works had been raised with great industry, and the garrison had been reinforced by regular troops. Others were mustering elsewhere, so that the slender British force of 8,000 men bade fair to be surrounded and cut off in an enemy's country; and now Admiral Lestock sent repeated messages to the general to the effect "that he could no longer expose the ships on an open coast at such a season of the year."

General Sinclair consequently abandoned the siege, after holding several Councils of War, and spiking his mortars and the two heavy iron ship-guns, he retreated to the seaside in good order, and re-embarked on the 30th; but the troops had undergone considerable hardship during the few days they had been on shore.

It was at first resolved to proceed to Ireland; but during the re-embarkation of the troops, Admiral Lestock, on the 1st of

October, received a letter from Captain Leke, of the *Exeter*, 60 guns (who had been sent to sound Quiberon Bay), in which he gave so favourable an account of the anchorage that the admiral, notwithstanding the adverse opinion of a Council of War, resolved to proceed with the fleet and army to that place. The town of Quiberon, in Morbihan, is situated on a long narrow peninsula of the same name, which, with some islands, forms one of the largest bays in Europe.

With the exception of some of the transports and store-ships, which, by stress of weather, had been compelled to bear away for England, on the 2nd the armament came to anchor off Quiberon; when they found that on the preceding day Captain Leke, in the *Exeter*, with the *Pool* and *Tavistock*, sloop, the one of 44 and the other of 10 guns, had engaged in the bay and in sight of the town a French sixty-four-gun ship, *L'Ardente*, and forced her on shore, where she was afterwards burned. She belonged to the Duke d'Anville's squadron, and had just returned from America in great distress.

Another landing was at once resolved on. Lieutenant-Colonel John Munro went on shore with 150 of the Black Watch, and took possession of the long isthmus; while General Sinclair, with the rest of the Highlanders and the 1st battalion of the Royal Scots, stormed an eighteen-gun battery, driving out the enemy sword in hand ("Records of the 1st and 42nd Regiments"). They now fortified the isthmus; more troops were landed, and all were cantoned in the villages and farm-houses, from which the scared inhabitants fled.

The next proceeding of the invading force was to assault the fort on the Isle of Houat, which lies six miles north-east of Belleisle-en-Mer, and is three miles long. Several insulated rocks secure it on the south; and on the east, where the fort stood, lie the Bay d'Enfer and Port Navalo. Here the troops landed, and speedily carried the works.

The adjacent isle of Hoedic, which was defended on the south by Fort Pengarde, and on the southwest by a tower, armed with cannon and having a broad ditch, was also reduced. The fortifications were then destroyed, the cannon spiked, the habitations of some 600 fishermen, who occupied both isles, and all the houses on the isthmus, were laid in ruins; after which the troops re-embarked and returned to England, and the fleet came to anchor in the Downs on the 24th of October.

This expedition to the Morbihan, though a somewhat puerile affair, was resented by the entire French nation as one of the greatest insults they had ever sustained; but it demonstrated the possibility of injuring France seriously, by means of an armament vigorously conducted,, secretly mustered, and well-timed. But nothing could be more absurd and precipitate than the duty on which the Ministry dispatched General Sinclair, to invade France with only 8,000 men, without draught-horses, tents, or a proper train of artillery, from a fleet that lay of, an open beach, exposed to tempestuous weather, in the most uncertain season of the year.

General Sinclair was subsequently employed as Ambassador to the Courts of Vienna and Turin, with Hume, the historian, as his secretary, in which capacity the latter wore a military uniform. On the death of his brother, the general became Lord Sinclair, in the peerage of Scotland, and died at Dysart, in Fifeghire, in 1762.

CAPE FINISTERRE, 1747

THE NAVAL transactions of the year 1747 were more favourable to Great Britain, and more brilliant than any others during the war which arose out of the Pragmatic Sanction. Beyond all example was her success, but more advantageous perhaps than glorious, as she had manifestly the superior force in every engagement.

The *London Gazette* of May 16th records that the British and French fleets encountered each other in the beginning of the month off Cape Finistère, on the Galician coast, and so called from its having been deemed before the discovery of America the western extremity of the globe.

Led by Admiral, afterwards Lord, Anson, and Sir Peter Warren, who had displayed great bravery at Louisbourg, in 1745, the British fleet consisted of seventeen sail, including one fire-ship, the whole mounted with 930 guns. Eleven of Anson's vessels were sail of the line, and his blue flag was hoisted on board the *Prince George*, 90 guns; Sir Peter Warren, as Rear-Admiral of the White, was on board the *Devonshire*, 66 guns.

The French squadron was under the Marquis de la Jonquiere and M. de St. George, and consisted of only thirty-eight sail (of these were afterwards taken six), ranging from seventy-four to forty-four guns, having in all battery to the number of 344 pieces of cannon, and manned by 2,819 seamen and marines.

There was thus a considerable disparity of force; but it should be- borne in mind that in Anson's squadron the *Namur*, *Devonshire*, *Yarmouth*, *Defiance*, *Pembroke*, *Windsor*, *Centurion*, and *Bristol*, all, however, line-of-battle ships, alone engaged the enemy.

The French admirals had under their convoy thirty valuable ships, laden with stores and merchandise, bound for America and the East Indies.

Every war had conduced to add to the skill, strength, and efficiency of the British navy. In 1734 by royal proclamation, all British seamen serving foreign powers were recalled for home service; in 1740 an Act was passed to prevent the press-gangs from seizing seamen who were above fifty years of age; and in January, 1746, the Parliament voted 40,000 seamen and 12,000 marines for the naval service. In the following year a uniform clothing was first appointed to be worn by admirals, captains, lieutenants, and midshipmen. The idea of it is said to have been first suggested by George II, when accidentally meeting the Duchess of Bedford (Diana, daughter of Charles Earl of Sunderland, and grand-daughter of John Duke of Marlborough) on horseback, in a riding-habit of blue faced with white. He commanded the adoption of those colours, but the order was never gazetted, though a subsequent one, in 1757, distinctly refers to it; hence we may assume that in the battle off Cape Finistère, on the 3rd of May, 1747, the uniform which became so identified with the naval glories of later years was for the first time worn under fire.

Frampton's Regiment, now the 30th Foot, served as marines on board the fleet on this occasion, "and received the approbation and thanks of both admirals for their general behaviour."

On the British squadron coming in sight, the war-ships of the Marquis de la Jonquiere immediately shortened sail, triced up their ports, and promptly prepared for action, forming line of battle; while the store-ships, under the protection of six; frigates, bore on their course with all the sail they could carry.

The British squadron had also formed line of battle as it drew near the enemy; but Sir Peter Warren, perceiving that the latter were beginning to sheer off as soon as the convoy had attained a considerable distance, advised Admiral Anson to haul in the signal to form line, and hoist that for giving instant chase and engaging, otherwise the whole French fleet might escape them under favour of the night.

The suggestion was at once adopted. All sail was made in pursuit; and about four in the afternoon, when the sun was shining redly on the mountain peak called the Nave- of Finistère, Captain Denis, in the *Centurion*, 50 guns, brought the sternmost ships to action.

Vessel after vessel now shortened sail, and opened fire as those in chase came up; the French fought with equal conduct and valour. The efforts of the *Centurion* were nobly seconded by those of the *Namur*, *Defiance*, and *Windsor*, and they continued pouring round shot and grape into each other, with a blaze of small-arms from the tops, poops, and forecastles, till sunset

Cape Finisterre.

began to steal over the sea; and, overpowered by the weight and force of the British, the French squadron struck their colours at seven in the evening, and were taken as prizes, but not until they had 700 of their men killed and wounded. Among the former was one captain, and the Marquis de Jonquiere, who received a musket-ball in the shoulder. He was in his seventieth year. At the moment he was wounded he had just run through the body a man who was about to strike the colours.

The British had 250 killed and wounded, according to Schomberg; 500 according to Smollett. Among the latter was Captain Thomas Grenville, of the *Defiance*, a sixty-gun ship. He was only in his twenty-eighth year, and was deemed an officer of great promise. He was the nephew of Viscount Cobham, who had been so recently serving at Culloden. "Animated with the noblest sentiments of honour and patriotism, he rushed into the midst of the battle, where both his legs were cut off by a cannon-ball. He submitted to his fate with the most heroic resignation, and died universally lamented" (Smollett). Lord Cobham erected an elegant column to his memory, in the gardens at Stowe. Captain Edward Boscawen, son of Viscount Falmouth, in after years a distinguished officer, was wounded by a musket-shot in the shoulder.

The admiral now detached the *Monmouth*, *Yarmouth*, and *Nottingham* (two sixty-fours and one sixty-gun-ship) in pursuit of the fugitive convoy, with which they came up and took nine sail, three of which were East Indiamen. The rest escaped under cloud of night.

Upwards of £300,000 were found on board the captured ships of war. The treasure was put into twenty wagons, and conveyed under military escort to London. One of the captured ships, *Le Rubis*, 52 guns, was commanded by Macarthy, an Irishman. "I have 4,000 prisoners now on board my squadron," says Anson, in his dispatch to the Duke of Bedford. "The French compute their loss at £1,500,000 sterling; and I believe it must be considerable, for we found £300,000 in specie, and out of the *Invincible* alone took £80,000. They all behaved well, and lost their ships with honour and reputation."

It is related that M. de St. George, in allusion to the names of two of the vessels taken, his own, *L'Invincible*, 74 guns, and *La Gloire*, 44, Captain de Salesse, said, while presenting his sword to Admiral Anson -

"Monsieur, vous vaincu L'Invincible, et La Gloire vous suit."

Anson brought his prizes safely to Spithead; and when he appeared at Court after this victory, the king was graciously pleased to say to him -

"Sir, you have done me a great service. I request you to thank in my name all the officers and private men for their bravery and good conduct, with which I am well pleased."

On the 13th of June Admiral Anson was created a peer of Great Britain, and Sir Peter Warren received the Order of the Bath. He died in 1752, and was buried in Westminster, where a monument was erected to his memory.

The 9th of August subsequent to this victory saw Admiral Sir Edward Hawke, K.B., who had shown such bravery when captain of the *Berwick*, at Toulon, cruising off Cape Finistère, with a squadron of fourteen sail of the line and several frigates, mounting 854 guns, with 5,890 men.

As Rear-Admiral of the Red, his flag was hoisted on board the *Devonshire*, 66 guns. His special orders were to intercept a fleet of French merchant-ships which were expected to sail from the Basque Roads, under the convoy of a strong squadron of vessels of war, commanded by M. de Letendeur.

He had cruised for some time along the coast of Brittany, and at last the French expedition sailed from the Isle of Abe, at the *embouchure* of the Charente; and on the morning of the 14th of October the two squadrons came in sight of each other,

Surrender of M. St. George.

as the dispatches have it, "in the latitude of seventeen degrees forty-nine minutes north, and the longitude of one degree two minutes west of Cape Finistère."

Admiral Hawke instantly hoisted the signal to "give chase," and fired a gun; but on observing several large ships drawing out from the convoy, he changed his plan, and signalled to form line of battle.

M. de Letendeur, whose squadron carried, 556 guns and 5,416 men, at first mistook the fleet of Hawke for some of his own convoy from whom he had been separated in the night; but on nearer approach he discovered his error, and ordered the *Content* and some of the frigates to make their way seaward with all the merchantmen, while he formed the remainder of his force in order of battle.

Hawke instantly detected the design of the chef d'escadre, and, resolving to baffle it, made signal for a general chase. This was at eleven in the forenoon, and in half an hour after the stern-most ships of the French fleet were compelled to shorten sail, and reply to the fire of the *Lion* and *Princess Louisa*, two sixty-gun ships, under Captains Scott and Watson, who sailed right through the squadron, passing along the whole line to the van, exchanging fire with every ship in succession.

These two ships were speedily supported, as the rest soon came up, and a severe general action ensued, and was continued with great obstinacy during the whole afternoon, many vessels having every tier of guns on both sides engaged.

By four o'clock in the afternoon four of the enemy's ships had been so riddled and wrecked by shot that they had struck; and by seven two more had followed their example.

Le Tonnant, the ship of the chef d'escadre, and *L'Intrepide*, commanded by the Count de Vandrieul, the one an eighty, and the other a seventy-four-gun ship, to avoid sharing the fate of their companions, made all the sail they could to escape into the darkening night; but were quickly pursued by the *Nottingham*, *Yarmouth*, and *Eagle*, the crews of which during the chase were refitting their shattered gear, carrying the wounded below, and throwing their dead overboard.

In an hour they were overtaken, and the engagement was renewed, when there was scarcely light by which the men could train their guns; but Captain Philip Saumarez, of the *Nottingham*, a gallant officer, who had served under Lord Anson in the Pacific, being killed by a stray shot, the lieutenant, who succeeded to the command of the ship, hauled his wind, which favoured the escape of the enemy, who gradually disappeared in the offing.

It is undeniable that the French maintained this conflict with the greatest bravery. Every ship that was taken was dismasted, save two, and their casualties were considerable. Of all ranks, they had 800 men placed *hors de combat*. Of these no less than 1.60 were killed on board *Le Neptune*, including her captain, M. de Fromentiére, and she had 140 wounded. The British loss was 154 killed and 558 wounded.

A plain monument was erected to Captain Saumarez in Westminster Abbey.

When the night had fairly set in, Admiral Hawke brought to, to muster his fleet. Next morning, at a Council of War, it was agreed that the pursuit of those vessels which had escaped should, be abandoned.

The admiral then steered for England, and on the 31st of October anchored with his prizes at Spithead.

Soon after he received the Order of the Bath, as a reward for his services.

- C H A P T E R   X I V -

TORTUGA, 1748

I N THE summer of the preceding year, it was ordered that all ships of war from fifty to those of a hundred guns were to carry as many marines as they mounted guns; ships of fifty guns and under were to have ten marines more than the number of their guns; and all sloops of war were to have twenty marines on board.

In the autumn of 1748, Rear-Admiral Sir Charles Knowles, an officer who had greatly distinguished himself when a captain, particularly in the attacks made on the Spanish settlements in the West Indies, was cruising off the Tortuga Bank in the hope of intercepting the Spanish Plate fleet - then the great object of ambition to our seamen - which was expected at the Havanah from La Vera Cruz.

His flag was on board the *Cornwall*, an eighty-gun ship. His squadron consisted of seven sail of the line, carrying 246 guns and 2,900 men.

On the 30th of September, he was joined by the *Lennox*, under Captain William Holmes (who was afterwards killed at the siege of Pondicherry), who reported that the day before, while having under his convoy the homeward-bound trade fleet from Jamaica, he fell in with and was chased by a Spanish squadron of seven ships of war. He added that he ordered the convoy to "shift for themselves," and proceeded to give the admiral earliest notice of the enemy being at sea, doubtless to protect the eagerly looked-for Plate fleet from La Vera Cruz.

This squadron of Spanish ships was commanded by Rear Admiral Spinola, and carried 420 guns, with 4,150 men; consequently his numerical force was superior to that of

Admiral Knowles, who on the 1st of October discovered the enemy ranged in order of battle.

They lay near Tortuga, an island so called by the buccaneers from its fancied resemblance to a tortoise - a rocky and rugged place, covered with lofty trees, some ten miles north from the coast of Dominica.

Rear-Admiral Knowles instantly formed his line and bore down upon the enemy; and at half-past two in the afternoon the battle began. Captain Innes, in the *Warwick*, 60 guns, and Captain Edward Clarke, in the *Canterbury*, also of 60 guns, being at some distance astern, or unable to make up their leeway in time, gave the Spaniards at first the advantage.

Thus in half-an-hour the British flag-ship had her maintopmast and foretopsail-yard shot away, and was otherwise so considerably damaged that she was obliged to quit her place in the line, with her decks encumbered by dead and dying men, and all slippery with blood.

Her place was soon supplied by other ships, whose commanders closed in, maintaining a rapid and heavy cannonade, which very soon drove the *Conquistadore*, 64 guns, commanded by Don de St. Justo, so fairly out of the line that she fell away to leeward of the *Cornwall*.

Rear-Admiral Knowles, in the latter, had by this time repaired the damage she had sustained, and shipped spare spars aloft. Then bearing down upon the *Conquistadore*, he attacked her with renewed fury. Her crew fought bravely and made a most obstinate resistance, but on the fall of St. Justo her flag was struck, and she surrendered, but not until she was dreadfully shattered by round and cross-bar shot.

Meanwhile, Captain Holmes, in the *Lennox*, had been gallantly fighting almost yard-arm and yard-arm with the *Invincible*, 74, which carried the flag of Admiral Spinola, till the arrival of the *Warwick* and *Canterbury* made the action more general and furious; and the roar of so many hundred pieces of cannon, borne by the breeze and water, could be distinctly heard amid the forests and wild volcanic mountains of Dominica.

At eight in the evening the Spanish admiral slackened his fire, and ultimately "hoisting everything that would draw," bore away for Havanah, which was fully 700 miles distant from Tortuga. Along the coast of Cuba the fugitive Spaniards were pursued by Admiral Knowles and his squadron, which fired on them whenever they came within range. However, they all got safe into Havanah, save the *Africa*, 74 guns, the ship of the vice-admiral, who had been killed, and lay dead in his cabin.

Her masts had been shot away, so her crew let her anchors go within a few leagues of the Moro Castle, where she was soon discovered by the inexorable British squadron. To prevent her being taken, the crew set her in flames, and fled in their boats; and just as they were half way between her and the shore, her shattered hull blew up with a hideous crash.

In this protracted action the Spaniards had one admiral, 3 captains, 14 other officers, and 72 men killed, and 197 of all ranks wounded. The British squadron had 180 killed and wounded.

Admiral Knowles still persevered in cruising off the mouth of the Havanah, in hope of intercepting the expected Plate fleet, till there was brought into his squadron a Spanish advice-boat, whose commander informed him that the preliminary articles for a general treaty of peace had been signed in Europe.

At home all parties had grown weary of the useless and protracted war; and the preliminaries for a complete pacification had by this time been fully made at Aix-la-Chapelle, and by the 7th of October hostilities ceased everywhere.

These tidings are said to have caused the deepest dejection on board of Knowles' squadron, whose prospect of the riches they would have shared had the Plate fleet come a day or two sooner now vanished, and he bore up for Jamaica. Some dissensions that had prevailed among the officers of the fleet were now much increased. The admiral taxed some of his captains with misconduct, and a court-martial was the result of their mutual accusations. Those who adhered to their commander, and others whom he impeached, showed against each other the most rancorous resentment.

Smollett states that the admiral himself did not escape without censure. Two of his captains were reprimanded; but Captain Holmes, who had displayed uncommon courage, was honourably acquitted. The admiral fought a bloodless duel with Captain Paulett, of the *Tilbury*; but Captains Innes and Clarke met by appointment in Hyde Park, with a case of pistols each. The former was mortally wounded, and died next morning; the latter was tried and condemned for murder, but received His Majesty's pardon,

On the peace a general reduction of the armaments took place; thus in 1748 all cavalry regiments were disbanded to the present 14th Hussars, and all regiments of infantry to the present 49th Foot.

- C H A P T E R   X V -

SEA-FIGHT OFF CAPE FRANÇOIS, 1757

URING THE war with France our cruisers kept at sea amid all the severity of the winter, for the double purpose of protecting the commerce of the kingdom and annoying that of the enemy. Great were their activity, vigilance, and success; so the trade of France was almost destroyed. A gallant exploit was performed by a Captain Bray, who commanded the *Adventure*, a small armed vessel, which fell in with the *Machault*, a large privateer of Dunkirk, near Dungeness. He ran on board of her, and lashed her bowsprit to his capstan, and after a close, and hot engagement compelled her to submit. A French thirty-six-gun frigate was taken by Captain Parker, in a new fire-ship of much inferior force. Many privateers of the enemy were taken, burned, or sunk, and a vast number of valuable merchant ships were made prizes.

The great success of our ships of war was not confined to the Channel. In the month of October, 1757, there was a brilliant action fought off the island of Hispaniola, between a French squadron and three ships belonging to the fleet which had sailed for Jamaica under the flag of Admiral Cotes.

Captain Arthur Forest, an officer of distinguished merit, with the *Augusta*, 60 guns, had sailed from Port Royal, accompanied by the *Dreadnought*, 60, and the *Edinburgh*, 64, commanded respectively by Captains Maurice Suckling and William Langdon, with orders to cruise off Cape François, on the northern coast of Hispaniola, in sight of Port Dauphin and the headland of Monte Christo. This service they literally performed in the face of the French squadron, under Admiral de Kersaint, which had lately arrived from Africa, to convoy a number of merchant vessels assembling there for Europe.

Piqued to find himself insulted by the presence of these three ships, De Kersaint resolved to come forth and give them battle, to the end that he might either take, or sink, or drive them out to sea, so as to afford free passage for the merchant shipping in his care. Hence he took every precaution to ensure success. His squadron consisted of seven vessels, as follows: - *L'Intrepide*, 74 guns, 900 men, De Kersaint; *La Sceptre*, 74 guns, 800 men, M. Cleveau; *L'Opiniatre*, 64 guns, 680 men, De Moliau; *Greenwich*, 50 guns, 500 men, De Fau-cault; *L'Outarde*, 44 guns, 400 men; *Le Sauvage*, 32 guns, 300 men; *La Licorne*, 32 guns, 300 men. Total, 370 guns, 3,880 men.

Though he had but three English ships to contend with, carrying in all only 184 guns and 1,232 men, he reinforced his squadron by several store-ships, mounted with guns and completely armed for the grand occasion; he took on board seamen from the merchant ships, and a body of troops from the garrison, and on the 21st of October stood into the offing.

The French were no sooner perceived to be under sail, than Captain Forest held a brief Council of War with the two other captains.

"Gentlemen," said he, "you know our own strength, and see that of the enemy; it is far more than double ours. Shall we give them battle ?"

Both officers replied in the affirmative.

"Then fight them we shall!" said he, confidently and exultingly. "Return to your ships, and clear away / or action."

Without further hesitation, the three British men-of-war bore down on the enemy; and as the latter found their honour at stake, were confident in their vast and superior strength, and knew that the coast was lined with, spectators expecting to see them return in triumph, it is but fair to admit that the French fought with even more than their customary bravery.

By nine in the morning the *Dreadnought*, which had first seen the enemy in motion, according to the dispatches, tacked to join her consorts and prepare-for battle. "The *Edinburgh* being to leeward, very properly tacked too, and made a trip to gain her station; while Captain Forest also tacked, reefed his topsails, and made the signal for the line ahead, standing from them under easy sail, just sufficient to preserve the wind, draw them from the coast, and permit them to come up. The French now pursued with great pride, forming a line of seven sail, the tenders plying about their chief; and the whole came up very fast."

The three British ships having fully secured the weather-gage and plenty of sea-room, now hauled up their foresails, letting the enemy see that they awaited them. The moment this

View in Jamaica.

138

little evolution was performed, the French squadron tacked and stood in-shore; on which the three British ships bore down upon them under a press of canvas.

Captain Suckling having requested that he might take the lead, it was accorded to him. "In about a quarter of an hour after, the enemy tacked again, and stood towards us to the northward; forming an extensive line as before, with this difference, that their commodore now led. We continued our course till abreast of the third ship, when the squadron wore in a sweep, the *Dreadnought* still keeping the lead, and lasking (sic) for the headmost ship."

The smaller sails were now furled, and the three vessels stood on under only their foresails and topsails. M. de Kersaint now ordered his frigates out of the line, and sent *Le Sauvage* ahead. "This last action having left their spaces open a little; their commodore very foolishly brought to with his foretopsail to the mast, and lost command of his ship."

When the *Greenwich* (a captured ship), under Captain de Faucault, shot too near the commodore, she nearly fell on board of him. This caused De Kersaint to fill and let fall his foresail, by which *Le Sauvage* was thrown out of her station, and the *Greenwich*, being compelled to back her sails, made a great gap in that part of the line.

At a quarter-past three the French commodore opened fire on the *Dreadnought*, which sprung her luff in order to steer with him as he set sail. The fore-courses were soon after hauled up on both sides, and being then within musket-shot, the fire was given and returned with equal fury.

"Captain Forest, by the opening I have described," wrote Rear-Admiral Cotes to the Admiralty, "was obliged to bear more immediately down upon his opponent, and suffered in the manner the *Dreadnought* might have expected, before she approached near enough to return the enemy's fire. This likewise obliged the

Edinburgh either to have taken a large sweep, or lie as she did for some time at the beginning of the action, without being able to do all the service she could have wished; so that the *Augusta* had now the whole weight (i.e., fire) of the rear to sustain."

The cannonade soon became general on all sides, and the *Dreadnought* getting on the bow of *L'Intrepide*, kept the helm hard-a-starboard to rake her fore and aft, or, if she proceeded, to fall on board of her in the most advantageous position possible; but the commodore chose to bear up, and continued to do so during the whole of the action, till his stately seventy-four was disabled and began to drop astern.

"By this bearing short upon her own ship," continues the dispatch, "those astern were thrown into fresh disorder, from which they never thoroughly recovered; and when *L'Intrepide* dropped (relieved by *L'Opiniatre*, 64), the *Greenwich*, still in confusion, got on board of her, while the *Sceptre* pressing on these, the whole heap were furiously pelted by the *Augusta* and *Edinburgh*, especially *L'Intrepide*, having then flying a signal for relief, lying muzzled in a shattered condition. A frigate soon after endeavoured to take her in tow, but from some cause unknown she was prevented. *L'Outarde*, 44 guns, before this had got into the action, and played very briskly upon the enemy, both upper and lower decks."

The ships were now very close together - muzzle to muzzle in some instances - and we are told that "never was a battle more furious than the beginning. In two minutes there was not a rope or sail whole in either ship. The French use a shot which we neglect, called langridge, which is very serviceable in cutting the rigging."

Captain Forest, on perceiving the shattered condition of the *Dreadnought*, sensible of the damage his own ship, the *Augusta*, had sustained, and satisfied with what the enemy had suffered, thought proper to discontinue the action without pursuing them farther in-shore, since, in the condition of the three British ships, after being subjected to the united fire of so many, it was impossible to take any of them. The lower-masts of the *Dreadnought*, *Augusta*, and *Edinburgh* were all more or less wounded, and the loss of one of these, if any pursuit was attempted, would place the disabled ship completely at the mercy of the enemy's frigates, and also of the *Greenwich*, which was at the close of the action the most serviceable of the enemy's squadron. Captain Forest therefore hailed the *Dreadnought*, as he passed to windward of her, ordering her to make sail, but she continued the engagement for some time after, until she bent some fresh canvas "wherewith to haul up," when her antagonist, *L'Opiniatre*, wore round on the heel and stood away. The *Edinburgh*, after the *Augusta* hauled off, was warmly and closely engaged with the *Intrepide*, *Sceptre*, arid *Outarde*, for nearly half an hour, after which she filled her sails to the yard-heads, at a quarter-past six o'clock, and stood after the *Augusta*; so the battle and the day ended together.

Our losses and damages in the action were as follows: - The *Augusta* had her first lieutenants and eight men killed, twenty-nine wounded, twelve dangerously; her masts, sails, boats, and rigging rendered almost useless. The *Dreadnought* had nine killed and thirty wounded, twenty dangerously. She had her mizzentopmast, mizzen-yard, maintopmast, and top shot away; every other mast, yard, rope, and sail were rendered perfectly unserviceable by the showers of round, chain, and langridge shot that had swept her. The *Edinburgh* suffered least; she had five killed and thirty wounded. She was considerably shattered aloft, and had several shot in her hull.

The *Augusta* and *Dreadnought* were both lightly-metalled ships, and one French seventy-four was considered equal to them both in weight of shot. The French lost, killed and wounded about 600 men.

Our ships were so much damaged that Captain Forest and his consorts were obliged to bear up for Jamaica; and Admiral de Kersaint, finding the sea clear, sailed for Europe with his convoy. In the Channel a dreadful storm overtook his squadron. Many vessels were disabled, and *L'Opiniatre*, *Greenwich*, and *L'Outarde*, having anchored in Conquet Roads, parted their cables, were driven ashore, and totally wrecked. The *Greenwich* had been taken early in the year by a French squadron in the West Indies, when her commander was Captain Roddom.

It is impossible to close this chapter without referring to the future brilliant services of Captain Forest, before the close of the year 1757.

On the 14th of December, Rear-Admiral Cotes being on a cruise off Cape Tiburon with the *Marlborough*, *Augusta*, and *Princess Mary*, when beating up to windward took two French privateers, from the crews of which he learned that a rich convoy was preparing at Port-au-Prince to sail for Europe, under the protection of two armed vessels.

Cherbourg.

To ascertain if this was true, he ordered Captain Forest to cruise off La Gonaive, an island on the western side of Hispaniola; to remain there for two days, and if he could see nothing of this convoy, to rejoin him at Cape Nicholas. Accordingly, Captain Forest, in the *Augusta*, proceeded into the bay of Port-au-Prince, with the intention of executing a scheme which he had conceived in his own mind, and the first craft he saw were two French sloops. Lest they should take him for a British cruiser, he hoisted Dutch colours, and disguised the *Augusta* by spreading tarpaulins over some portions of her hull. Moreover, he forbore chasing. At five in the evening seven more sail were seen steering to the westward; and still to avoid creating suspicion, Captain Forest kept the Dutch ensign flying, and hauled from them till after dark, after which he set all sail and bore towards them. About ten o'clock he sighted two vessels, one of which fired a gun; the other then parted company, and steered-for Leogane, a bay in the island of Hispaniola.

Captain Forest now reckoned eight sail to leeward, near another port named Le Petit Goave. Overhauling the ship which had fired the gun, he hailed her, told her captain who he was, and running out two of his heaviest guns, threatened to sink her with all on board if her crew gave the least alarm. They at once submitted. He put a lieutenant with thirty men on board in place of her crew, with orders to steer for Le Petit Goave, and intercept any of the fleet which might attempt to reach that harbour.

He then made sail after the rest, and by daybreak found himself amidst the whole convoy, on each of which he turned his guns in quick succession. They returned his fire for some time, as all the vessels were well manned and armed.'At length three struck their colours; prize-crews were put on board, and these aided him in securing five other vessels. Thus, by a well-conducted stratagem, was a whole fleet of vessels taken by a single ship, in the vicinity of five harbours, where they could have found shelter and security. They were as follows: - *Le Mars*, 32 guns, 108 men; *Le Theodore*, 18 guns, 44 men; *La Solide*, 12 guns, 44 men; *Le St. Pierre*, 14 guns, 40 men; *La Marguerite* 12 guns, 44 men; *Le Maurice*, 12 guns, 30 men; *La Flora*, 12 guns, 35 men; *La Brilliante*, 10 guns, 20 men; *La Monet*, 12 men.

The total capture amounted to 112 guns, 409 men, and 3,070 tons, The prizes were conveyed to Jamaica, and there sold for the benefit of the crew of the *Augusta* "who may safely challenge history to produce such another instance of success" says Smollett.

Captain Forest served long in the West Indies, and died when commodore, at Jamaica, on the 26th of May, 1770.

OFF BREST, 1778

A BOUT THE time our colonies revolted, formidable preparations were made in France for the sudden invasion of Britain, and a scheme for the execution of such a movement had been carefully prepared ten years before by Grant of Blairfinly, a Jacobite refugee, who was a colonel of French light infantry. According to his plan, 6,000 dismounted dragoons, 40,000 infantry, and 4,000 light troops were sufficient for the purpose; so the year 1778 saw 50,000 Frenchmen marched towards the Channel ports from Havre to St Malo, while England had an equal number of militia under arms.

"The better to arrive at that end (i.e., the conquest of Britain), I believe it would be necessary," added Colonel Grant, "to induce King Charles Edward, who is at Rome, to come forward once more."

The advanced division of the French army was commanded by the Count de Rochambeau, and their main body by the Marshal Duke de Broglie. The great object was to enable the fleet which was lying at Brest, under Count d'Orvilliers, to effect a junction with the Spanish fleet; and an immediate descent on the English coast was threatened, for the purpose of compelling our fleet to keep near it own shores.

The command of the Channel squadron was conferred on Admiral the Hon. Augustus Keppel, who captured Goree, and had distinguished himself at Belleisle and the Havanah; and on the 13th of June he sailed from St. Helen's to cruise in the Bay of Biscay, with a fleet consisting of thirty sail, twenty-one of which ranged from sixty-four to a hundred guns. He had discretionary power to act, for as yet no deed of hostility had been committed by France, though her leaguing with the rebel subjects of the crown might have been deemed sufficient.

On the 17th, when about twenty-four miles southwest of the Lizard, the admiral gave chase to four sail, which were seen to be reconnoitring our fleet; and in the evening the *Milford*, 28 guns, Captain Sir W. Chaloner Burnaby, came up with and brought in the *Licorne*, a French frigate, of 32 guns and 230 men. Admiral Keppel ordered Lord Longford, in the *America*, a sixty-four-gun ship, to stay by her all night. In the morning her crew were observed to be setting fresh sail on her, as if she intended to make off, on which a shot was fired over her, as a hint that she must keep her course with the fleet. In an instant her ports were triced up, her guns run out, and she poured a whole broadside of round shot and small-arms into the *America*, at the very moment when Lord Longford was standing on the poop, remonstrating in a friendly manner with the French captain - for the vessels were within speaking distance.

Four of the *America's* crew fell; and this atrocious piece of bravado was followed by the Frenchman instantly hauling down his colours, probably to save himself from a broadside of the *America*, which must infallibly have sent him to the bottom. However, Lord Longford, with a magnanimity that did him honour, restrained his just resentment, and satisfied himself with ordering the *Licorne* to keep under the stern of Admiral Keppel's ship, the *Victory*.

Meanwhile another French frigate, *La Belle Poule*, had been pursued quite out of sight of the fleet by Captain Samuel Marshal, in the frigate *Arethusa*, a name well known in naval song and story, with the *Alert*, cutter. At night "the saucy *Arethusa*," as the sailors were fond of naming her, came up with *La Belle Poule*. Captain Marshal informed her commander that he had orders to conduct him to the British admiral. With these the French captain peremptorily and contemptuously declined to comply, on which a shot was fired over his deck. As on the previous occasion, the reply was an entire broadside; so both frigates shortened sail, and an obstinate and close engagement ensued for two hours. By this time they had drifted in close to the coast of France, and *La Belle Poule* stood into a small bay, where a number of armed boats came out and towed her into a place of safety; while the *Arethusa*, having had her mainmast carried away, was so disabled that it was with difficulty she was kept from drifting ashore.

In this encounter she had forty-four killed and wounded, and *La Belle Poule* ninety-seven.

On the following day the *Pallas*, a French frigate of thirty-two guns, was overtaken, brought into the fleet, and searched; and from papers found in her and the *Licorne*, Admiral Keppel obtained such accurate information of the strength and destination of the armament at Brest as determined him to return to port for a reinforcement. Accordingly, he came to anchor at St. Helen's on the 27th of June; and with such dispatch were the measures for adding to his force carried out, that he was again at sea by the middle of July, with the addition of ten line-of-battle ships.

In the meantime the French fleet, under Count d'Orvilliers, had crept out of Brest, and immediately on its safe departure general letters of reprisal against the King of Britain and his subjects, grounded on the capture of the *Licorne* and *Pallas*, were issued by the Court of France. As an augur of success, the fleet of D'Orvilliers captured the *Lively*, the same frigate whose guns had been so active at Bunker's Hill. Having been left to watch the motions of the enemy, a fog overspread the sea, and on its clearing she found herself in the centre of them, and had at once to strike her colours.

On the 23rd of July the hostile fleets came in sight of each other.

Admiral Keppel led thirty ships of the line, carrying 2,288 guns and 19,088 men, with nine frigates and fire-ships, in three divisions.

Count d'Orvilliers led thirty-two ships of the line, having on board 2,270 guns, and 21,850 men.

Admiral Keppel threw out the signal for forming line, but his fleet were so much dispersed that night came on before they were in their several stations; and when grey dawn began to steal over the sea and the distant hills of Bretagne, it was found that the French had contrived to get the weather-gage, and that, moreover, they manifested no desire for fighting, their great object being to effect a junction with the Spanish fleet

For four successive days Admiral Keppel continued to pursue the enemy by chasing to windward, seeking to bring them to action. At length, on the morning of the 27th, the British fleet, by redoubling its efforts, by spreading every inch of canvas, and trimming every ship to perfection to profit by a slight variation of the wind in its favour, was enabled "to fetch the enemy."

Suddenly, however, black clouds came banking up from the windward, and a black squall swept over the summer sea, compelling an instant reduction of canvas; and when the weather cleared up, about half an hour after, the French fleet was perceived to have fallen away to leeward, and was now so near the leading ships of the van, commanded by Sir Robert Harland, Bart, (whose father had been a distinguished naval captain of 1704), that a cannonade began, and was furiously maintained, though the late squall had left a great swell upon the sea, and the ships were rolling heavily.

This was maintained for nearly two hours, while the fleets passed each other on opposite tacks. As soon as they had completely passed the firing ceased, and Admiral Keppel wore his ship to bear down once more upon the enemy, and made a signal for the whole to form in line. But observing that the

148

Formidable, 90 guns, and some other ships of the division of Sir Hugh Palliser, Vice-Admiral of the Blue, from the damages they had sustained, were incapable of obeying the signal, and in danger of being cut off as they fell away to leeward, he bore down to join them, and formed his line of battle ahead.

By this time in Palliser's division there were 133 men killed and 365 wounded. Of these, 65 were on board the *Formidable* alone; and many of the vessels had suffered considerably in their hulls and spars.

The result of this luckless battle roused public indignation keenly against Admiral Palliser. The latter retorted upon Keppel, who received the thanks of both Houses for his services; while Palliser, for disobedience of orders, was tried and reprimanded, compelled to resign his seat in the House of Commons, and vacate all his offices.

In 1782 the admiral was created Viscount Keppel, and died in October, 1786.

- C H A P T E R   X V I I -

SEA-FIGHTS OFF USHANT AND GRENADA, 1779

ON THE morning of the 6th of October, 1779, His Majesty's ship *Quebec*, 32 guns, commanded by Captain George Farmer, the cadet of a family of that name long seated at Youghal, in the county of Cork, in company with the *Ramble*, cutter, under Lieutenant George, being fifteen leagues to the south-west of the isle of Ushant, or Ouessant, discovered about daybreak a large French frigate, which proved to be *La Surveillante*, carrying twenty-eight eighteen-pounders and twelve six-pounders, and attended by a heavily-armed cutter.

Captain Farmer was a brave officer, who had distinguished himself on many occasions, and had been the officer commanding at Port Egmont when the Spaniards took possession of the Falkland Islands in 1770, during a time of peace, and the "Universal Magazine" states that "he acquitted himself then, as on every other occasion, with a dignity which did honour to his character and his country."

By ten o'clock in the forenoon the frigates were close alongside of each other; their courses were hauled up, and a furious engagement with cannon, and small-arms from their poops, forecastles, and tops, began. This lasted for three hours and a half till both were totally dismasted, their tops falling into the sea, with the wounded, the dead, and dying in them;

The two ships then fell foul of each other; and as the crew of the *Quebec* were compelled to fire through her fallen sails, which lay in heavy folds over her port-holes, she unfortunately caught fire; and *La Surveillante* was towed out of the danger by the crews of her own boats, otherwise she must have perished too.

In spite of every effort made by Captain Farmer and his crew to extinguish the flames, they could not be suppressed; and they continued to sheet the ship with fire till six in the evening, when she blew up, with her ensign still flying over the stern; and her brave commander, who had been frequently solicited, but in vain, to leave her, perished, with most of his officers and men. Another account states that Captain Farmer threw himself into the sea, when, having been before severely wounded, he was soon drowned.

Previous to this catastrophe, the *Ramble*, cutter, had brought the French cutter to action by eleven o'clock, and continued a close fight with her till two in the afternoon, when the Frenchman set all his canvas and bore away, leaving the *Ramble*, whose sails and rigging were very much cut up, unable to pursue; and Lieutenant George, seeing the disabled state of the two frigates, and that the *Quebec* was on fire, hastened to her relief. But having fallen away to leeward a considerable distance during her share in the battle, and there being but little wind and a heavy swell, she was unable, being crippled aloft, to do more than send a boat to the *Quebec*, and thus saved two midshipmen and fourteen seamen.

Thirteen more were saved by the crew of a Russian vessel, which providentially chanced to be near.

In his dispatch, Lieutenant George mentions incautiously, as a reason for not saving more of the crew of this unfortunate frigate, that the enemy's ship fired on his boat as it passed between the *Quebec* and the cutter. But this circumstance "was afterwards cleared up, much to the honour and humanity of a brave and generous enemy, who, while in the act of towing their ship to windward out of reach of the flames, saved the lives of Mr. Roberts, the first-lieutenant, the second-lieutenant of marines, the surgeon, and thirty-six of the crew."

Lieutenant George evidently, amid the smoke, which, from

the conflagration, covered all the sea, mistook the guns of the *Quebec*, which went off as they became heated, for those of *La Surveillante*.

For the bravery and resolution of Captain Farmer in this frigate battle, his eldest son was created a baronet by George III, on the 26th of October, 1779; and an annuity of £200 per annum was settled upon his widow, with £25 yearly to each of her seven children.

SEA-FIGHT OFF GRENADA

On the 6th of January this year, Vice-Admiral the Hon. John Byron, who had served in the *Wager*, under Anson, in 1740, arrived in the West Indies, with nine sail of the line, and joined Rear-Admiral the Hon. Samuel Barrington, off St. Lucia. After various encounters among the Leeward Isles by single ships, towards the middle of June, a considerable fleet of merchant-men from different parts of the West Indies having rendezvoused at St. Christopher's, Admiral Byron was induced to consider it an object of the greatest importance that they should be convoyed clear of those waters, and escorted safely so far on the way to Britain. Towards the end of the month, he therefore sailed on this duty, with his whole disposable force.

On his return to St. Lucia, on the 1st of August, he received intelligence that the island of St Vincent had been captured by the French and Caribs from seven companies of our regular troops, without a shot being fired; a circumstance ascribed to the dread of a general insurrection among the natives, who had never been reconciled to British rule. He learned further that the French admiral, the Count d'Estaing, on being joined by a reinforcement under M. de Motte Piquet, had still further improved the opportunity of his absence by sailing from Fort Royal, with twenty-six ships of the line, eight large frigates, and a squadron of transports, having on board 9,000 troops, and capturing the island of Grenada, compelling the governor, Lord Macartney, with his little garrison of 150 men, to surrender at discretion, and give up 100 pieces of cannon, 24 mortars, and £40,000 worth of shipping.

A writer in the "Scots Magazine" for that year states that the little force of Macartney was surprised in the dark by a detachment of the Irish Brigade, who, "by speaking the same language, were admitted into the intrenchments as friends, and they immediately overpowered our troops by numbers,"

To attempt the recapture of this place, the most beautiful isle of the Antilles, became now the first object of Admiral Byron, who at once sailed towards it.

At daybreak, on the morning of the 6th of July, the enemy's fleet was seen under sail coming out of St. George's Bay, a spacious inlet on the western side of Grenada, and stretching out to the seaward. Their force could not be exactly ascertained at that time, but their white canvas could be seen distinctly

Grenada.

towering up against the greenness of the high land which overhangs the bay. It consisted of twenty-two large vessels, ranging from *La Languedoc*, 96 guns, to *L'Amphion*, 54, armed in all with 1,568 pieces of cannon, with a vast force of seamen, troops, and marines.

The fleet of Admiral Byron consisted of twenty-one sail of the line, carrying 1,516 guns, with 11,641 men on board, including the 4th and 46th Regiments, acting as marines; but the *Conqueror*, 74 guns, under Rear-Admiral Parker, and four sixty-four-gun ships did not engage. The orders were for the *Suffolk*, 74 guns, under Rear-Admiral Rowley, to lead with the starboard tacks on board, and the *Grafton*, 74 guns, Captain Thomas Collingwood, with the larboard; the *Aridane*, frigate, to repeat signals.

From the manoeuvres of the French admiral, who evidently displayed no desire for battle, and whose ships being faster sailers than ours gave him the advantage, should he be compelled to engage, in the mode of attack; Admiral Byron, whose flag was on board the *Princess Royal*, 90 guns, in the centre of the British line, seeing that D'Estaing meant to avoid him, threw out the signals for a general chase, and for the ships to open fire and form as they could get up.

As the French drew into line of battle, their strength and superiority were plainly perceptible; but as the signal for chase was yet flying on the breeze, together with that for close battle, the action commenced partially about half-past seven in the morning, between Vice-Admiral Barrington (an officer who died at Bath, in 1800), in the *Prince of Wales*, 74 guns, supported by the *Boyne*, *Sultan*, *Grafton*, *Cornwall*, *Lion*, and *Monmouth*, all stately three-deckers, with the whole line of the French fleet, whose very superior sailing enabled it to elude every effort of Admirals Byron and Parker to bring on a close and general, and,- consequently, more equal engagement.

In this unequal conflict between a single British squadron and the entire force of the enemy, the *Grafton*, Captain Collingwood; the *Cornwall*, Captain Edwards; the *Lion*, Captain the Hon. W. Cornwallis (afterwards an admiral); and the *Monmouth*, Captain Thomas Fanshawe, an officer of singular bravery, sustained the whole fire of the French fleet as they passed it on the opposite tack, and were dreadfully disabled.

The *Lion* was so battered and pierced that she was afterwards sunk as unserviceable at St. Lucia. Her captain, Timothy Edwards, had been posted for his bravery in the action with the *Valeur*, and was popularly known in the fleet as "Old Hammer and Nails," from a habit he had of nailing his colours to the mast before going into action. Once he was knocked down by a splinter, and so much stunned that he was supposed to be dead; but on hearing some of the sailors bewailing his fate, he sprang up, crying -

"It's a lie. Stand to your guns and fire away, my lads !"

"The French squadron tacked to the southward about three o'clock in the afternoon,"says the admiral, in his dispatch to Mr. Stephens, "and I did the same, to be in readiness to support the *Grafton*, *Cornwall*, and *Lion*, that were all disabled, and a great way astern; but the *Lion*, being likewise much to leeward, and having lost her main and mizzen-topmasts, and the rest of her rigging and sails being cut in a very extraordinary manner, she bore away to the westward when the fleets tacked, and, to my great surprise, no ship of the enemy's was detached after her. The *Grafton* and *Cornwall* stood towards us, and might have been weathered by the French if they had kept their wind, especially the *Cornwall*, which was farthest to the leeward, and had lost her maintopmast, and was otherwise much disabled; but they persevered so strictly, in declining every chance of close battle, notwithstanding their great superiority, that they contented themselves with firing upon these ships when passing

The French fleet off Grenada.

barely within gunshot, and suffered them to rejoin the squadron without one effort to cut them off. The *Monmouth* was so totally disabled in her masts and rigging, that I thought it proper to send directions in the evening for Captain Fanshawe to make the best of his way to Antigua, and he parted company accordingly."

Captain Robert Fanshawe was an officer who at a future time greatly distinguished himself in the action with the French fleet on the 12th April, 1782.

When Byron's armament was close in-shore, the French colours could be seen flying upon the fort and batteries at St George's Bay, which left him no doubt of the enemy being in full possession of the island; and he did not think it practicable to attempt to dislodge them at that time.

As evening fell Admiral Byron formed up the remaining ships of his fleet in line of battle, fully expecting that the Count D'Estaing would attack him next morning; but during the night that officer having crept into the Grenada coast, and got his squadron under the guns of the batteries, thinking it more prudent to preserve his new conquests than to seek to gather laurels, Admiral Byron proceeded with the fleet to St. Christopher's.

The total number of killed and wounded in our fleet was 529 of all ranks. The greatest number of casualties occurred on board the *Grafton*, which had 35 killed, and 63 wounded. There were four officers in each list. The French loss was very great; the lowest estimate makes it 2,700, of which the slain were 1,200. A slaughter so great was attributable to the large number of troops who were crowded on board, and exposed, helpless, to be decimated at long range by cannon-shot.

- CHAPTER XVIII -
FLAMBOROUGH HEAD, 1779

IN THE autumn of 1779, there was fought a battle between His Majesty's ship *Serapis* and another armed ship against a superior force, and at serious odds; and the conflict took place within sight of Flamborough Head, that magnificent range of limestone rocks which extends for miles along the Yorkshire coast, in some places rising perpendicularly to the height of 150 feet.

It chanced that on the 23rd of September, Captain William Pearson, of the *Serapis*, 40 guns, and the *Countess of Scarborough*, 20 guns, commanded by Captain Percy, being close in with the town of Scarborough, the bailiff of the corporation sent off a messenger by boat to inform Captain Pearson that a flying squadron of the enemy's ships had been seen from the peninsular height on which the old castle stands the day before, and that they were standing under easy sail to the southward. Though the captain had the homeward-bound Baltic fleet with him, he resolved to go in quest of the enemy.

He made a signal for the convoy to bear down on his lee; but though he repeated it more than once, they still kept stretching out from under Flamborough Head till between twelve and one o'clock, in the day, when the headmost ship got sight of the enemy, who was in full chase of them.

The ships of the convoy then tacked, and stood in towards the coast of Yorkshire, letting fly their topsail-sheets and firing guns; while Captain Pearson made all sail to windward, to get in between the convoy and the enemy's men-of-war.

The latter were no other than the squadron of the notorious corsair, Paul Jones, one of the most remarkable naval adventurers of the age. A native of Kirkcudbright, in Scotland, the son of a humble gardener, and originally by name John Paul, he had early evinced a strong predilection for the sea, and ere long became an officer under the Congress, and with a single armed ship, the *Ranger*, kept the whole coast of Scotland and part of England in constant trepidation and alarm; and now, after many delays and disappointments, he had obtained from the French Government the command of the ship *Duras*, 40 guns and 375 men, on board of which he hoisted the American flag, changing her name to *Le Bon Homme Richard*. With a squadron of seven ships, he had sailed from St. Croix on the 14th of August, 1779; and, after being deserted by four of them, he appeared in September in the Forth, opposite Leith, but was prevented by a sudden change of wind from either landing on the coast or attacking the ships of war in the roads, the latter being evidently his chief design. Failing these, he had now come in quest of the homeward-bound Baltic fleet.

At one o'clock his vessels were descried by the look-out man at the masthead of the *Serapis*, and at four they were visible from the deck, and were found to be three large vessels and a brig. The *Countess of Scarborough* being close in-shore with the convoy, Captain Pearson signalled for her to join him, and let the convoy make the best of their way alone.

By half-past five, Captain Percy having joined him, Captain Pearson tacked, and laid the ships' heads in-shore, for the better protection of the now fugitive convoy as long as possible.

The enemy still bearing down, Captain Pearson, says Schomberg, perceived their force to be, not what he had thought at first, but "a two-decked ship and two frigates." By twenty minutes past seven, when twilight was darkening on the sea and the bluffs of Flamborough, the largest ship, which proved to be *Le Bon Homme Richard*, brought-to on the larboard bow of the *Serapis*, within musket-range. As neither of them had hoisted their colours, Captain Pearson hailed, by asking what ship she was.

"The *Princess Royal*" replied Paul Jones, treacherously, or some one else for him, in English, and using the name of a vessel actually in the service.

Dissatisfied with this answer, Captain Pearson asked a few other questions, to which evasive replies were given. He then fired a shot at her. She replied by another, and the American colours were then run up.

As all Pearson's crew we're at quarters, and standing by their guns, a few broadsides were promptly exchanged, after which the Chevalier Jones, as he called himself, backed his topsails, and dropped within pistol-shot of the *Serapis'* quarter. Then, suddenly filling again, he made a resolute attempt to board her, but was driven back by bayonet and pike.

The twilight was deepening fast, and Captain Pearson, in order to get square with the enemy again, backed his topsails; a movement which was no sooner perceived by Jones than he filled, put his helm a-weather, and laid the *Serapis* athwart hawse, where she continued for some little time, the small-arms from the tops, waists, and poops of each ship flashing redly through the dusk the while, till the jib-boom gave way; and then both ships fell round alongside of each other head and stem, so close, that aloft the yard-arms locked and swayed, and below the muzzles of the guns actually knocked against each other, and some of the port-lids were torn off.

In this close situation, almost within arm's length of each other, the action was continued with blind fury long after absolute darkness had settled on the sea; and the red flashing of the cannon was visible to many on the Yorkshire coast till about half-past ten at night.

During that time the *Serapis* was set on fire no less than twelve times, by burning combustibles that were flung on her deck; and it was only with the greatest difficulty and exertion,

160

while the shot swept her deck, that, stumbling over dead and dying men, the crew could get the flames extinguished.

About half-past nine, it chanced that either from a hand-grenade being thrown in through one of the lower-deck ports, or some other accident unknown, a cartridge of powder for one of the guns was set on fire. The explosion was instantly communicated from cartridge to cartridge, and thus blew up every officer and man stationed abaft the mainmast, burning and scorching them dreadfully; and by this dreadful catastrophe all the guns in that part of the ship were useless during the remainder of the action.

All this while it must be borne in mind that the largest of the two frigates was sailing round and round the *Serapis*, raking her with such fatal effect that every man on the quarter and main-decks was either killed or wounded.

At ten o'clock the enemy began to cry for "quarter." Surprised at this, Captain Pearson hailed, asking if they had struck. No answer was given, on which he issued the order -

"Boarders away!"

With pike and cutlass a body of his crew sprang on board; but the moment they were there they discovered that a trap had been laid for them, for a superior force of the enemy were seen crouching in the dark between the guns and under the bulwarks, ready to spring upon them with pikes and pistols.

On this, with a shout of rage, the crew of the *Serapis* retreated to their own ship, and once more flew to their guns. But the remorseless frigate backed her mainyard, while steadily pouring a whole broadside into the stern of the *Serapis*, with the most terrible effect; and the mainmast falling at the same moment rendered Captain Pearson totally incapable of getting a single piece of ordnance to bear upon her in return.

Captain Pearson was now under the necessity, which must ever prove painful and humiliating to a British seaman, of ordering the colours to be struck, on which the firing ceased; and with his first lieutenant he was escorted on board *Le Bon Homme Richard*, where he was received with the courtesy his courage merited, by the famous Paul Jones.

The frigate which had also engaged the *Serapis* was the *Alliance*, 40 guns and 300 men; so every way the contest had been most unequal. Upon Captain Pearson going on board *Le Bon Homme Richard*, he found her in a very distressed condition - her quarters and counter were driven in; the whole of the guns on her lower-deck were dismounted, the carriages having been knocked to pieces by sheer dint of round shot. Her decks were strewn with mangled bodies, and splashed with blood and brains; she was on fire in two places, and had seven feet of water in her hold, where it kept increasing upon them so much that the next day they had to betake themselves suddenly to their boats, as she sunk, with the greatest portion of her wounded on board: and the cries of these poor creatures, as the waves rushed in the lower-deck ports and breaches made by the shot of the *Serapis*, were terrible in the extreme, till the water flowed over her decks, and their voices were silenced for ever.

She had 306 men killed or wounded, only 59 remaining untouched. The loss of the *Serapis* was 117 killed and wounded.

While this obstinate and bloody contest had been waged between the latter and her two adversaries, Captain Percy, in the *Countess of Scarborough*, had been quite as hotly engaged with the *Pallas*, a French frigate of thirty-two guns and 275 men, and the *Vengeance*, 12 guns and 70 men; till, perceiving another frigate bearing down through the gloom, he too was compelled to surrender, after bravely defending the king's ship for more than two hours, and having four-and-twenty killed and wounded.

The enemy carried their prizes into the Texel. Upon Captain Pearson's return to England, His Majesty conferred upon him the honour of knighthood, in consequence of the bravery and vigour of his defence. The Royal Exchange Assurance Company presented him with a piece of plate valued at a hundred guineas, and another of fifty to Captain Percy; while the French were so elated by a victory from which they reaped no honour, that the King of France presented Paul Jones with a superb gold-hilted sword, bearing an appropriate inscription, and, through his Minister, requested the permission of Congress to invest him with the military Order of Merit. He performed in after years many brilliant actions in the service of America and Russia; and, after all, was permitted to close an adventurous and extraordinary life in obscurity and penury, at Paris, in 1792.

RODNEY IN THE LEEWARD ISLES, 1780

THIS YEAR saw our warlike operations so much on the increase all over the world, that ne less than 85,000 men, including 18,779 marines, were voted for the fleet. About this time the new gun called a carronade, or "smasher," came into use for ships and batteries. They were cast at the Carron Iron Works, in Scotland, hence their name, and were the invention of General Robert Melville, an officer who had served under Lord Rollo at the capture of Dominica and elsewhere. They were peculiarly constructed, being shorter and lighter than other cannon, and having a chamber for powder, like a mortar. They were cast in enormous numbers at Carron, and were employed throughout the fighting and mercantile marine of all Europe and America till nearly about the time of the Crimean War. The first of them was presented by the Carron Company to the family of the general, who still preserve it; and an inscription on the carriage records that they were cast for "solid, ship, shell, or carcass shot, and first used against the French fleet in 1779."

During the progress of the war in the West Indies, Sir George Rodney, K.B., an officer who had served with distinction at the bombardment of Havre, in 1759, at the captures of Martinique and Grenada, after defeating Don Juan de Longara and relieving Gibraltar, joined Rear-Admiral Sir Hyde Parker at Gros Islet Bay, in the isle of St. Lucia. There he learned that the enemy's fleet, consisting of twenty-five sail of the line and eight frigates, had for several days been hovering in sight of that beautiful shore, which a traveller has described as "a checkered scene of sombre forests, smiling plains, and towering precipices, with shallow rivers and deep ravines," and where the giant Pitous, or sugar-loaf mountains, are clothed from the waves to the clouds with evergreen foliage.

Sir Hyde Parker, who was afterwards drowned in the *Cato*, when going to command our fleet in the East Indian seas, reported to Sir George that only a few hours before his arrival the French fleet had retired into Fort Royal Bay, in the isle of Martinique.

Rodney hastened the equipment of his armament, and on the 2nd of April appeared off Fort Royal with his whole force, consisting of twenty-three sail, mostly of the line, ranging from ninety to fifty guns, with five frigates, offering the enemy battle; but Admiral the Count de Guichen, Lieu-tenant-General of the Naval Forces of Louis XVI, did not choose to venture out, notwithstanding that his fleet was far superior in force. Sir George, after two days of defiance, left a squadron of copper-bottomed ships to watch his motions, and returned with the rest to the anchorage in Gros Islet Bay.

On the night of the 15th, the French admiral put suddenly to sea; on the following day his fleet was discovered to the north-west of St. Lucia. Sir George Rodney instantly made the signal for a general chase; and by five in the evening the count's force was seen to consist of twenty-three sail of the line, one ship of fifty guns, three frigates, and two other vessels.

On board of these could be seen many troops, some in white uniforms, others in red. The former were companies from the Regiments of Champagne (or 2nd of the French Line), Touraine (98th), En-ghien (100th), Viennois, and Ausenois; the latter, the corps of Dillon (94th) and Count Walsh (of the Irish Brigade), together with the Regiment of Martinique, the Volontaires de Bouillie, and some companies of artillery.

Night coming on, Sir George formed his fleet into line of battle ahead, keeping the while a sight of the enemy, who, by their manoeuvres, evidently wished to avoid a battle; though the count, in his dispatch to the King of France, states that he "employed every manoeuvre that appeared to him most advantageous to draw near the enemy, who had the advantage of the wind, which did not permit him to attack them so soon as he could have wished."

When day dawned the British fleet certainly had the weather-gage; and at ten minutes to twelve the admiral made a signal for every ship to bear down, steer for and engage, yard-arm and yard-arm if possible, her opposite craft in the enemy's line.

On came the British fleet, under a press of canvas; by one the action began, and ere long the roar of 3,400 pieces of cannon, together with small-arms, reverberated over the waves.

Admiral Rodney, in the *Sandwich*, 90 guns, bore into the heart of the French fleet, pouring a dreadful cannonade from his tiers of artillery; his port and starboard guns being both engaged at once, spouting fire and death, as he set a noble example to his officers by crippling and beating in succession the *Couronne*, 80 guns, bearing the flag of M. de Guichen; the *Triomphant*, 80, under Chef d'Escadre the Count de Larde; and the *Fendant*, 74, Captain the Marquis de Vaudrieul, and driving them fairly out of the line; on which the first-named vessel set all her sails and bore right away before the wind, an example which was speedily followed by the whole fleet, the crippled state of some of our ships, particularly the *Sandwich* (after a conflict so unequal with three ships in succession), which for twenty-four hours was with difficulty kept above water, preventing a pursuit. Of this engagement, which lasted till four in the evening, the French give a very different account: - -

"The Count de Guichen was in hopes that the combat would terminate in a more decisive manner, his position to the leeward leaving no resource to force the enemy, who was master, to push on the action with vigour, or to slacken it. The surprise of the

French admiral was great indeed when, at half-past four, he saw Admiral Rodney set his mainsail and haul his wind, which was also done by all his fleet. Half an hour after, the foretopmast of the *Sandwich* was seen to fall. The ship seemed to be much disabled, and it was perceived that the admiral had shifted his flag on board of another. The king's ships kept their lights burning, and made their signals by firing guns; but on the 18th at break of day they saw nothing of the enemy, who were not discovered until the 19th, when they were to leeward."

According to Sir George (afterwards Lord) Rodney's dispatches, every exertion was made to put the fleet in order to pursue the French, of whom they got sight on the 20th, and

Admiral Rodney.

whom they pursued for three successive days. The great object of the Count de Guichen seemed to have been shelter in Fort Royal Bay, Martinique; but finding it impossible to obtain that without another action, he took shelter under Guadaloupe; while Sir George returned to St. Lucia to refit, fill his water-casks, and put ashore his wounded, who were 353 in number, while his loss in killed amounted to 120 - in the former list were nine officers, in the latter six. On the 6th of May Sir George received intelligence that the enemy's fleet had left Guadaloupe, and were seen standing to windward of Martinique. He instantly put to sea, and on the 10th discovered them about nine miles to windward of him, their force being the same as in the preceding action, with the addition of 600 grenadiers, whom the Marquis de Bouillie had embarked on board *La Courageuse*, a thirty-six-gun frigate, commanded by the Chevalier de la Rigoudière.

Still the French admiral studiously eluded coming to general action; but, aware of his superiority in sailing, he frequently bore down upon the British with all his ships abreast in line of battle, and then brought them to the wind again, before he came within range of cannon-shot.

Mortified to find that he could not get to windward of this cautious and vigilant enemy, and thereby force him to fight, on the 15th Rodney signalled his fleet to make "all sail possible on a wind," which led the count to think he was retiring; and this emboldened him, when next he bore down, to come much nearer than he intended. Rodney quietly permitted them to enjoy the flattering delusion, until their van ship had come abreast of his centre, when, by a lucky and sudden shift Of the breeze, which he knew would enable him to weather the enemy, he signalled for the third in command (who then led his van) to tack and beat to windward of the enemy.

The moment this movement was perceived, the French fleet wore, and literally fled with all sail crowded to their trucks, another change in the wind enabling them to recover their advantage. By seven in the evening Captain Bower, in the *Albion*, 74, which had a party of the 5th Foot on board acting as marines, reached the centre of the French line, and opened a furious cannonade, supported by Rear-Admiral Rowley, in the *Conqueror*, 74, and the rest of the van; but as the enemy were still flying under a press of sail and firing as they fled, none of the rest of the British fleet could take part in the action, which was renewed again on the 19th, when the Count de Guichen, seeing that his rear could not escape being engaged, appeared to have taken the resolution of risking a general action.

Lord Cornwallis.

As soon as his van had weathered the British, he bore away along their line to windward, and opened a heavy cannonade, but at such a distance as to do little execution; though by one shot Ensign Curry, of the 5th Foot, was killed; a second mortally wounded Captain Watson, of the *Conqueror*; Lieutenant Douglas, of the *Cornwall*, lost a leg; and an officer of the 87th Foot was severely injured on board of the *Magnificent*. But when the van, under Commodore Hotham (who was afterwards created a peer), closed in with the enemy, they ran out their studding-sails to escape, and sailed so swiftly that by the 21st they were completely out of sight, and after that Rodney steered for Barbadoes.

The total loss of the British fleet in these affairs amounted to 188 killed and 567 wounded; while that of the French was 158 killed and 820 wounded, eleven officers being among the former, and twenty-eight among the latter.

- C H A P T E R   X X   -
DEFENCE OF YORK TOWN, 1781

B
Y THE preparations of General Washington, it soon became evident that they were directed in reality against our army in Virginia. The situation of the Earl of Cornwallis was becoming indeed most hazardous. Washington, at the head of 8,000 American troops, and the Count de Rochambeau, with the same number of French, were rapidly approaching to surround him by land; while the French fleet, under the Count de Grasse, was preparing to blockade him by sea. Hence his lordship selected York Town, at the mouth of the river York, as the best point for at once securing his own troops, and the shipping by which they were attended.

In the month of August the army entered the town, and immediately commenced to fortify it. He determined to occupy the double post of York and Gloucester, on-each side of the river, at a point where it narrows to the extent of about a mile across, being both above and below not less than three in width. To reach this station it was necessary that both infantry and cavalry should be embarked, and conveyed with the artillery and stores up the course of the river. No confusion occurred in this movement; the horses were cast overboard into deep water, but swam ashore without injury.

These operations lasted from the 6th to the 22nd of August, by which date the whole army was assembled; and the morning of the 23rd beheld strong working parties cutting out the line of entrenchments, which the engineers had previously devised.

In the meanwhile the cavalry, with a party of mounted infantry, scoured the open country, and swept it of flour, forage, grain, and other necessaries that a blockade might render useful; and the time had now come in which the tides of war and fortune, which had never run much in our favour since this unhappy strife began, were destined to turn, "and Lord Cornwallis, after long and vigorously prosecuting an offensive strife, was doomed to combat, not for glory, but for existence."

Of the capabilities of the two posts selected on the York river, natural as well as acquired, we find a description in the narrative of one who bore a distinguished part in the strife we are about to relate.

"Gloucester is situated on a point of land on the north side of the York river, and consisted at that time of about a dozen houses," says Colonel Tarleton. "A marshy creek extends along part of the right flank. The ground is clear and level for a mile in front; at that distance stands a wood. The space which it occupies is narrowed by the river on the left, and a creek on the right. Beyond the gorge the country is open and cultivated...... York Town, again, before the war was a place of considerable trade. Great part of the houses form one street, on the edge of a cliff which overlooks the river; the buildings stand within a small compass, and the environs of the town are intersected by creeks and ravines. Different roads from Williamsburgh enter York in several directions, and the main route to Hampton passes in front of it."

Hence the facilities for strengthening the post were ample; and a few redoubts commanding the open country, and securing by cross fires the creeks and ravines, placed it beyond the chances of an assault. Colonel Tarleton proceeds to relate that many houses were demolished, and a chain of connected works formed round the town, with their flanks resting on the river. It was a post, he continues, "in every respect convenient for the King's troops. The right rested on the swamp which covered the right of the town; a large redoubt was constructed beyond it, close to the river road from Williamsburgh. The *Charon* and *Guadaloupe*, two small frigates, were moored opposite to the swamp; and the town batteries commanded all the roads and causeways which approached it."

From the records of the Royal Welsh Fusiliers, we find that the large redoubt in question was constructed by them; and the defence of it was specially entrusted to them by Lord Cornwallis.

Two other redoubts were placed on the right, at the head of the morass, one on each side of the road to Williamsburgh. The centre was protected by a thin wood, which was felled to form an abattis, with the branches thrown outward. A field-work, armed with guns, commanded the Hampton road. Abattis, fleches, and batteries were constructed at every point deemed vulnerable. The distance between the heads of the swamp and creek, which embraced the flanks of the town, did not exceed half a mile. In front of the line, the face of the country was broken near the centre by a morass; and excepting this break, the ground was open for 2,000 yards. At every point the field-guns were placed to the greatest advantage by Captain Rochefort, who commanded that arm of the service.

While these defences were in course of erection, the Marquis de la Fayette took up a position near the Chickahominy river, six miles from Williams-burgh, where he quietly awaited the development of plans to which every day lent a more terrible interest. In furtherance of these, a powerful French fleet, under the Count de Grasse, entered the Chesapeake, and proceeded to block up the York river, after sending 3,000 men to succour the Americans who watched the entrance of the bay. The marquis, on this, broke up his camp, and advanced as far as Williamsburgh, to cut off the water communication with New York.

It was now suggested to Lord Cornwallis, that the best hope for the future of himself and his gallant little army lay in instantly taking the field, but he rejected the proposal, in consequence of a communication from New York, in which Sir Henry Clinton assured him of ample support the moment the fleet of Admiral

Digby arrived on the coast. He, therefore, instead of attacking La Fayette, continued to complete his line of defences. On the 25th of August, Admiral Sir Samuel Hood, with our fleet from the West Indies, arrived off the Chesapeake Bay - a large arm of the sea, between Capes Henry and Charles, on the Virginian coast - and thence proceeded to Sandy Hook, where he was joined by Rear-Admiral (afterwards Lord) Graves, who had five sail of the line; and then took upon him the command of the fleet, which sailed in quest of the enemy.

On the morning of September the 5th, the French fleet was discovered at anchor across the Chesapeake, extending from Cape Henry to the Middle Ground. As soon as the Count de Grasse saw the British, he stood out to sea, forming his line of battle as his ships stretched out from under the lee of the land.

The fleet of Graves consisted of nineteen sail of the line, carrying 1,340 guns, and manned by 11, 318 seamen and marines, in three divisions. His flag was on board the *London*, 98 guns; that of Sir Samuel Hood was flying on the *Barfleur*, 98 guns; and that of Admiral Francis Drake on the *Princessa*, 70 guns. The battle which ensued was very indecisive, and served but to raise for a time, and to no purpose, the hopes of Lord Cornwallis and his slender army.

The following is the account of the action translated from the *Paris Gazette*.

It states that after the Count de Grasse threw out the signal for battle, "the captains executed their manoeuvres with such celerity that, notwithstanding the absence of nearly 90 officers and 1,800 men, who were landing troops, the fleet was under sail in less than three-quarters of an hour, and the line formed. *La Languedoc*, commanded by the Sieur de Montreuil, Commodore of the White and Blue, being directly ahead of the *Ville de Paris*, and the Count de Grasse seeing there were no general officers to his rear division, gave him verbal orders to take command of it.

The enemy came from the windward, and had kept it in forming their line, close-hauled on the starboard tack.

"At two o'clock they wore, and stood on the same tack with the French fleet; but the two squadrons were not ranged in parallel lines, the rear of Admiral Graves being greatly to windward of his van. At three the headmost vessels of the French fleet found themselves, by the variety of the winds and currents, too much to windward for their line to be well-formed. The Count de Grasse made them bear away, in order to give all his ships, the advantage of mutual support, and when they had borne away sufficiently they kept the wind.

"The van of the two fleets now approached each other within musket-shot. At four o'clock ours (the French), led by the Sieur de Bougainville, opened a very brisk fire, and the centre ships joined in succession.. At five the wind, having varied considerably, again placed the French van too much to windward.

"The Count de Grasse earnestly wished the battle to become general, and ordered his van to bear away a second time. That of Admiral Graves was very roughly handled; and he profited by the advantage of the wind, which rendered him master of the distance, to avoid being attacked by the French rear, which exerted every effort to come up with his rear and centre.

"The setting sun terminated the combat. The British fleet kept the wind; and having also preserved it the-next day, employed it in repairing."

The battle was most indecisive. Admiral Graves' losses were 336 killed and wounded; but the *Princessa*, 70, the *Shrewsbury* and *Montague*, two 74's, and the *Intrepid*, 64, sustained so much damage that it took a considerable time to put them in a state for service again. The *Ajax* and *Terrible*, two 74's, were so leaky and battered that on the 10th the admiral took out the crews and scuttled them.

For five days the fleets remained within sight of each other, without the Count de Grasse showing any disposition to renew the attack; and on that officer being joined by seven more ships of the line, under the Count de Barras, Admiral Graves, after holding a Council of War, returned to New York. , Though not defeated, our fleet had utterly failed in forcing the navigation of the bay. The army thus found themselves abandoned; blockaded by sea, as they would speedily be by land, as Washington was in full march towards the south by the Elk river and Baltimore.

On the 14th he was at Williamsburgh. His troops, with those brought by the Count de Grasse, and those Under the Count de Rochambeau, made altogether 7,000 French and 12,000 Americans; while those in York Town, under Cornwallis, did not exceed 5,950 men, and only 4,017 were fit for duty.

On the 28th the combined forces made their appearance; and Earl Cornwallis, having the same evening received assurances' of speedy succour from Sir Henry Clinton, withdrew his troops

York Town.

176

from the outer works, which were on the following day occupied by the enemy, and then York Town was completely invested, as Washington began to break ground before it.

On the 6th of October the enemy began their first parallel, and on the 9th their batteries opened fire upon our left. Other batteries opened at the same time against a redoubt that was advanced over the creek on the British right. It was defended by only 130 men of the 23rd Regiment and Royal Marines, who, as Lord Cornwallis states in his dispatch, held it with valour and resolution. "Soon after, 3,000 French grenadiers, all volunteers, made a vigorous attempt to storm the right advanced redoubt, but were repulsed by only 130 officers and soldiers of the Royal Welsh Fusiliers, and 40 marines. Two other attempts were made by the French to storm the redoubt, which were also unsuccessful."

During the first four days, a fire was poured upon this redoubt till it was reduced to a heap of sand. A general storm was now essayed; the redoubts were carried, and their guns turned on other parts of the intrenchments. One of these redoubts had been manned by some of the Fraser Highlanders; and although the defence of it had been as desperate as any of the rest, the regiment deemed its honour so involved by the loss of the work, that a petition was drawn up by the privates, and taken by the colonel to Lord Cornwallis, praying that they might be permitted to recapture it, or die in the attempt. "There was no doubt of the success of the undertaking by the men; but as the retaking was not considered of importance in the existing state of the siege, the proposition was not acceded to."

The situation of the besieged was now become very critical. The whole encampment was open to assault, exposed to a constant enfilading fire, and numbers were killed while carrying on the common duties of the garrison; and sickness within, was now added to the peril of shot from without. A sortie was made by 200 men, under Lieutenant-Colonel Abercrombie, with the hope of impeding the formation of a second parallel, against which, it was evident the new works on the left could not stand long, as the guns in that quarter had been already silenced.

This force, composed of detachments from the Guards and the grenadiers of the old 80th, or Royal Edinburgh Volunteers, under Lieutenant-Colonel Leeke, of the Guards, with some light infantry, under Major Armstrong, had orders to carry the two batteries that seemed in the greatest state of forwardness. This was on the 16th of October.

They succeeded in storming the redoubts, in spiking eleven pieces of cannon, and in killing or wounding above 100 Frenchmen, and rejoined the lines with a trifling loss. The enemy, however, carried on their advances with such activity that they had, ere long, too pieces of ordnance mounted in battery, which effectually prevented the British from showing a single gun.

Reduced to dire extremity now, Earl Cornwallis determined upon that measure of retreat which, if attempted at an earlier period, must have proved eminently successful. He made up his mind to leave all sick and wounded behind, and, with the *élite* of his fighting men, to cut a passage through the lines of General Choisé, and endeavour to reach New York.

To draw off the garrison by the Gloucester side of the river, where Choisé's force was small and might easily be overpowered, was now the plan; and some large boats were, on other pretences, ordered to be in readiness at night. In these a detachment of the Welsh Fusiliers and of some other corps embarked; but at this most critical moment there suddenly came on a dreadful storm of rain and wind, that drove all the boats, with the drenched troops on board, down the river. Fortunately they were all enabled to return in the course of the forenoon; but the design of drawing off the garrison was completely frustrated. Not a cannon-shot could now be fired, and all the bombs had been expended. The enemy's batteries had opened at daybreak; the defences were in utter ruin, and assailable at many points. Our small force in York Town looked forward to the future in silent and sullen despair.

Circumstanced thus, Cornwallis came to the mortifying resolution of opening a communication with Washington, with a view to capitulate. On the 17th the flag of truce went out, and the terms, such as the British general thought he had a right to demand, were proposed, but were accepted only in part. Washington would not consent to grant to the garrison of York Town, other honours than those which the garrison of Charlestown had received; and as his circumstances had now become desperate, the earl was compelled to submit.

After a loss of all ranks amounting to 472 men, he and his forces surrendered as prisoners of war on the 18th of October, 5,000 or so laying down their arms in presence of 20,000 of the enemy. York, with all its artillery and stores, as well as the harbour, passed, the former, into the possession of the Congress; the latter, into that of the King of France. The officers were in many instances permitted to return to Europe on parole, and to retain their private property. Two officers of the Royal Welsh Fusiliers availed themselves of these privileges to save the two colours of their regiment by wrapping them round their, bodies. One of these was Captain (afterwards Lieutenant-General) Thomas Peter; the name of the other is not given in the Regimental Record.

Few corps distinguished themselves more than this Welsh battalion at York Town. "Even the French general officers," we are told, "gave the Royal Welsh Fusiliers their unqualified approbation and praise, for their intrepidity and firmness in repulsing their attacks on the redoubt, and could not easily believe that so few men had defended it."

Most of the prisoners were marched to the back settlements

of Virginia, and confined in barracks surrounded by a stockade. Many soldiers of all regiments, the Fraser Highlanders excepted, violated their oath of fidelity by joining the American army. This blow at York Town was decisive, and thirteen of our colonies were now virtually separated for ever from the mother country.

The blow of this affair - if blow there was - Lord Cornwallis laid to the failure of succour expected from Sir Henry Clinton, who in turn equally blamed the plan and its execution.

- C H A P T E R   X X I -
GIBRALTAR, 1781-2-3

W E HAVE already detailed the capture of this famous fortress, now undoubtedly the greatest in the world, by Sir George Rooke, in 1704, and the futile attempt to recapture it in 1728; thus it now remains to us to depict, if possible, the terrors and the glories of that memorable siege, when it was defended with such consummate skill and valour for nearly three years, against the combined powers of France and Spain by land and sea.

When the Spaniards declared their intention of revengefully taking part in that war which separated the American colonies from our empire, the siege of Gibraltar was one of the earliest measures by which they evinced their ambitious desires and hostile disposition. So early as the 21st of June, 1779, all communication between Spain and Gibraltar was closed by an order from Madrid.

So little did the garrison anticipate anything hostile, that two days before that event the governor-general, George Augustus Elliot, accompanied by all his field-officers, paid a visit to General Mendoza, within the Spanish lines at San Roque, to congratulate him upon recent promotion; but these gentlemen remarked that their reception was cold, and that the Spanish officers seemed embarrassed.

Ere long came tidings that Admiral d'Orvilliers, with twenty-eight French sail of the line, was cruising off Cape Finistère to form a junction with a Spanish fleet from Cadiz; the mail from the garrison was refused on the land side; British officers resident in San Roque, with their families, were in some instances expelled, in others made prisoners; and all communication being closed, a Council of War was summoned, and preparations made privately for defence of the garrison, as war seemed certain now.

The garrison at this juncture consisted of a body of artillery, under Colonel Godwin, the 12th, 39th, 56th, 58th, and old 72nd Regiments (Royal Manchester Volunteers); Hardenberg's, Reden's, and De la Motte's Hanoverian Corps; with a company of engineers or artificers, under Colonel Green, making a total force of 5,382 men, including officers of all ranks, sergeants, and drummers.

It may be necessary to remind the reader that the promontory of Gibraltar is a tongue of land, consisting of a very lofty rock, rising abruptly to the height of 1,300 feet, presenting a face almost perfectly perpendicular, and at its northern extremity being quite inaccessible. The west side, however, and the southern extremity consist of a series of precipices. The town is built on the former side. From north to south, along the summit of the mountain, there runs a ridge of bristling rocks, that forms an undulating line against the clear blue Spanish sky. The whole western breast of the promontory is covered with fortifications. It is said to have been well wooded of old, but few trees are seen there now. A great part of the rock is hollowed out into caverns, some of which are magnificent in their dimensions, particularly one named the Cave of St. George, which, though having an entrance of only five feet, expands into an apartment of two hundred feet in length by ninety in breadth, with a roof covered by stalactites.

To attempt a description of the fortifications of Gibraltar would be to write a volume; but it was then, and is now, without doubt, the most complete fortress in the world. A century ago it was accounted by our best officers as impregnable. "No power whatever," says Colonel James, in his "History of the Herculean Straits," "can take that place, unless a plague, pestilence, famine, or the want of ordnance musketry, and ammunition, or some unforeseen stroke of Providence should happen."

An improvement which has especially added to its security is the formation of numerous covered galleries, excavated in the living rock, with embrasures through which to fire down on both the bay and the isthmus which connects the mountain with Spain.

The governor at this important juncture was one well suited for the task before him. The future Lord Heathfield, long and popularly known in the I army as "The Cock of the Rock," was the ninth I son of Sir Gilbert Elliot, of Stobs, in Roxburghshire, where he was born in 1718. After being educated at Leyden, and attending the military school of La Fère, in Picardy, and serving as a volunteer with the Prussians, he joined, also as a volunteer, the 23rd Welsh Fusiliers, at Edinburgh, in 1736, and afterwards became adjutant of the Scottish Horse Grenadier Guards, with whom he served, and was wounded at Minden. He subsequently served as brigadier in France and Germany, and was second in command at the Havanah; and, from being the commander-in-chief of His Majesty's forces in Ireland, was, at his own request, recalled, and sent to take care of the great fortress of Gibraltar.

At this time it was enacted by the regulations of the service that every sergeant and corporal" must carry a mould to cast bullets, and a ladle to melt lead in, with three spare powder-horns (for priming), and twelve bags for ball;" and that an officer when dressed for duty should have his hair queued, his sash and gorget on, with his espontoon (except in fusilier corps, the officers of which carried fusils), buff gloves, black linen gaiters with black buttons, black garters and uniform buckles."

Foreseeing the impending storm, General Elliot was now unremitting in his preparations to defend Gibraltar to the last cartridge.

According to the History of the Siege published by Major Drinkwater, of the old 72nd or Manchester Regiment, depôts of earth were collected in various places, empty casks were procured and filled, to strengthen or repair the fortifications; while, on the other side, the Spaniards were busy intrenching, and mounting their batteries. Elliot employed 300 Jews and Genoese in levelling heaps of sand near the gardens on the Neutral Ground, to preclude the enemy from having protection from our lower batteries, if they approached; and on the 3rd of July, 180 picked Linesmen were selected to join the Royal Artillery, to be instructed in the use of the great guns.

Ten days after, two line of-battle ships, with the Spanish flag flying, were seen cruising behind the Rock. Next, the port was blocked up by a squadron consisting of two seventy-four-gun ships, two frigates, five xebecs (i.e., armed vessels, with lateen sails), and a number of row-galleys, so judiciously arranged as to keep a vigilant look-out; and from that time the garrison was closely blockaded.

From the fortress the officers could see by telescope the busy Spanish camp, near the pretty white town of San Roque, being daily reinforced with additional regiments of horse and foot; and that numerous fatigue parties were landing enormous quantities of ordnance and stores at Point Malo, till the whole

Spanish battering ships - port and starboard.

isthmus. bristled with the *matériel* of war; and by the middle of August the garrison became confirmed in the opinion that, as the blockade by sea and land was so strict, the object of the Spaniards was to reduce Gibraltar by famine.

A picked company of sixty-eight marksmen, selected from all regiments, was now formed by General Elliot, under the command of Lieutenant Burleigh, 39th Regiment; the engineers were formed into three divisions, and some experiments were made with red-hot shot.

All this while the Spaniards worked without intermission at the batteries; daily, and nightly too, as the number of lights indicated, not less than 500 shovels were busy in the trenches, and filling up with sand the ditch of Fort St. Philip. General Elliot kept a watchful eye on these operations, molesting them as much as possible from Willis's Battery, while proper precautions were taken in the town to render a bombardment less distressing when it began;, thus, all the pavement in the northern streets was removed, the towers of all conspicuous buildings were taken down, and traverses thrown up, to render communication more secure.

In October the force in possession of the isthmus consisted of sixteen battalions of infantry and twelve squadrons of cavalry, under Lieutenant-General Don Martin Alvarez de Sota Mayor; but long ere this Elliot's guns had been firing on every object that presented itself within range.

As winter drew on, provisions of every kind became very scarce and dear, and the most common vegetables were with difficulty to be got at any price, and bread was the article most wanted. It was at this period that General Elliot made trial of how small a quantity of rice would suffice a single person for twenty-four hours, and actually subsisted himself on four ounces of rice per day. Coals next became scarce, and the fuel issued was wood from ships broken up; but so strongly had the timber imbibed salt water, that fires were made of it with the greatest difficulty.

To eke out this pittance of rations, the Hanoverian Brigade fell upon a most ingenious method of hatching and rearing chickens by artificial heat, and actually taught capons to sit upon the young broods, with all the care and tenderness of mother-hens. But scarcity of vegetables made scurvy now common in the garrison, whom actual want began to stare in the face; when, in the middle of January, 1780, a brig laden with flour stole into harbour, with the joyful news that the gallant Admiral Rodney was coming to their relief, and had captured, off the coast of Portugal, a Spanish sixty-four-gun ship, with five frigates and seventeen merchantmen, and that, with a fleet of twenty-one sail of the line and a large convoy of store-ships, he should soon be in the bay. His success was quickly followed by another. In the same month a Spanish squadron, consisting of eleven sail-of-the-line, was discovered near Cape St. Vincent, and after a conflict of many hours was completely defeated. Seven were taken, one blew up, two were driven ashore and lost; so that only four were brought into Gibraltar, which was fully relieved by Sir George Rodney, who sailed soon after, leaving in the harbour only two ships of the line and two frigates. No sooner had he left the bay than the Spaniards attempted to burn these ships, but without success, though the garrison was again more closely blockaded than ever.

The garrison was now provisioned, relieved of the burden of many invalids, women, and children, whom Elliot sent home with the fleet, and further strengthened by the 2nd battalion of the 73rd Regiment, or Lord Macleod's Highlanders, who landed at the New Mole, 1,052 strong of all ranks, and marched into the casemates of the King's Bastion, with pipes playing and colours flying. By this time the garrison was in a most perfect state for defence, save that scurvy was still prevalent; the stores and magazines were full, and the arrival of the strong Highland regiment had put the troops in the highest spirits; but by the month of August the provisions became bad and decayed. The blockade was more strict and vigilant than ever. Chains of small cruisers covered all the entrance to the Straits, at the entrance of the bay and on every side of the Rock; while the scurvy began to gain ascendancy over every effort of the surgeons; and when a Dane from Malaga, laden with lemons and oranges, came close in-shore during a fog, the governor gladly distributed her whole cargo among the soldiers.

In the growing desperation of their affairs, the officers of the garrison drew up a memorial to the king, setting forth their total inability to subsist upon their pay during this blockade, and the exorbitant rate of exchange; adding that even with strictest economy it was almost impossible to live; concluding with a request" that His Excellency would be pleased to lay their prayer in all humility at His Majesty's feet."

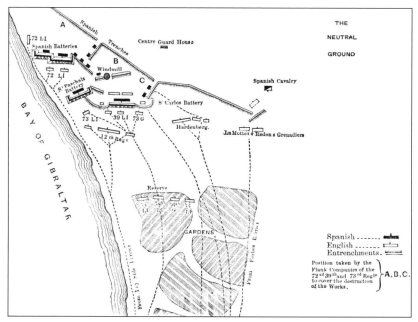

Sortie from Gibraltar.

Whether this was ever done we are not told; the memorial was followed by a second, but no answer was ever returned to either; but daily the scurvy and starvation grew side by side, while shot and shell were exchanged between the bastions on one side and the fast-growing earthworks on the other. By March, 1781, bread was so scarce that biscuit crumbs were sold at one shilling per pound, and for many days at a time the soldiers were without even these; and matters were in this state when, on the 7th of April, the *Eagle*, a Glasgow privateer of fourteen guns, beating off a xebec, a fourteen-gun sloop, and no less than eleven gunboats, gallantly fought her way into the bay, with tidings that the fleet under Admiral Darby was close at hand. Then once again the cheers resounded through Gibraltar, and every officer and man worked harder than ever at the batteries.

Perceiving by this new relief that it was hopeless to try to starve the garrison into capitulating, the Spaniards resolved to attempt the reduction of the place by an extraordinary effort. Their works were pressed with new vigour; the batteries were supplied with guns of the heaviest metal, and 200 pieces of battering cannon, with 80 mortars, were got into position against the fortress, while the most eminent engineers from France and Spain were brought to superintend the approaches of the besiegers. These guns and mortars poured a most dreadful and incessant fire upon Gibraltar; the troops were resolved that this last desperate effort of the Spanish Monarchy should be unparalleled, and the Duke de Crillon, the conqueror of Minorca, was appointed to lead the siege. A number of floating-batteries were constructed, upon a model which, it was imagined, would secure them from being either sunk or fired. In every other respect the preparations were enormous, and all the artillery of Spain appeared to be collected for this single purpose.

More than eighty gun-boats and bomb-ketches were to second the efforts of the floating-batteries, with a cloud of

188

frigates and smaller vessels; while the grand combined fleet of France and Spain, amounting to fifty ships of the line, was to cover and support the attack. Many Spanish princes of the blood and the flower of the French *noblesse* - a *noblesse* as yet unbroken by the Revolution - repaired to De Crillon's camp to witness that which they vauntingly deemed inevitable - the fall of Gibraltar; and on the 13th of September, when the Rock was to be beaten to powder, the adjacent hills of Andalusia were covered by thousands of spectators, as if all Spain had been gathered to see the sight.

But when the sun went down the Union Jack was still floating defiantly on the tower of O'Hara.

Prior to the grand attack a most brilliant sortie was made from Gibraltar on the night of 27th of November, 1781, under General Ross. The following are the heads of the Garrison Orders issued for this occasion:-

"Gibraltar, Nov. 26th, 1781.

Countersign. Steady.

"All the grenadiers and light infantry of the garrison, and all the men of the 12th and Harden-berg's Regiments, and non-commissioned officers now on duty, to be immediately relieved, and to join their regiments, to form a detachment consisting of the 12th and Hardenberg's Regiments complete, the grenadiers and light infantry of all other regiments (which are to be completed to their full establishment from the battalion companies), one captain, three lieutenants, ten noncommissioned officers, and 100 artillery, and three engineers, seven officers, and twelve non-commissioned officers, overseers, with 146 workmen from the Line, and forty from the artificer company. Each man to have thirty-six rounds of ammunition, with a good flint in his piece, and another in his pocket. No drums to go out, except two with each regiment. No volunteers will be allowed. The whole to be commanded by Brigadier-General Ross; and to assemble on the

Red Sands at twelve o'clock to-night, to make a sortie upon the enemy's batteries. The 39th and 58th Regiments to parade under the command of Brigadier-General Picton, to sustain the sortie if necessary."

The officer named was the uncle of the gallant Picton of future years, and was then colonel of the 12th Foot, which, by a singular coincidence, fought side by side with the Regiment of Hardenberg at Minden, and was now brigaded with it for the sortie from Gibraltar.

At midnight the detailed troops were under arms in deep silence; and, on being joined by 100 seamen under Lieutenants Muckle and Campbell, were formed in three columns, the right being under Lieutenant-Colonel Trigge, the left under Lieutenant-Colonel Hugo, and the centre under Lieutenant-Colonel Dachenhausen. The whole sortie party were only 2,225 of all ranks.

The right column was to march against the extremity of the enemy's parallel; the centre to follow, through the Bay Side Barrier, to destroy the mortar batteries; the left to bring up the rear, and advance upon the gun-batteries, all observing the most profound silence.

By the time all was arranged the morning of the 27th was far advanced, and as the moon had then nearly finished her nightly course, her light was waning on the hills and sea. At a quarter before three the sortie began to issue by files from the right of the rear line; but, notwithstanding the profound silence observed, the Spanish advanced sentries detected them amid the gloom of the hour and the sound of the waves upon the beach, and, after challenging, fired upon them.

"Forward !" was the immediate response; and Colonel Hugo, on finding that an alarm had been given, pushed forward his column at a rush for the extremity of the parallel, where he found no opposition, and the pioneers at once fell to the work of filling up, overturning, and dismantling, with shovel and pickaxe. Part of Hardenberg's Regiment, which was under Hugo, mistook the route of the grenadiers, owing to the darkness of the morning, and suddenly found themselves in front of the San Carlos Battery. In this dilemma they had no alternative but to assault it, which they did gallantly, after receiving the fire of the trench-guard. They stormed the great earthen parapet, driving back the enemy; but now Colonel Dachenhausen, with the flank companies of the 39th, finding them in the battery, supposed them, in the gloom, to be the enemy. They were thus fired upon by their own comrades, and many fell severely wounded, the countersign, "Steady," alone preventing further mischief.

The flank companies of the Macleod Highlanders were equally successful, and stormed the gun-batteries with an ardour that was irresistible; the trench-guards gave way on every side, abandoning those works which had cost so much expense and so many months of perilous labour. The woodwork of the batteries, the fascines and platforms, were set in flames, and columns of fire and smoke rolled through the grey sky of the early morning. Trains were laid to the magazines, which were blown up, the greatest exploding with a crash that shook the waters of the bay, and threw into the air masses of blazing timber.

In his anxiety General Elliot came out in person to aid General Ross; and in one hour, with the loss of only four privates killed, Lieutenant Tweedie, of the 12th Foot, and twenty-four others wounded, the sortie was complete, and the detachment returned, after demolishing the works and spiking ten thirteen-inch mortars and eighteen twenty-six-pounders, effecting destruction to the value of £2,000,000 sterling.

National pride, no less than national interest, were now enlisted in the desire to reduce a place which baffled every attack.

Under the direction of D'Arcon, a celebrated French engineer, the floating-batteries already referred to were constructed. They were ten in number, and deemed invulnerable. Their bottoms were of thick timber, their sides of wood and cork, which had been soaked in water, with a hollow space between, filled with wet sand; and, to prevent them from being burned by red-hot shot, numerous ducts of water went through them. A sloping roof, formed of strong rope netting, covered with wet skins, preserved the men on board from the falling shells; and each of these batteries, which earned from ten to twenty-eight pieces of cannon, was manned by picked crews of resolute Spaniards. Guns to the number of 1,000 and 12,000 of the finest infantry of France, came to second then-efforts, under the Duke de Crillon.

"It appeared," says Drinkwater, "that they meant, previous to their final efforts, to strike, if possible, a terror through their opponents, by displaying an armament more powerful than had ever been brought before any fortress. On the land side were most stupendous batteries and works, mounting 200 pieces of heavy ordnance, managed by an army of nearly 40,000 men, commanded by an active and hitherto victorious general, and animated by the immediate presence of two princes of the blood-royal of France (the Count d'Artois and Duke de Bourbon), with other dignified personages, and many of their own nobility. In their certainty of success, however, the enemy seemed entirely to have overlooked the nature of that force which was opposed to them; for though the garrison scarcely consisted of more than 7,000 effective men, including the marine brigade, they forgot they were now veterans in this service, had long been habituated to the effects of artillery, and were, by degrees, prepared for the arduous conflict that awaited them."

After weeks of incessant but minor cannonading, the grand attack was made on the 13th of September, 1782, when the floating-batteries, under Bueno-ventura de Moreno, a distinguished Spanish officer, were brought into the requisite position to act in unison with the guns of the ships and shore batteries; and at a quarter to ten the firing began on all sides, exhibiting a scene of which neither pen nor pencil can give the slightest idea. Suffice it to say that 400 pieces of the heaviest artillery were thundering at once against Gibraltar, the defenders of which found the floating-batteries quite as formidable as they had been represented.

The heaviest bombs rolled from their flexible roofs, and thirty-two-pound shot failed to make any impression on their hulls. They were frequently on fire, but the flames were speedily extinguished. Artillery salvoes more tremendous, if possible, than ever were now directed from Gibraltar; incessant showers of red-hot balls of every calibre, of flaming carcases, and shells of every species, flew from all quarters; and as the great masts of the stately ships went crashing by the board, and their rigging became cut and torn, the consequent confusion in the fleets gave fresh hope to the garrison.

By evening the ship cannonade began to slacken; rockets, as signals of distress, were seen soaring into the air, while boats were rowed around the disabled men-of-war, in which our artillery must have made the most dreadful havoc, for, during the short intervals of cessation, a strong, indistinct clamour, the mingled sound of groans, and cries, and shrieks, came floating upward to the ears of the garrison.

By midnight one great battering ship was in flames from stem and stern. The light thus thrown around enabled our artillery to point their guns with the utmost precision, while the giant Rock, with all its grim batteries, was brilliantly illuminated, and the ships and floating wreckage in the bay were distinctly visible. From the depressed guns the red-hot globes of iron seemed to.streak the air with red lines as they went on their errand of destruction; and by four in the morning six other battering ships

The grand attack on Gibraltar.

were also in flames, adding to the sublimity and terror of the scene.

The magazines began to explode, and men were heard shrieking amid the flames for pity and assistance; others were seen imploring relief, with gestures of despair. Of these crews only 400 men (out of 5,260) were saved by the humane efforts of the garrison, and chiefly by those of Captain (afterwards Sir Roger) Curtis, of the Royal Navy.

To reply to all the batteries of the enemy, the garrison had only eighty, pieces of cannon, with some mortars and nine howitzers. Upwards of 8,000 rounds (more than half of which were red-hot shot) and 716 barrels of powder, were expended by our artillery. What quantity of ammunition the enemy expended could never be ascertained.

Notwithstanding their defeat, they recommenced their cannonade from the isthmus, expending during the remainder of the month from one to two thousand rounds every twenty-four hours, and shelling all night.

The captured prisoners were sent to their own camp, and a captain of the marines (rescued from a battering ship) who died of his wounds, was honourably interred by the grenadiers of the 39th, who fired three rounds over his grave.

Hourly now bodies were cast ashore from the burned wrecks and shattered pinnaces, and many of them were horribly mutilated and scorched. The combined fleets still remained in the bay, being determined to oppose any relief of the garrison; while additional works were raised on shore, and the fighting continued almost without cessation, till the long blockade was terminated by the announcement of the signature of the preliminaries of a general peace, on the 2nd of February, 1783. The men in the Spanish boat who bought these joyful tidings made their appearance with ecstasy in their countenances, exclaiming, as they went ashore -

"We are all friends! We are all friends!"

It was not, however, till the 10th of March that free intercourse was re-established by the arrival from England of the official intelligence that peace had been concluded; and thus ended the great siege of Gibraltar, which lasted three years seven months and twelve days, from the commencement of the blockade till the cessation of hostilities.

During these long and terrible operations, the garrison lost 1,231 men of all ranks, expended 8,000 barrels of powder, and 205,328 cannon-balls.

On the 18th of March the Duke de Crillon presented General Elliot with a beautiful grey Andalusian horse; and some days after, attended by a brilliant staff, paid him a visit. He was received by a salute of seventeen guns; and our soldiers, with that fine spirit which is so truly British, received him with three hearty cheers. This is said to have greatly perplexed him, till the spirit in which it was done was explained, and then he seemed highly pleased.

He was much impressed by the ruined aspect of the town. The officers of the garrison were introduced to him by corps.

"Gentlemen," said he, to those of the artillery, "I would rather see you here as friends than on your batteries as enemies, where you never spared me."

He was greatly impressed by the general strength and nature of the works, and particularly by a gallery six hundred feet long, above Farringdon's Battery.

"Those works," he exclaimed to his suite, "are worthy of the Romans !"

After dining with the officers of the garrison, he passed through the camp to Europa, each regiment turning out in succession without arms, and giving him again three cheers. The extreme youth and good appearance of our troops excited his surprise and admiration. To General Elliot he said -

"You have exerted yourself to the utmost of your abilities in your noble defence; and though I have not been successful, yet I am also happy in having my sovereign's approbation of my conduct.

On his return to England, General Elliot was created, in 1787, Lord Heathfield and Baron Gibraltar, and died thirteen years after, at the ripe age of seventy-seven, when on a visit to the baths at Aix-la-Chapelle.

Sir Roger Curtis, who brought home his dispatches after the siege, was knighted by the king, and subsequently made a baronet.

After the peace which followed the independence of America and the successful defence of Gibraltar, all our troops were disbanded to the 73rd, now styled the Perthshire Regiment.

It was during this peace that "county designations "were first given to corps of infantry, in some instances without any apparent reason, as the 55th Regiment, which was raised in Scotland, and chiefly at Edinburgh, in 1755, was called "the Westmoreland;" and many other instances might be cited.

IN THE INDIAN SEAS, 1782-3

WE MUST not omit to record that prior to the Peace of 1783 the war in the Carnatic had raged by sea as well as land. In January, 1782, Admiral Sir Edward Hughes, K.B., an officer who fought no less than five very sanguinary battles with the French in Indian waters, after carrying into execution a design he had formed for the complete reduction of the Dutch settlement at Trincomalee, consisting of a town, fortress, and harbour in Ceylon, sailed thence on the 31st, and on the 8th of February came to anchor in Madras Roads. On that day he received advice from Lord Macartney, the governor, that a French squadron, consisting of thirty sail, was at anchor twenty leagues to the northward of that port.

On the 9th he was joined by three ships of war and an armed transport. Every possible expedition was used to get on board the stores and necessary provisions; but before all was complete the enemy's squadron appeared in the offing, and came to anchor about four miles outside the roadstead.

The fleet under M. de Suffren (styled in France, "Bailli de Suffren de Sainte Tropez, Lieutenant-General of the Naval Forces of His Most Christian Majesty") consisted of seventeen sail, eleven of which were ships of the line, with nine *flûtes* or transports. On board were 7,072 seamen and 870 guns, with 3,457 soldiers, belonging to the Regiments D'Austerie, L'Isle de France (89th of the Line), D'Artillerie, the Legion de Lausanne, the Volunteers of Bourbon, and some sepoys.

Sir Edward Hughes, on the sudden appearance of this armament, immediately placed his ships, with springs upon their cables, in the most advantageous position to defend themselves and the numerous merchant shipping which lay within them in the roads. For the information of the non-nautical reader, we may mention that a spring is a rope put out at either side of a vessel, and made fast to her cable, while at anchor, for the purpose of changing her position, or steadying her, as may be required.

At four in the afternoon M. de Suffren suddenly weighed, and stood away to the southward. A detachment, consisting of 300 men of the 98th Regiment, was placed on board the fleet of Sir Edward Hughes, to reinforce the marines. His fleet consisted of eleven sail, carrying 628 guns and 5,120 officers, seamen, marines, and soldiers; but one, of the vessels, the *Seahorse*, was a corvette of twenty guns, and the *Manilla*, armed transport, carried only fourteen. Nevertheless, Sir Edward weighed directly, and under easy sail pursued the French all night

At daybreak next morning he found that the squadron had separated in the dark, for their sails were seen scattered over the horizon. The ships of the line were chiefly about four leagues to the eastward of the British fleet; while the frigates and transports were to the south-westward, and steering directly for Pondicherry. Sir Edward threw out the signal for a general chase in that quarter, in order, if possible, to cut off their transports, which might be the means of compelling M. de Suffren to give battle, by bearing down to the protection of his convoy. In the course of the exciting chase, the copper-bottomed ships overtook and captured six sail of the convoy, five of which proved to be British ships taken by the enemy, when to the northward of Madras, with all their crews on board. The sixth was a large and heavily-armed French transport, *Le Lauriston*, which was taken by the Hon. Captain Lumley, of the *Isis*, a fifty-gun ship, and proved to have on board 300 men of the Legion de Lausanne, and was moreover deeply laden with shot, gunpowder, and other stores, all destined for the aid of Hyder Ali.

As soon as M. de Suffren perceived that the convoy was in

peril, he bore down with every inch of canvas he could spread; and by three o'clock four of the best-sailing line-of-battle ships were within three miles of the sternmost of the British, who were too much scattered for effective service, in consequence of the chase. Sir Edward Hughes made a signal for the pursuing ships to join him, which they did by seven o'clock, after which the hostile squadrons kept each other in view all night.

When day broke on the 17th, the weather proved squally; the sea and sky were alike a gloomy grey colour, the former flecked with white foam, and the winds were baffling and uncertain. Hence the squadrons could not approach each other till the afternoon, when, after several manoeuvres, a favourable squall enabled M. de Suffren to bear down with his whole force on the centre and rear of the British, who, not having the wind, were unable to form in sufficiently close order.

Sir Edward Hughes was now attacked by eight of the enemy's finest ships, about four in the afternoon. The *Exeter*,

Madras, from the sea.

200

64, carrying the flag of Commodore King, the sternmost ship, was a slow sailer, and being somewhat detached from the rest of the squadron, was furiously cannonaded by three French ships. M. de Suffren, in the *Hero*, a stately seventy-four, opened fire with great spirit upon the *Superb*, 74, which was Sir Edward's flag-ship. Meanwhile the van of the British lay all this time helplessly becalmed, and unable to render the least assistance; yet the unequal action was maintained with great resolution till six o'clock, when a sudden breeze gave the British the advantage of the wind, and they in turn became the assailants, and opened so sharp a fire of cannon and musketry that in twenty-five minutes the enemy hauled their wind, stretched every inch of canvas to the yard-heads, and bore away to the north-east, "after having visibly suffered severely."

It had evidently been the chief object of M. de Suffren to disable the *Exeter* and *Superb*. These vessels had ninety killed and wounded on board. The mainyard of the latter was cut in two at the slings: and she had four feet of water in the hold, where it continued to rise till the shot-holes were plugged. The *Exeter* was reduced to a mere wreck, having been cannonaded by no less than five ships. But for the prompt assistance given her by Captain Wood, of the *Worcester*, she must have sunk, with all her wounded on board.

Towards the close of the action, two large ships of the enemy were seen bearing down to renew the attack upon the crippled *Exeter*, and the master asked Commodore King what was to be done now. "Done!" exclaimed the commodore. "There is nothing to be done but to fight till she sinks."

In the morning the enemy had disappeared. The masts of the *Superb* and *Exeter* were so severely wounded that it was dangerous to carry sail on them; and the shot-holes in all the ships that had been engaged were so far under water as to make it impossible to stop them at" sea. The admiral therefore stood for Trincomalee, as the only place where the squadron could be refitted.

The total loss in killed and wounded was 127 of all ranks. Among the former were Captains Stephens, of the *Superb*, and Reynolds, of the *Exeter*.

After having his squadron refitted, Sir Edward Hughes sailed from Trincomalee on the 4th of March, and eight days after came to anchor in Madras Roads, without seeing anything of the enemy: On the 30th he was on his way back to Trincomalee with a reinforcement for the garrison, where he was joined by the *Sultan*, 74 guns, and the *Magnanime*, 64, but though the crews of these vessels were sickly, he continued his voyage "without seeking or shunning the enemy."

On the 6th of April he fell in with a French ship from the Mauritius, which had on board dispatches from France, for their commanders by land and sea. The admiral drove her ashore near the Danish settlements of Tranquebar, where the crew burned her and escaped with the dispatches.

At noon on the 8th the enemy's squadron was discovered to leeward, consisting of eighteen sail. The admiral still continued his course, and for three successive days the hostile fleets were in sight of each other. On the nth the coast of Ceylon came in sight, about fifteen leagues to the windward of Trincomalee, for which place he bore away. By this change of course the enemy won the weather-gage of the British squadron, and by daybreak next morning they were seen to crowd all the sail they could carry, as if in pursuit, As the copper-sheathed ships were coming fast up with his rear, Sir Edward determined to fight them; accordingly, at nine a.m. he drew his squadron into line of battle ahead on the starboard tack, each ship being two cables' lengths (i.e., 240 fathoms) apart.

By this time the enemy, bearing north-by-east, were distant six miles to windward, with all their canvas bellying out upon the breeze. They continued to manoeuvre their ships and to change their positions in the line, till fifteen minutes past twelve, when they triced up their port-lids and bore down on our fleet. Their five van ships stretched along to engage that of the British; while M. de Suffren, with seven other sail, steered directly down on the *Superb*, whose second ahead was the *Monmouth*, 64 guns, and her second astern the Monarch, 70 guns.

By half-past one the battle had begun in the van of both fleets; and very soon after De Suffren, in the *Hero*, 74 guns, her second astern being *L'Orient*, 74 guns, Captain de Pallière, engaged the *Superb* within pistol-shot range, and for nine minutes continued to give and to receive the most dreadful fire. The *Hero*, greatly damaged, then forged ahead to attack the *Monmouth*, which was already closely engaged with another French ship. This made space sufficient for the enemy's rear to bear up and attack the British centre, where the battle raged with the greatest violence, and all the ships were soon shrouded in smoke to their cross-trees.

View of Bombay.

By three o'clock the *Monmouth*, after her crew had sustained with splendid courage the attack of two large ships, had her mizzenmast shot away; soon after her mainmast, with all its top-hamper, went crashing over the side. She was thus compelled to bear out of the line and drop away to leeward, and would have been taken by the enemy, had not Sir Edward Hughes, followed by the *Sultan* and *Monarch*, borne down to her relief.

At forty minutes past three, as the wind still blew from the northward, the admiral became apprehensive that the ships might become entangled with the shore;'he consequently made signal "to wear, and haul their wind in a line of battle ahead, still engaging the enemy."

Two hours later, the squadron being in fifteen fathoms' water, Sir Edward, fearful that the *Monmouth* in her disabled state might drift ashore, made the signal to prepare for anchoring. On this the French squadron, sorely battered, crippled, and in great disorder, bore away to the eastward; and so ended this battle, off the coast of Ceylon, where the fleet anchored.

The *Hero*, M. de Suffren's ship, was so much damaged that he had to shift his flag into the *Hannibal*, 74. Just after dark the French frigate *La Fine*, 40 guns, having been ordered to reconnoitre the British squadron, came so close for that purpose that she fell on board the *Isis*, commanded by Captain Lumley, who compelled her to strike her colours; but owing to the darkness of the night, and the disabled state in which the *Isis* had come out of the action, she contrived to get clear off, and escaped.

On the 13th, at dawn, the enemy's squadron was seen at anchor five miles to the seaward of ours, in much disorder, and apparent distress; with the crew of every ship busy in the task of repairing and refitting both rigging and hulls. The two fleets remained in sight of each other thus till the 19th, when the enemy got under sail with the land breeze, and stood out to sea close-hauled.

By noon the wind came from the sea, on which they tacked, and Stood directly for the British squadron, which cleared away for action. However, M. de Suffren seemed to change his mind, for, without coming within gunshot, he tacked again, bore away to the eastward, and by evening his whole squadron had disappeared from the horizon. Sir Edward then bore away for Trincomalee.

The loss he sustained in this action amounted to 137 billed and 430 wounded. The brunt of the fighting fell chiefly on the *Superb* and *Monmouth*. The casualties of the former were 155, of the latter 147. In this action Captain James Alms, an officer who greatly distinguished himself in the *Monmouth*, lost his only son, a lieutenant, who was slain on board the flag-ship. He was in after years captain of the *Repulse*, which was totally wrecked on the coast of Holland.

The losses of the French are stated at 503. At Cuddalore M. de Suffren took on board 400 French troops to act as marines, and 300 artillerymen to aid in working his guns; and on the 23rd of June Sir Edward Hughes, having completely refitted his ships, plugged all shot-holes, and set up new spars, sailed from Trincomalee to have another bout with the French. Next day he came to anchor in the roadstead of Negapatam, a seaport on the Coromandel coast, of which we had possessed ourselves in the preceding year.

There he was informed that the enemy were at anchor off Cuddalore, and that they had captured the *Raikes* and *Resolution*, two armed transports, laden with the munition, of war. At one o'clock in the afternoon of the 5th of July the enemy's squadron appeared off Negapatam. It consisted of eighteen sail, carrying 854 guns, and in the evening came to anchor eight miles to windward of Sir Edward Hughes, who immediately got under weigh; and by three o'clock his entire squadron was at sea, and stood to the southward during the whole evening and night, to get the weather-gage of the enemy.

By daylight on the 6th, the admiral having gained this point, formed his line of battle abreast, and bore away towards the enemy, who weighed and formed their line of battle as they stood to the westward; upon which Sir Edward Hughes signalled his fleet to form line ahead, and for each ship to bear directly down upon any one of the enemy that might be opposite to her, and engage her closely.

Promptly were these orders obeyed, and for a considerable time the battle was warmly and sternly maintained on both sides. The firing had commenced in the French line at twenty minutes before eleven o'clock, but was not replied to by the British till they were sufficiently near for their shot to have a deadly effect; and then, from van to rear, the action was general till thirty-five minutes past twelve, by which time the enemy's ships appeared to have suffered greatly in their masts and hulls, the latter showing a multitude of shot-holes, and vast breaches and scars, whence showers of splinters had been knocked away.

The van ship had been compelled to bear away out of the line, and the *Brilliant*, 64, which seconded the flag-ship of M. de Suffren, had her mainmast carried away. At this critical moment the sea breeze set in with unusual violence, and threw both fleets into great disorder. Several of the ships in the British van and centre were taken aback, and "paid round on the heel" (i.e., stern-post), with their heads the contrary way; while those in the rear, whose rigging had suffered least in the action, were able to continue on their former tack, particularly the *Burford*, 70 guns, and the *Eagle* and *Worcester*, two sixty-four-gun ships, which were nearing the enemy's squadron very fast. The latter, during the disorder into which the sudden shift of the breeze had thrown the British, had time to collect, and come to the wind on the larboard tack; those ships that were least disabled forming a line to windward, to protect those which had suffered most

To remedy the confusion in his fleet, Sir Edward Hughes hauled down the signal "for the line," and hoisted one to "wear," intending to follow it by one for "a general chase;" but at that moment Captain John Gell, who afterwards commanded under Lord Hood in the Mediterranean, hailed the admiral to state that all the standing rigging of his ship, the *Monarch*, 70, had been shot away, and that consequently she was quite ungovernable. The *Hero*, 74, being on the contrary tack, was hauling in with the land, with signals of distress out; while the enemy were endeavouring to cut off the *Eagle*, which was hard pressed by the fire of two of their ships.

Under all these circumstances, he made the signal to "wear" only, and form the line ahead on the larboard tack; while the engagement was still partially waged by those ships that were within range of each other, gun after gun continued to boom over the water, and the work of wounds, death, and destruction continued.

At two o'clock, M. de Suffren stood in-shore, and collected his ships in a close body, while the British remained much dispersed, and some were so mauled aloft that they failed to obey the helm, so the admiral had to relinquish his hope of renewing the engagement. At half-past four he hauled down the signal for battle, and an hour after came to anchor between Negapatam and Nagon, in the Bay of Bengal, while the French anchored nine miles to leeward.

All night the men in both fleets were busy in securing the lower-masts, sending aloft new spars, and refitting generally; and by nine next morning the British had the mortification to see the enemy get under sail, and return to the roads of Cuddalore, their disabled ships ahead, the most serviceable, with the frigates, covering their retreat.

On this morning Sir Edward Hughes sent Captain James Watt, of the *Sultan*, 74 (an officer who afterwards died of a wound received in a subsequent action), with a flag of truce and a letter to M. de Suffren, alongside whose ship he ran in the *Rodney*, a disarmed brig, to demand the French king's ship, *Le Sévère*, 64 guns, which had struck her colours to the *Sultan*, but which, while that ship was wearing, had rehoisted them, poured a raking fire into the *Sultan*, and then stood away. M. de Suffren returned, however, an evasive answer, and alleged that her colours had not been struck, but that the halliard had been cut by a shot.

The loss sustained by the British amounted to 77 killed and 233 wounded. Among the former were Captain Jenkinson, of the 98th Regiment, and the Hon. Dunbar Maclellan, of the *Superb*, a soil of Lord Kirkcudbright. The total Josses of the enemy were 779. "The death of Captain Maclellan, of the *Superb*," says the admiral's dispatch, "who was shot through the heart with a grape shot early in the engagement, is universally regretted by all who knew him. I had experienced in him an excellent officer in every department of the service." Major Gratton, of the 100th Foot, served under him as a volunteer in the *Superb*.

Finding it impossible to repair at sea the damages sustained by his fleet in the late action, and that the stores of every kind were nearly exhausted, Sir Edward Hughes sailed for Madras, which he reached on the 20th of July.

There he was joined by the *Sceptre*, 64 guns, which had left England with Sir Richard Bickerton, Bart., an officer who was knighted by George III when steering his barge, in 1773, at a great naval review at Portsmouth. On the 31st of July, to secure Trincomalee from any desultory attempt which the enemy might make in that quarter) Sir Edward Hughes dispatched the *Monmouth* and *Sceptre* with a reinforcement of troops for the garrison; and by the 10th of August these ships rejoined him.

On the 1st of the same month, M. de Suffren, having refitted his squadron, sailed from Cuddalore to join the Sieur d'Aymar, who he heard had arrived at the Point de Galle, in the Isle of Ceylon, in the *St. Michael*, 64 guns, accompanied by *L'Illustre*, 74, having under convoy the second division of the Marquis de Bussy's troops and artillery. So difficult was it to procure correct intelligence, that the admiral could know nothing of the movements of the enemy till the 16th, when he was joined by the *Coventry*, frigate, 28 guns, commanded by Captain (afterwards Admiral Sir Andrew) Mitchell, who, on the 12th, off the Friar's Hood, on the coast of Ceylon, had fallen in with and attacked the *Bellona*, French forty-gun frigate. He fought her for two hours and a half, till she sheered off and made sail. Captain Mitchell gave chase, but the *Coventry* had suffered so much aloft that he was unable to come up with her till, to his astonishment, he found himself lured almost into the midst of the whole French fleet, which he suddenly discovered at anchor in Batacalo Roads. Two line-of-battle ships instantly gave chase to the *Coventry*, which contrived to elude them. In her conflict with the *Bellona*, she had 15 men killed and 29 wounded.

Immediately upon receiving this intelligence, Sir Edward Hughes hastened his preparations for sea; and by the 20th he was steering southward towards Trincomalee, full of apprehension that, during the absence of his squadron, the enemy might make themselves masters of the harbour. As the wind blew strong from the southward, he did not arrive off Trincomalee till the night of the 2nd of September; and on the following morning, to the intense mortification of the admiral and every man in his fleet, the French squadron, consisting of thirty sail, was at anchor in the bay, and the French colours were flying on the town and all the forts.

He then found that Captain Hay Macdowal, of the 2nd battalion of the 42nd Highlanders, the commandant of

Trincomalee, had been compelled to surrender, by capitulation, on the 30th of August - only five days before - to M. de Suffren and the Baron d'Agault. The Highlanders marched out with the honours of war, with two six-pounders and one mortar in front They had been conveyed to Madras; and in 1786 were constituted the 73rd Highland Regiment, in which the future Duke of Wellington was an ensign in the following year.

On the appearance of the British squadron off the bay, on the morning of the 3rd, M. de Suffren got under weigh, and, with fifteen ships of the line, three frigates, and a fire-ship, stood out of the Back Bay with the land breeze, which placed him to windward of the British. Sir Edward immediately signalled to form line of battle ahead at two cables' distance between each ship, and, shortening sail, he edged away from the wind, that all might get the more speedily into their respective stations.

The armament of the French carried 1,092 guns; that of the British, consisting of twelve line-of-battle ships and four

Point De Galle, Ceylon.

frigates, with one fire-ship, carried 946 guns. On board were detachments of the 78th or Seaforth Highlanders, and the 98th Regiment, to act as marines.

At twenty minutes past eight o'clock the enemy began to edge down towards the British line; and Sir Edward Hughes, in order to render the battle a decisive one, endeavoured, by steering away under his topsails, to lure them as far as possible from Trincomalee, until half-past eleven. At half-past two the French cannon opened on the line of our ships; heartily it was returned, and the conflict became general. Two vessels of the enemy made a furious and especial attack upon the *Worcester*, the rear ship. She made a brave resistance, under her captain, Charles Wood, who was mortally wounded; and was nobly supported by the *Monmouth*, her second ahead, which, with all her sails thrown aback, poured in so close and heavy a fire upon them that the attack entirely failed on that side. Five of the enemy's ships now bore down on the *Exeter* and *Isis*, and, by an incessant and powerful cannonading, drove the former, much disabled, out of the line; they then tacked, and, while keeping their wind, fired on the *Isis* and other ships in the van as they passed.

"In the meantime," says Sir Edward, in his dispatch to the Admiralty, "the centres of the two fleets were warmly engaged, ship to ship. At twenty-eight minutes past three the mizzenmast of the French admiral's second astern was shot away, and his second ahead lost her fore and mizzentopmasts. At thirty-five minutes past five the wind shifted suddenly from south-west to east-south-east. I made the signal for the squadron to wear, which was instantly obeyed in good order, the ships of the enemy either wearing or staying at the same time; and the engagement was renewed on the other tack, close and vigorously on our part."

A little after six o'clock M. de Suffren's mainmast was shot away, and soon after his mizzen went crashing to leeward also. The *Worcester* about the same time lost her maintopmast; and at seven o'clock the whole French squadron hauled their wind to the southward, and for fully twenty minutes were exposed to a severe and galling fire from all the vessels of the British rear, and as they passed away the action gradually ceased. After an encounter so long and desperate, the British were in no condition to pursue the enemy, who by daylight next morning were quite out of sight.

Our total loss in killed and wounded was 334. Among the former were Captain Watt, of the *Sultan*; Captain Clugstone, of the marines on board the *Monarch*; Lieutenants Murray, Ord, Barrett, and Edwards, of the marines; Captains Wood, of the *Worcester*, and Lumley, of the *Isis*. Among the latter were two officers of the 78th Highlanders - the Hon. Captain Maitland, son of the Earl of Lauderdale; and Lieutenant Hugh Sandilands, son of Lord Torphichen.

The crippled state of the squadron, more particularly of the *Superb*, *Burford*, *Eagle*, and *Monmouth*, compelled the admiral to return to Madras, where he arrived on the 9th.

The French squadron returned to Trincomalee on the night of the action, and such was their hurry and confusion lest they should be pursued, that *L'Orient*, one of their finest seventy-four-gun ships, ran on shore in the dark, and became a total wreck. M. de Suffren was so much dissatisfied with the conduct of some of his captains, that he sent no less than six of them under arrest to the Mauritius. The losses he had sustained were not published in the usual manner at once; but it became afterwards known that they were undoubtedly severe, as the slain amounted to 412, and the wounded to 676. The *Hero*, the admiral's own ship, had on board 1,200 men when she entered the action; and of these 380 were killed or wounded.

As the monsoon was at hand, Sir Edward Hughes ordered the

Sea-fight with the Mahrattas.

213

line-of-battle ships to Bombay; but ere they could clear the Bay of Bengal they encountered a terrific hurricane. "Several boats were lost, with their crews, who were waiting for the officers from the shore; and nothing could equal the scene of horror and distress which soon presented itself. The beach for several miles was covered with wrecks, and with the bodies of the dead and dying."

During these wars one of our last conflicts in Indian waters occurred with the Mahrattas. A treaty of peace having been concluded and proclaimed with that people, the Company's snow, *Ranger*, 12 guns, commanded by Lieutenant Pruen, sailed from Bombay on the 5th of April, 1783, having on board Colonels Norman Macleod, of the 42nd Highlanders, and T. Mackenzie Humberstone, of the 78th Highlanders, Major Shaw, and several other officers, who were on their way to join their regiments in Bengal. On the morning of the 8th they found themselves near the Mahratta fleet belonging to Geriah, and consisting of two ships, a ketch, and eight gallivats. These vessels, without hailing or the least ceremony, surrounded and attacked the *Ranger*, firing on her with the greatest fury. Lieutenant Pruen made a desperate defence, and fought his little vessel against this vast odds with the greatest bravery for four hours and a half.

For the last hour the two ships and the ketch were lashed alongside the *Ranger*, and in this situation the action was maintained by musketry alone; and the resolute valour of the crew and those officers who were passengers on board, prevented the enemy from boarding till, from the number of killed and wounded, and many of the muskets becoming unserviceable, the fire from the deck of the *Ranger* became so much reduced that further resistance was useless, and Lieutenant Pruen struck his colours.

The instant they were down the exulting enemy swarmed

on board, uttering shrill and terrible yells, and commenced an indiscriminate slaughter of all on deck. Major Shaw was shot dead; Colonel Macleod received two wounds in his left hand and shoulder, and a ball through the body. Lieutenant Stewart, of the 100th Regiment, was literally hacked to pieces. Lieutenants Taylor and Seton, of the Bombay Army, and Lieutenant Pruen, also received severe sword wounds; and Colonel Mackenzie Humberstone was shot through the lungs.

The *Ranger* was carried into Geriah, where the subahdar disowned all knowledge of the peace till the 7th of May, when he permitted her to sail with the wounded survivors for Bombay. Prior to this Colonel Humberstone had expired, in his twenty-eighth year. He was one of the most distinguished of our officers in India; in 1781, with only 1,000 Europeans and 2,500 sepoys, he had undertaken to carry on the war in the kingdom of Calicut, and covered himself with honour in many of the actions against Hyder Ali.

- CHAPTER XXIII -

THE MAGICIENNE AND LA SIBYLLE, 1783

O N THE 18th of January this year, His Majesty's ship *Magicienne*, 48 guns, under Captain Thomas Graves, was seen to steer into the harbour of Kingston, in Jamaica, without a single mast standing, and in a sorely battered condition, with a few tattered sails spread on jury spars; after having been in action with two French vessels, during which the most courageous conduct was displayed by her officers and crew. For a narrative of this brilliant affair, we are chiefly indebted to the journal of one of her officers, in a West Indian print of the time, and the *Gazette de France*.

The *Magicienne* formed one of the convoy escorting Brigadier Stewart and 1,600 troops, bound from Charleston, after its evacuation, for service in the West India Isles.

At daylight on the morning of the 1st of January, the *Magicienne* sighted two strange sail in rear of the convoy, and soon afterwards saw His Majesty's ship *Endymion*, 44 guns, Captain E. T. Smith, in chase. She made sail towards them, and repeated to the *Emerald*, 32 guns, the *Endymion's* signal for two strange craft being visible to the north-east. At half-past six the *Endymion* signalled, "A fleet in sight," and hoisted French colours to denote its nationality; and by nine o'clock she brought-to one of the chase, a ship under the Gallic ensign. Soon after the *Magicienne* came abreast of the *Endymion's* prize, the *Celerity*, taken shortly before, and valued at ‚£20,000. She hoisted out and manned her barge, to assist in taking out the prisoners. At half-past nine the *Endymion* signalled, "Chase north-east;" as the French fleet were making all the sail they could spread, to escape the

British, except five, which, says the journalist, "hauled their wind toward us."

As the *Magicienne* approached them, her captain perceived the two headmost ships of war, the largest carrying a commodore's pennant at the main-topgallantmast-head, that of the Count de Kerigarian de Locmaria, post-captain, and commander of a king's frigate; so Captain Graves took in his royals and studding-sails, to let the *Endymion* come up with him, as he had no intention of rashly engaging these two ships single-handed, and she was then five miles astern.

He slung his lower-yards, stopped the topsail-sheets, and cleared away fore and aft for action. Three of the ships that were now farthest to leeward, were seen to bear up and follow the convoy, then to wear, and follow the two French ships, *La Sibylle* and the *Railleur*, which were standing straight for the *Magicienne*, with colours flying, ports triced up, and all their canvas bellying out upon the wind.

The *Endymion* now signalled, "Make more sail in line, headmost ship;" but as the *Magicienne* came within cannon-shot, the Count de Kerigarian and his consort wore, and made all the sail they could from her, firing at the same time their stern-chasers, which they continued to work till brought to close action.

The *Magicienne* now ran up her royals, set her studding-sails, and gave phase, firing her bow-guns as they bore on the enemy, whose ships kept dose together, the lesser on the larboard quarter of her commander. The *Endymion* was still five miles astern, and though using every effort to come up with the *Magicienne*, was fast being left behind.

By twenty minutes past twelve the latter was abreast of the sternmost ship; and after a few rounds of cannon and small-arms, her ensign being down and her fire silenced, Captain Graves hailed to know whether she had struck, as her pennant was still streaming out upon the wind. But he could receive no distinct answer; her officers and crew were all in confusion, as she lay aback, with her studding-sails and smaller sails flying about in extreme disorder.

Ere long the *Magicienne* was on the larboard quarter of the headmost ship, and brought her to close action. This lasted for an hour and three-quarters, with her studding-sail booms locked in, the sides frequently touching, the cannon being literally muzzle to muzzle; the men hurling grape and other shot by the hand, and frequently striking at each other through the port-holes with their half-pikes and rammers.

The smaller vessel, taking advantage of this state of matters, made sail, rehoisted her colours, and made off, firing her guns at the *Magicienne* as long as she was within range. At a quarter past two, when the enemy's fire was nearly silenced, and there was every appearance of her becoming a prize, the main and mizzen-topmasts of the *Magicienne* came down; and as they unfortunately fell clear of the enemy's ship, she had thus an opportunity of increasing her distance.

Five minutes after the foremast followed; and the *Magicienne*, deprived thus of all means of pursuing the enemy, lay like a helpless log upon the sea.

"The *Magicienne* had already lost her mizzen-mast," says the *Gazette de France* of the 13th of May, "when a volley of langridge shot scoured the quarter-deck of *La Sibylle*, killing eleven men, and striking down the Count de Kerigarian, who for some time was thought to be dead. The Sieur Descures, post-lieutenant, then took command in his place, re-established the battle which this event had relaxed, and had the satisfaction to see the main and foremasts of the *Magicienne* fall in succession."

La Sybille, now had her canvas spread to the yard-heads, and made off with all speed; while every gun that could be brought to bear upon her stern was fired at her. At half-past three the *Endymion* passed in full chase, her crew cheering vociferously; the enemy being then distant two miles on the starboard beam.

On board the *Magicienne* there were killed three officers and sixteen seamen; wounded, three officers, twenty-nine seamen, and five marines.

Until eight in the evening the *Endymion* continued to pursue *La Sibylle*, which had thirteen men killed and twenty-nine dangerously wounded, with eight more slightly. The count, her commander, had previously sent a solemn challenge to one of our frigates on the North American station.

In the following month there occurred a curious instance of the capture and recapture of one of our frigates.

On Monday, the 10th of February, His Majesty's ship *Argo*, commanded by Captain Butchart, sailed from Tortola, one of the most mountainous and rocky isles of the Virgin group, with General Shirley on board, bound for Antigua. Eight days after Captain Butchart found by the chart that, owing to strong lee currents and head winds, he had got no farther than Sombriero, a desert island in north latitude 18° 36'and west longitude 63° 28'. Then a heavy gale came on, a high sea was running; the *Argo* sprung (i.e., cracked, or split) her main topmast, and just at that crisis two French frigates hove in sight and ran up their colours.

Captain Butchart gave orders to clear away for action instantly; by eleven o'clock, a.m., the headmost frigate was abreast of the *Argo*, and the fighting began with great ardour. Captain Butchart perceived the other frigate, which was a heavy one, coming up very fast with him; and finding it impossible to use his lower-deck guns, from the very high sea that was running, after having attempted to open the ports once or twice, when the waves came rushing in so heavily as to endanger the safety of the ship, he deemed it expedient to make a running fight of it, in hopes of the enemy losing something aloft, by which means he might escape to Tortola.

In the space of about an hour and a half the other frigate came up with the *Argo*, and both now being close to her, the fire of cannon and small-arms became very hot and destructive; but, notwithstanding the superior force of the enemy, Captain Butchart and his crew fought with the courage and resolution of British seamen. Till four in the afternoon the *Argo* faced these two ships, till Captain Butchart finding that thirteen of his men were killed, and a vast number lying wounded and helpless about the main-deck, unwilling to sacrifice the lives of others, and seeing the futility of further resistance, reluctantly struck his colours. By this time his mainmast had been severely injured by a crossbar shot, the maintopmast had gone by the cap, the mizzenmast was fractured, and much of his rigging had been shot away.

The frigates proved to be the *Amphitrite* and *Nymphe*, the latter carrying forty-eight guns, eighteen-pounders on the main-deck and nine-pounders on her poop; the former having thirty-six guns, six and twelve-pounders. The *Argo* continued in their possession still five o'clock next morning, when suddenly His Majesty's ship *Invincible*, 74 guns, Captain Saxton, hove in sight, as she was beating up for Jamaica. This occurred a little to windward of Porto Rico.

She recaptured the *Argo* - the two frigates escaping - and carried her into Spanish Town on the 24th of February.

General Shirley had remained on deck with the marines during the whole of the action.

From the violence of the weather, the French had done nothing towards repairing the *Argo*; so she was retaken in exactly the same condition she was in when Captain Butchart struck his colours.

- C H A P T E R   X X I V   -
A FRIGATE BATTLE IN 1795

ONE OF the most spirited of the many gallant actions between frigates, during our long war with France, was that fought between the *Blanche*, a British twelve-pounder thirty-two-gun frigate, commanded by Captain Robert Faulknor, and the *Pique*, a French thirty-six-gun frigate, Captain Conseil, off the Isle of Guadaloupe, in 1795.

The captain of the *Blanche*, when serving at the capture of Martinique, was tried by a court-martial (but acquitted) for killing one of his quarter-masters for disobedience during the engagement. He was the son of Captain Robert Faulknor, who took *La Courageux*, 74 guns, in 1761.

About daybreak on the morning of the 4th of January, the *Blanche* discovered the *Pique* lying at anchor just outside the harbour of Pointe-à-Pitre, the commercial emporium of Guadaloupe, on the south-west coast of the Grande Terre district.

At seven a.m. the *Pique* got under weigh, and began to make an offing by letting fall her topsails; backing the mizzen occasionally to keep near a schooner which accompanied her. At half-past eight the *Blanche* cleared away for action, and made sail to meet them both, until nearly within gun-shot of Fort Fleur d'Espée, when, finding the *Pique* disinclined to leave the cover of its batteries, the *Blanche* which had been defiantly hove-to, made sail to board a second schooner, which was seen running along the well-wooded shore of Grande Terre.

At half-past twelve, when the two frigates were about three miles apart, the *Pique* filled her yards and made sail towards the *Blanche*, which shortly after had brought-to the schooner., The latter proved to be an American, laden with wine and brandy, from Bordeaux, and bound to Pointe-à-Pitre, which, with all the Isle of Guadalonpe, was then in our possession. Taking the schooner in tow, the *Blanche* steered towards the Saintes, a group of rocky isles that lie between Guadaloupe and Dominica.

At two in the afternoon the *Pique* crossed the *Blanche* on the opposite tack, and, displaying the tricolour, fired four shotted guns.

Considering this as a deliberate challenge, the British frigate fired a single shot to windward. At half-past two, when the sky was bright and the sea smooth, finding that the *Pique* was standing towards her, the *Blanche* shortened sail, as if awaiting her; but at half-past three the former tacked and stood away.

Lord Howe.

Tired of this coquetting, and hoping to induce the *Pique* to follow him, Captain Faulknor, an officer of bravery and experience, trimmed his ship under her topsails and courses, and stood away towards Marie-Galante (one of the Little Antilles), the brown barren mountains of which were barely visible at the horizon.

At seven p.m., observing the *Pique* still lingering under Grande Terre, Captain Faulknor wore his ship and stood towards Dominica. An hour after the French frigate was descried astern, about six miles distant, standing in pursuit of the *Blanche*, which instantly cast off the American schooner she had in tow, and, tacking, made all sail to close with her.

Midnight had barely passed when the *Blanche*, on the starboard tack, passed under the lee of the *Pique*, which was then on the port tack, when every rope and spar could be seen distinctly under the clear starry light of a West Indian sky. The ships exchanged broadsides in passing, but they were as yet too far apart to do damage.

At half-past twelve, having got nearly in the long white wake of her antagonist, the *Blanche* tacked suddenly; and before one o'clock on the morning of the 5th, when within musket-shot of the starboard quarter of the *Pique*, the latter wore, i.e., turned her head away from the wind, with the intention of crossing her opponent's bows and raking her ahead. To prevent this, Captain Faulknor gave orders to '"wear ship" also; and then the two frigates, in the first hour of the morning, became closely engaged, broadside to broadside.

The *Blanche*, after fighting her guns for an hour and a half, shot ahead, and was in the act of luffing up to port to rake the *Pique* ahead, when the main and mizzen-masts of the former, having been wounded, went crashing over her side to leeward. The *Pique* next ran foul of the *Blanche's* larboard quarter, and made several attempts to board. These the British crew resisted

223

with success; and the larboard quarter-deck guns, and such of the main-deck guns as could be brought to bear, were fired with terrible effect into the *Pique's* starboard bow.

Meanwhile the small-arm men of the latter, perched in the tops and lower rigging, were blazing away in the starlight, while a fire was returned from some of her quarter-deck guns run in amidships, fore and aft. Amid this truly infernal scene of destruction, the carnage, in a space so small, was very great; and at three in the morning, while assisting with his own hands Second Lieutenant Milne and others of the crew to lash with such ropes as were at hand the bowsprit of the *Pique* to the capstan of the *Blanche*, so that escape should be impossible, preparatory to a more secure fastening by means of a hawser, a musket-shot pierced the heart of the young and gallant Faulknor, who fell to rise no more.

On the death of the captain becoming known, a yell came from the crew of the frigate, and more resolutely and grimly than ever did they work their guns to avenge him.

Cape St. Vincent.

Soon after his fall the lashings broke loose, but the *Pique* again fell foul of the *Blanche* upon her starboard quarter. In an instant, with cheers of triumph and derision, the British sailors lashed her bowsprit to the stump of their own mainmast. Clutched in this fashion, the *Pique* was towed before the wind by her resolute enemy, now commanded by Lieutenant Frederick Watkins, afterwards Captain of the *Néréide*, and the captor of Curacao. Again and again, with axe and cutlass, did the Frenchmen seek to slash through this second lashing; but standing shoulder to shoulder the marines of the *Blanche* poured a storm of bullets on the spot and swept them away.

The fire of musketry that came from the forecastle and tops of the *Pique*, together with that of her quarter-deck guns levelled forward, proved very destructive to the *Blanche*, which was without stern ports on the main deck. In vain had her carpenters striven to cut down the upper transom beam, so no alternative remained but to blow it away by dint of cannon-shot. Bucket in hand, the firemen were summoned to the cabin, where the captain lay dead and still amid the roar of conflict about him, and two guns were levelled against the stern frame.

This discharge made a clear breach on both sides of the rudder-case, and the firemen soon extinguished the blaze it had occasioned in the woodwork; and thus two twelve-pounders from an unexpected point played havoc along the deck of the *Pique*.

At a quarter-past three in the morning the mainmast of the French frigate (her fore and mizzen-masts having previously come down) fell over the side. In this utterly defenceless state, without a gun which, on account of the wreck of her masts, she could now bring to bear, the *Pique* sustained the raking fire of the *Blanche* until quarter-past five a.m., when some of the French crew from the bowsprit-end called aloud for quarter. "The *Blanche*," continues James, in his "Naval History," "immediately ceased her fire; and every boat in both vessels having been destroyed by shot, Lieutenant Milne, followed by ten seamen, endeavoured to reach the prize by means of the hawser that still held her, but their weight bringing the bight of the rope down in the water, they had to swim a part of the distance."

So ended this most spirited and gallant duel between these two frigates.

Besides her thirty-two long twelve and six-pounders, the *Blanche* mounted six eighteen-pounders; and having sent away in prizes two master's mates and twelve seamen, had on board only 198 men and boys. Of these she lost Captain Faulknor, Midshipman Bolton, and six seamen killed, and twenty-one wounded.

The *Pique* had two carriage-guns, six-pound carronades, less than her complement, thirty-eight in all; but along her gunnel were a number of brass swivels. The strength of her crew is variously given. Vice-Admiral Benjamin Caldwell states it at more than 360, while the French affirm it to have been no more than 360; however, "head money" was paid for 265 men taken. The *Pique* had, it appears, 76 officers and men killed, and no wounded, "a loss," says James, "unparalleled in its proportion."

Among the wounded mortally was Captain Conseil, of the *Pique*, which, it must be admitted, her crew fought in a most gallant manner, only surrendering when their ship was a defenceless hulk, and themselves reduced to a third of their original number. "On the part of the British officers and crew," says our naval historian, "consummate intrepidity was displayed from the beginning to the end of this long and sanguinary battle. Indeed, a spirit of chivalry seems to have animated both parties; and the action of the *Blanche* and *Pique* may be pointed to with credit by either."

The master of the former frigate, David Milne, was afterwards captain of *La Seine* (as her name imports, a prize), and captured, after a gallant action, *La Vengeance*, a French frigate of fifty guns.

The *Blanche* was afterwards totally lost, in the year 1799, when conveying troops from the Helder.

OFF L'ORIENT, 1795

ON THE 16th of June, 1795, a squadron of ships under the flag of the Hon. William Cornwallis, Vice-Admiral of the Blue, was cruising off" the coast of France. He was an officer who had greatly distinguished himself on many occasions, particularly in the action off Grenada, in 1779, in the following year off Monte Christi, and elsewhere.

Being in with the land near Penmarch Point, the promontory of Audierne Bay, in the department of Finistère, the *Phaeton*, thirty-eight-gun frigate, under the Hon. Robert Stopford, having been sent ahead to look out, signalled, "A fleet in sight."

Upon the *Phaeton* bringing-to, the vice-admiral made the signal to haul to the wind on the starboard tack. By this time thirty sail were in sight; and, according to a signal from the scouting frigate, among them were thirteen line-of-battle ships, fourteen frigates, two brigs, and a cutter. They were to leeward of the British squadron, and sailing on a wind with all their canvas set.

The squadron of Admiral Cornwallis consisted of only eight sail of the line, two frigates, and a sixteen-gun brig, so it was impossible to face this French fleet, which gave immediate chase; but, owing to the lightness of the wind, they did not get within gun-shot during the whole day.

The *Brunswick* and *Bellerophon*, two seventy-four-gun ships, the first commanded by a Scottish peer, James Lord Cranstoun (who distinguished himself as captain of the *Belliqueux*, in the actions between Hood and the Count de Grasse), and the latter under Lord C. Fitzgerald, afterwards Baron Lecale, in Ireland, being very dull sailers, were repeatedly in danger of being intercepted and cut off; but the admiral ordered the *Mars* and

Triumph, under Sir Charles Cotton and Sir Erasmus Gower, to keep between them and the enemy, and bring up the rear, as he was determined not to abandon any of His Majesty's ships, even before a force so superior.

Next morning, when day dawned, the enemy had got well up with our little fleet, and were found upon both quarters, as if determined to make a vigorous attack; however, it was not until nine o'clock that one of their leading ships opened a fire upon the *Mars*, together with a frigate which kept more to leeward than the rest, and when she ranged up on the port quarter of the *Mars* she yawed and fired frequently.

From her stern-chasers, the *Mars* replied to them both by a well-directed cannonade, the shot in many instances passing through the enemy from stem to stern; thus in about half an hour the van ship of the French dropped the action, but another took her place, and the line-of-battle ships that were to leeward came up in succession, maintaining a harassing fire all day, till seven in the evening, when show was made of a more serious attack on the *Mars*. This determined the admiral to bear up with the whole squadron to her support; when, to the surprise of all, the French armament, just as the sun was setting, bore away and made all sail for France, declining to engage.

This unexpected retreat is said to have been hastened by a ruse of Admiral Cornwallis, who caused signals to be made as if a superior British fleet was in sight, which caused the French admiral to relinquish a pursuit which the British were quite ready to turn into a close battle.

"Indeed," says Cornwallis, in his dispatch, "I shall ever feel the impression which the good conduct of the captains, officers, seaman and marines, and soldiers in the squadron has made on my mind; and it was the greatest pleasure I ever received to see the spirit manifested by the men, who, instead of being cast down at seeing thirty sail of the enemy's ships attacking our little squadron, were in the highest spirits imaginable. I do not mean the *Royal Sovereign* alone; the same spirit was shown in all the ships as they came near to me: and although (circumstanced as we were) we had no great reason to complain of the conduct of the enemy, yet our men could not help repeatedly expressing their contempt of them. Could common prudence have allowed me to let loose their valour, I hardly know what may not have been accomplished by such men."

The damage sustained by our squadron was trivial; none were killed, and only twelve men on board the *Mars* were wounded. But though the French fleet relinquished the pursuit of Admiral Cornwallis, who came to anchor in Cawsand Bay, they did not return to port, but continued at sea; and this affair formed the preface to the severe engagement which took place on the 22nd of the same month.

At dawn on the morning of that day, the *Nymph* and *Astræa*, the look-out frigates ahead of the Channel Fleet commanded by our Admiral of the White, Alexander Lord Bridport (the gallant Hood of previous naval battles), made the signal of the enemy's fleet being in sight.

The force under Lord Bridport was twenty-two sail, carrying 1,454 guns. His own flag was on board the *Royal George*, no guns: and among the officers serving under him were Curtis, of Gibraltar fame; Sir Alan Gardiner; Sir Snape Douglas, who, in the great battle of the 1st of June, 1794, had won the highest commendations for valour; Lord Hugh Seymour, Admiral of the Blue; and Captain (afterwards Sir Henry) Harvey, who commanded the *Ramillies* on the same occasion.

In Bridport's squadron were the *Queen Charlotte*, like the flag-ship, of no guns; five of ninety-eight guns; the *Sans Pareil*, 80 guns; five seventy-fours; six frigates; two fire-ships, and one hospital ship, the *Charon*.

Though superior in force, the French fleet, of thirty-two

sail, wished to avoid coming to action, which Lord Bridport observing, caused him to hoist the signal for a general chase. The weather being calm and the wind light, the pursuit and flight continued during the whole of that day and the ensuing night; and early on the morning of the 23rd the sax headmost ships, when the long low coast of the Morbihan and all its scattered islets, I were rising from the sea, rapidly came up with the enemy, bringing the wind with them.

These were the *Irresistible*, *Orion*, the *Russell*, and *Colossus*, all seventy-four-gun ships; the *Sans Pareil*, 80, and the *Queen Charlotte*, 110 guns, carrying the flag of Sir Roger Curtis, Rear-Admiral of the Red; and before six the action began, and was continued without intermission for three hours.

Ere long the hostile ships were close in-shore - so close that some forts from thence opened a cannonade upon the British, particularly on the *Queen Charlotte*, which her captain, Sir "Andrew Snape Douglas, an officer of high valour (the captor of the *Dumourier* and *St. Jago*, register ship, worth a million of money), steered in between the fire from the land and that of the enemy's leading line-of-battle ship, which he completely cut off, and compelled to strike, with the loss of only thirty-six of his men killed or wounded.

The soldiers of the 118th Regiment of the Line, a corps recently embodied, were scattered in detachments throughout the squadron, and did good service by the fire of musketry they maintained from every available quarter.

In this action the ships occasionally passed each other, as they got a start by a puff of wind. A Scotch sailor on board the *Colossus* played the bagpipes in the foretopmast-staysail netting during the whole battle, "the martial notes of the pipes sounding strangely over the water, with amusing and cheering effect," in the intervals of the firing.

Lord Bridport, in his dispatch, particularly mentions the

bravery and manly spirit of Captain William Domett, of the *Royal George*; and testifies "to the public zeal, intrepidity, and skill of the admirals, captains, and all other officers, seamen, and soldiers," during this short but sharp engagement, which ended at nine in the morning by the capture of *L'Alexandre* and *Le Formidable*, two splendid seventy-fours, and *Le Tigre*, 80 guns, with 500 killed and wounded men on board.

The rest of the enemy's fleet made all sail, escaped into the harbour of L'Orient, and came to anchor under shelter of the fortifications which defend it, and are of a somewhat formidable character.

The loss sustained by the British in this action amounted to only 31 killed and 113 wounded; of the former two were officers and of the latter nine.

The captured ships were added to the Royal Navy; and Lord Bridport, after distributing the prisoners among his squadron, found that the ships had suffered so little as to require no refitting, and consequently repaired once more to his post in the Channel.

CAPE ST. VINCENT, 1797

W HILE, THE armies of Republican France were proving almost everywhere triumphant on the Continent, the fleets of Britain rode victoriously in every sea; and by two brilliant victories in this year appeared more than ever to vindicate her old claim to the dominion of the ocean.

Admiral Sir John Jervis, K.B., who had for some time been blockading Cadiz, having received intelligence from Captain Foote, of the *Niger*, then stationed off Carthagena, that the Spanish fleet, under Don José de Cordova, had put to sea, sailed immediately in quest of it, with fifteen ships of the line, four frigates, a twenty-gun corvette, an eighteen-gun brig, and a ten-gun cutter.

He had with him old Trowbridge, of gallant memory, in the *Culloden*, 74; Admiral Parker, in the *Prince George*, 98; Captain (afterwards Sir Robert) Calder, in the *Victory*, 100, which carried his own flag; Sir Charles Knowles, in the *Goliath*, 74; Collingwood, in the *Excellent*, 74; and one whose name was yet to be greater than all, Horatio Nelson, as commodore, in the *Captain*, 74 guns.

The fleet bore altogether 1,414 pieces of cannon.

With high hope and gallant expectation in every heart, the seamen of Jervis, at dawn of day on the 14th of February, when on the starboard tack, Cape St. Vincent (known to the Portuguese as Cabo-de-Sao-Vicente) rising high and rocky against the horizon east by north, about twenty-four miles distant, descried the Spanish fleet, consisting of forty sail, extending from south-west to south, with all their canvas shining in the morning sun. After a time, the wind being west by south, the weather became hazy.

Among the Spanish ships were the *Santissima Trinidad*, 130 guns, a veritable floating castle; the *Conception*, *Salvador del Mundo*, *Manecano*, and *Principe de Asturias*, 112 guns each; one of eighty, and nineteen of seventy-four guns, with seven frigates and one twelve-gun brig.

At half-past six Captain Trowbridge, in the *Culloden*, signalled, "Five sail visible in the south-west quarter." At forty minutes past ten a.m., amid the deepening haze, Captain Charles Lindsay, in *La Bonne Citoyenne* (a French prize, of twenty guns) made a signal to Sir John Jervis, reporting the strength of the enemy, on which he ordered the ships to form in order of battle.

Formed in the most compact order for sailing, and in two lines, the fleet came on under a press of canvas, and with such speed that, as the admiral states in his dispatch, he "was fortunate in getting in with the enemy's fleet at half-past eleven o'clock, before it had time to collect and form a regular order of battle."

The five ships first discovered by the *Culloden* were at this period separated from their main body, which was bearing down in loose order to join them. It appeared to have been the first intention of Sir John Jervis to cut off those five ships before the main body of the fleet could arrive to their assistance. With this view he signalled the swiftest sailers to give chase; but on observing the near position of the main body, he afterwards formed his ships into a line of battle ahead, as most convenient.

At twenty minutes to eleven the admiral signalled to pass through the enemy's fleet, which was done. The separated ships attempted to form on the larboard tack, says Southey, in his "Life of Nelson," either with a design of passing through the British line or to leeward of it, and thus rejoining their friends. Only one succeeded in doing this, being so shrouded in smoke after the firing began as to be completely hidden.

Ten minutes after the passage through the line was effected, the *Culloden* began to fire on the enemy's leading ships to windward; and as ship after ship came up the action soon became general.

The regular and spirited cannonade of the British was but feebly returned by the enemy to windward; and they were completely prevented from joining their companions to leeward, and compelled to haul their wind on the larboard tack. "Admiral Jervis having thus fortunately obtained his first object," says Captain Schomberg, "now directed his whole attention to the main body of the enemy's fleet to windward, which was reduced at this time by the separation of the ships to leeward to eighteen sail of the line. A little after twelve o'clock the signal was made for the British fleet to tack in succession, and soon after the signal for again passing the enemy's line; while the Spanish admiral's design appeared to be to join the ships to leeward by wearing round the rear of "the British line."

Nelson, whose station was in rear of the latter, perceived that the Spaniards were bearing up before the wind with an intention of forming their line, going large (i.e., with the breeze abaft the beam), and joining their separated vessels, or else of getting away without an engagement. To prevent either of these schemes, he disobeyed the last signal without a moment of hesitation, and ordered his ship to be wore, and stood on the other tack towards the enemy.

In executing this bold and decisive manoeuvre, he found himself alongside of the Spanish admiral, Don José de Cordova, in the *Santissima Trinidad*. 130 guns; while close by were the *San Joséf*, 112; the *Salvador del Mundo*, 112; the *San Nicholas*, 80; the *San Isidoro*, 74; another ship of the same calibre, and a first-rate. Notwithstanding this terrible disparity of force, the gallant Nelson did not shrink from the contest.

Trowbridge, in the *Culloden*, immediately came up and supported him bravely; and for nearly an hour they maintained an unequal contest amid these mighty Spanish arks, which were crowded with men, and spouting fire and death from all their red portholes, while a blaze of musketry rolled incessantly along their upper decks.

The *Blenheim*, 90 guns, under Captain Frederick, now bore in between them and the enemy, and gave them a little respite, and time to replenish their lockers with shot, by pouring in her fire upon the Spaniards. The *Salvador del Mundo* and *San Isidro* were fired into with great spirit by Captain Collingwood, in the *Excellent*, 74 guns. The red and yellow standard of Castile and Leon descended from the high, gilded poop of the *San Isidro*, and Nelson thought that the *Salvador* had also struck. "But Collingwood," as he states, "disdaining the parade of taking possession of beaten enemies, most gallantly pushed up, with every sail set, to save his old friend and messmate, who was, to all appearance, in a critical situation."

For Nelson, in the *Captain*, was at that time under the concentrated fire of the *San Nicolas*, 80 (or 84), a seventy-four,

Battle of St. Vincent.

and three other first-rates. The *Blenheim* was ahead and the *Culloden* astern, sorely crippled. "Collingwood ranged up, and, hauling up his mainsail just astern, passed within ten feet of the *San Nicolas*, giving her a most tremendous fire, and then bore on for the *Santissima Trinidad*."

The *San Nicolas* luffing up, the *San Joséf* fell on board of her; then Nelson resumed his station abreast of them, and close alongside. His ship, after the dreadful cannonade she had undergone, was now incapable of further service, either in the line or in the chase. She had lost her foretopmast; her wheel was shot away, and not a sail, shroud, or rope was left. Finding her in this state, the commodore resolved on a bold and decisive measure; and this was, whatever might be the sequel, to board his opponent sword in hand. The boarders were summoned, and orders were given to lay the ship closer alongside the enemy.

Nelson's captain, Ralph Willet Miller, so judiciously directed the course of the ship that he laid her aboard the starboard quarter of the Spanish eighty-four, her spritsail-yard passing over the enemy's poop, and hooking in her mizzen shrouds. When the word to board was given, the officers and seamen destined for this perilous duty, headed by Lieutenant (afterwards Sir Edward) Berry, together with a detachment of the 69th or South Lincolnshire Regiment, then doing marine duty on board, led by Lieutenant Charles Pierson, all poured tumultuously into the enemy's ship, Berry dropping on the poop from the spritsail-yard, Nelson was aware that the attempt was hazardous, and thought that his presence might animate his brave shipmates, thus -he resolved to share in the enterprise. A soldier of the 69th, with the butt-end of his musket, smashed the upper quarter-gallery window, and jumped in, followed by the commodore, from the fore-chains of his own ship; and others came with pike and cutlass as fast as possible. The doors of the cabin were made fast, and the Spanish officers were resolutely firing their pistols at them through the window; but the doors were soon forced, and the Spanish brigadier fell while retreating to the quarter-deck. At the head of his boarders, seamen and soldiers mingled, Nelson rushed on, and found Captain Berry in possession of the poop, the Spanish ensign hauling down, and where he arrived just in time to receive the sword of the dying captain of the *San Nicolas*, who had been mortally wounded.

Passing onward to the forecastle, he met some Spanish officers, and received their swords. The British were now in full possession of the ship, and Nelson had been but a few minutes in taking measures for the security of his hard-won conquest, when suddenly a fire of musketry and pistols was opened upon her from the admiral's stern gallery of the *San José*. The two alternatives which instantly presented themselves to the decisive mind of Nelson were to quit the prize or board the three-decker; and, confident in the bravery of his seamen, he resolved on the latter. Placing sentinels of the 69th at the different ladders, he directed Captain Miller to send more men on board the prize, and gave instant orders for boarding the *San José* from the *San Nicolas*.

"Westminster Abbey or victory!" cried he, as, sword in hand, he led the way. Berry assisted him into the main-chains, and, as he was in the act of clambering up, a Spanish officer looked over the rail of the quarter-deck, and said -

"We have surrendered."

In less than a minute Nelson, at the head of his boarders, was on the poop, when the commandant advanced, and, inquiring for the British commander, knelt on one knee, presenting his sword by the blade, and apologising for the non-appearance of the admiral, who, he said, was lying dangerously wounded in his cabin.

At first Nelson could scarcely persuade himself of the reality of this second instance of good fortune; he therefore desired the Spanish commandant, who had the rank of brigadier, to muster the officers on the quarter-deck and to communicate to the crew the surrender of the ship. All duly appeared, and the commodore had the capture of the *San Joséf* confirmed by each officer delivering his sword in succession.

As he received them, one by one, he handed them, says Southey, "to William San Fearney, one of his old Agamemnons, who with the utmost coolness put them under his arm; 'bundling them up,' in the lively expression of Collingwood, 'with as much composure as he would a faggot, though twenty-two sail of their line were still within gunshot.' One of his sailors came up, and, with an Englishman's feeling, took him by the hand, saying he might not soon have such another place to do it in and that he was heartily glad to see him there."

Of the *Captain's* men, twenty-four were killed and twenty-six wounded. Nelson received only some bruises. The moment he returned to his own ship he signalled for boats to assist in disentangling her from the prizes; and, as she was rendered incapable of further service until entirely refitted, he shifted his pennant for a time on board *La Minerve*, frigate, and in the evening to the *Irresistible*, 74, where it remained until the *Captain* was again fit for service.

The Spaniards had still some eighteen ships which had suffered little or no injury, and that part of their fleet which had been separated from the main body in the morning was now coming up under a crowd of canvas; so Sir John Jervis hoisted the signal to bring-to.

He also ordered Captain Calder to lay his own ship, the *Victory*, on the lee quarter of the stem-most ship of the enemy, the towering *Salvador del Mundo*, and threw in so disastrous a fire that the Spanish commander, on seeing the *Barfleur*, 98, under Vice-Admiral Waldegrave, bearing down to enforce the attack, struck his flag. Meanwhile the van of the British fleet continued to press vigorously the *Santissima Trinidad*, and others which composed the rear of the now flying Spaniards. It was affirmed that the last-named ship had struck; she was, however, dreadfully shattered, and it was only with the utmost difficulty that she was towed into Cadiz.

It was four in the evening when Admiral Jervis signalled to bring-to; but the action was not over till five o'clock, as his dispatch states, and a strong line was formed for the protection of the disabled ships, and of the four prizes - the *Salvador del Mundo* and the *San Joséf* each of 112 guns; the *San Nicolas*, 84, and the *San Isidro*, 74.

The loss sustained by the British in this memorable battle amounted to exactly 300 officers and men killed or wounded; that of the Spaniards in the ships which were taken numbered 693. Those which escaped must have suffered considerably. Among the killed was the General Don Francisco Xavier Winthuyren, *Chef d'Escadre*, who had lost his right arm, when taken in the *Leocadia*, frigate, during the preceding war, by the *Canada*, Captain Sir George Collier.

When the firing ceased, Nelson went on board the ship of Sir John Jervis - that famous old *Victory* in which he was fated to breathe his last. He was received on the quarter-deck by the fine old admiral, who took him in his arms, and said that he could not sufficiently thank him. The sword of the Spanish rear-admiral, which Sir John insisted upon his keeping, he afterwards presented to the Corporation of Norwich, saying that "he knew no place where it could give him or his family more pleasure to have it kept, than in the capital of the county where he was bom."

In a narrative of the battle, published in June, 1797, we are told that not a gun burst on board the British fleet; and, as a sample of the heavy firing, the *Culloden* expended 170 barrels of powder, the *Captain* 146, the *Blenheim* 180, and all other ships in proportion.

The day subsequent to the action, while the British fleet was close under Cape St. Vincent, refitting and getting the prizes under sail, twenty-two Spanish ships of war suddenly hove in sight, and bore down in order of battle, as if resolved to engage again; but the British had barely beaten to quarters ere they hauled off, and made sail for Cadiz.

To secure his prizes and refit, Sir John Jervis was forced to put into Lagos Bay. There the squadron experienced the tail of a tempest, which, had the ships encountered it fully on the open sea, might have proved fatal to many a brave man who had escaped the perils of the battle off Cape St. Vincent. Captain Robert Calder brought home the dispatches, and received the rank of baronet. He was a native of Elgin, and had been born at Muirtown, his father's mansion, in the memorable year 1745.

Parliament voted thanks to the fleet; and the admiral was made a peer of Great Britain, by the titles of Baron Jervis of Meaford and Earl St. Vincent. Vice-Admirals Thompson and Parker were made baronets, and Commodore Nelson received the Order of the Bath, and the Freedom of the City of London in a gold box worth a hundred guineas. The victory was celebrated by a round of great guns from the Tower in London, and from the Castle in Edinburgh.

Very different were the emotions in Spain, and the awards to the Spanish fleet. Don José de Cordova was dismissed the service by Charles IV, and most of the flag-officers were degraded.

"I went this morning to visit the Spaniards," wrote the chaplain of the *Prince George*, three days after the battle, "and to witness a scene of desolation too melancholy to dwell on. Everything is shattered to pieces, and every countenance exhibits dismay and despair. One of the surviving captains, upon my expressing

Nelson receiving the swords on board the 'San Joséf'.

concern for the slaughter of his brother officers, assured me that he envied their lot, and that he should have welcomed death, under the pressure of such national disgrace. Individually no blame could attach to him or the other commanders of the ships we have taken; they defended themselves most gallantly, till they became mere water-logs, and no longer obedient to the helm. It would seem that they were wholly unprepared to receive us, and when they first descried us not a gun was loaded or a bulkhead knocked down.

"With regard to my own feelings during the action, which lasted five hours and a half, they were various. The cockpit is my appropriate station - a station which, in my opinion, demands more fortitude than any other in the ship. When the firing commenced, my sensations, I will acknowledge, were somewhat unpleasant; there was a solemnity which awed, if it did not frighten. We waited with anxious suspense, unknowing what was passing above, except the tremendous and incessant roar of the cannon, which stunned and deafened us. Our attention was soon called away to other objects. A seaman whose thigh had been dangerously wounded by a splinter was brought down to us, and he was shortly succeeded by others, wounded and dying. It was a scene I can never forget; but it is the most painful I have to remember. During the intervals I could be^spared from the amputations, I went upon deck, but there the scene was altogether different. Our seamen were in their element; they fought with the utmost contempt of danger and death, and the only difficulty was to restrain their impetuosity. Every lad," adds the letter, which appeared in the *Edinburgh Herald* for 1797, "seemed to take as much interest in the battle as the commander-in-chief himself; and when any of the enemy's ships struck, enthusiasm resounded through the whole fleet, and the cheers were repeated even by the wounded in the cockpit. I never felt myself so much an Englishman as on this proud day."

- C H A P T E R   X X V I I -
FRIGATE BATTLES, 1796

IN DECEMBER, 1796, the *Terpsichore*, frigate, commanded by Captain Richard Bowen, who in the same year so gallantly captured the Spanish ship *Mahonesa*, was cruising off Cadiz, when, at daylight on the morning of the 14th, he descried a large frigate lying on his weather-quarter; and as the wind was then blowing hard, and the sea running high, short, and covered with foam, he immediately turned and made sail, setting up his topgallant-masts and yards; and the moment the *Terpsichore* was ready, he tacked after the stranger in hope of bringing her to action.

The instant he was seen to tack, she made all sail and kept her wind, but as the latter headed the British frigate, he failed to come within gunshot of her. Soon after crossing her Captain Bowen tacked and chased with various success, sometimes gaining at others losing ground; while the wind was from the south-east, with sudden squalls, and very variable. About two in the afternoon she wore, and stood to the east-north-east, which brought her nearer the pursuer, who continued the chase under his courses only till two next morning, when, drawing in with the land about Cabo San Marco, Captain Bowen "wore ship, gave up the chase, and lay with head off shore."

About eight a.m., she was visible again from the masthead. He made all sail once more, tacked after her, and as the wind was round in the southwest, he had her on the lee bow, which gave him some hopes; but observing that she had made sail for Cadiz, he became doubtful of catching her before she got in, particularly as the fore and mainmasts of the *Terpsichore* had been sprung during the chase of the preceding day. However, Captain Bowen bore on, with all the canvas he could venture to spread, by ten o'clock, in the darkness of the December night, was alongside of her.

When the crew of the French frigate - for such she proofed to be - found that they had no hope of getting off, they hauled up their courses, hove-to, and ran out their guns, and allowing the *Terpsichore* to overtake her, quietly awaited her fire.

"When we came upon her weather quarter," wrote an officer who was on board, "we hailed her several times; not receiving any answer, and drawing up within ten yards, we 'tipped her a Terpsichore'(a technical term for our broadside), which laid about forty of those brave Republicans low."

She now hoisted the tricoloured flag, and a broadside of eighteen guns blazed out at once in reply; and for an hour and a quarter the cannonade and fire of small-arms was maintained in the dark between the two frigates, till the enemy suddenly struck.

When the firing had completely ceased, and the British were about to house their guns, the French treacherously fired a cannon double-shotted. Both the balls came up by the chess-tree of the *Terpsichore*, killing a boy, maiming four seamen, and dangerously wounding in the shoulder the captain's brother, Lieutenant George Bowen, who was also hurt in the head and feet by flying wood splinters.

The prize proved to be *La Vestale*, frigate, from Toulon, bound for Brest, of thirty-six twelve and thirty-six-pounders. She had her captain and forty seamen killed, and about a hundred wounded, besides twelve men that went overboard with her foremast, just as Captain Bowen's boat went alongside to take charge of her.

His loss was only four killed and eighteen wounded.

The affair of the *Terpsichore* and *Vestale* was deemed one of the best fought frigate actions during the naval campaign of the year, especially when it is -borne in mind that of his small complement of 250 men, he had two lieutenants, three midshipmen, the boatswain, and forty others absent, in hospital or away with prizes, while *La Vestale* had on board 300 men all told.

The master with eight sailors took charge of the prize; and, on being left to their own resources, found their situation somewhat perilous. The ship was in only four fathoms of water, upon a lee and rocky shore, the black waves running mountains high; all her masts and bowsprit gone, the gun-deck full of dead and dying men, no cables or anchor clear; the French prisoners, released from discipline, all drunk and disorderly: yet the master and those eight seamen made a shift to bring her up in less than three fathoms of water, and rode out the stormy night about two miles from shore, to the northwest of Cape Trafalgar, where the bottom was full of sharp rocks.

The *Terpsichore*, from her crippled situation and slender crew, all of whom were required to repair her own damages, could render the prize no assistance, but remained by her until she was moored; and when day dawned Captain Bowen anchored near, in hope of a favourable start to tow her off.

In the evening the wind began to abate a little, and the *Terpsichore* got under weigh with her prize in tow; but as the tow-rope got foul of a rock, it was cut to extricate both ships from imminent danger, and once more the prize, with the master and eight seamen, and all the French prisoners, was left to chance. The frigate stood off for the night, intending to pick her up in the morning; but the moment the *Terpsichore* was out of sight the prisoners, by a preconcerted plan, easily overpowered the slender prize-crew, set up a pair of sheers, and prepared to hoist out the launch and escape ashore.

Some Spanish boats now came off to them, and aided by the crews of these, they hoisted some canvas on the sheers, and steered along the shore for Cadiz, into which place the crew of the *Terpsichore*, when day dawned, had the mortification to see her towed with her colours flying. During all these operations Captain Bowen never had his uniform off. He remained on deck - where all his meals were brought to him - night and day, being without a single officer to assist him; his brother, Lieutenant Bowen, being in his cot dangerously wounded, and all the others out of the ship.

"I hope," wrote an officer of the *Terpsichore*, "we have only to lament her loss to us as a prize, and that our exertions will entitle us to as much credit as if we had brought her into Gibraltar. To have destroyed her was far more than we could manage without the wounded sharing in the calamity, and that would have been cruel and disgraceful to the English character. We had lost one of our cutters alongside of her, and had only another boat remaining serviceable; therefore our only alternative was to take the chance of the wind to bring her off, and that proved against us."

La Vestale was afterwards taken, in 1799, by Captain Cunningham, of the *Clyde*; but two years before that the gallant Captain Bowen fell in the attack on Teneriffe.

About the time of this encounter off Cadiz, Nelson fought one of his most gallant frigate battles off the Isle of Corsica. It is related that, in 1793, when the British and Spanish squadrons were off Toulon, Captain Nelson, on seeing the latter manoeuvre, remarked -

"If ever we should happen to have a war with Spain, I should not for a moment hesitate, with an English sixty-four-gun ship, to attack a Spanish three-decker, and be sure to take her;" and on the night of the 19th of December, 1796, Nelson showed that he could be as good as his word.

Having been dispatched by Sir John Jervis, in the *Minerva*, frigate, Captain George Cockburn, and with the *Blanche*, to Porto Ferrajo, to bring some naval stores which were left there to Gibraltar, on his way he fell in with two Spanish frigates, the *Sabrina* and *Ceres*, the former of forty guns, twenty-eight of these being eighteen-pounders, on the main-deck. Leaving the *Blanche* to attack the *Ceres*, Commodore Nelson ordered Captain Cock-burn to bear down on the larger vessel, which carried a poop-light.

At ten minutes to eleven the *Minerva* brought her antagonist to a close action, which was maintained resolutely till half-past one next morning, when the colours of the *Sabrina* were struck; but not until she had lost her mizzenmast, and had 164 killed or wounded out of 286, while the *Minerva* had only thirty-nine killed and wounded; but all her masts were shot through and her rigging much cut. Some of the 11th Regiment were serving on board as marines.

The commander of the *Sabrina*, who was her only surviving officer, and who proved to be Don Jacobo Stuart, a descendant of the Duke of Berwick, had barely been conveyed on board the *Minerva*, when another Spanish frigate came up and compelled her to cast off the prize, which she had taken in tow, and on board of which Nelson had placed Lieutenants Culverhouse and Hardy. Ordering these officers to steer southward, Nelson, at half-past four a.m., engaged this new adversary, which, by five, wore and hauled off; but now a Spanish squadron of two ships of the line and two frigates came in sight.'

When day dawned, the *Blanche*, Captain D'Arcy Preston, from whom the *Ceres* had slipped, was seen far to windward, and the *Minerva* escaped only by the anxiety of the enemy to recover their own ship.

Lieutenants Culverhouse and Hardy managed the prize with such judgment that, by steering a different course and hoisting British colours above the Spanish, they attracted the attention of the admiral, who pursued them with his squadron; and after a stout resistance of one of his frigates, the two officers were obliged to yield the prize, after her masts had gone by the board. Meanwhile, though frequently within cannon-shot, it required all the skill of Captain Cockburn to get off with the crippled *Minerva*. The *Blanche*, which in the interim had attacked the other frigate, and compelled her to haul down her colours, was obliged to sheer off on the approach of the two three-deckers and join the *Minerva*.

As soon as Nelson reached Porto Ferrajo, he sent his prisoner under a flag of truce to Carthagena, having previously returned to him his sword. This he did in honour of the great gallantry which Don Jacobo Stuart had displayed, and inspired perhaps by some emotion of respect for his royal and unfortunate Scottish ancestors.

"I felt it," said he, "'consonant to the dignity of my country, and I always act as I feel right, without regard to custom. He was" the best officer in Spain, and his men were worthy of such a commander."

By the same flag of truce Nelson sent back all the Spanish prisoners that were at Porto Ferrajo, for whom he received in exchange his own men that had been taken in the *Sabrina*.

Commodore Nelson, in his despatch, speaks in the highest terms of the bravery of Captain Cockburn and all his officers, and of the high state of discipline and efficiency on board the *Minerva*.

- CHAPTER XXVIII -
OFF THE SCILLY ISLES, 1796

ON THE morning of the 8th of June, 1796, two of our frigates - that fashion of ship which was the most beautiful and stately of "Old England's wooden walls" - were seen seventeen leagues westward of the Scilly Isles. They proved to be the *Unicorn*, 32 guns, Captain Thomas Williams, and the *Santa Margarita*, 36 guns, Captain Thomas Byam Martin, a vigilant and active officer, who at a subsequent period took, after a brilliant action, *L'Immortalité*, 40 guns, when commanding a ship of the same weight of metal.

As the dawn brightened three large ships loomed into sight, three miles distant on the lee-beam; and Captain Martin, who first made them out to be French frigates, signalled to Captain Williams to make all sail and join him, and to come within hail. The former then informed him of the strength of the enemy. "The statement of their superiority encouraged him in his eager pursuit," says Captain Martin, in his dispatch to Admiral Kingsmill, at Cork, "having said that he would attack the largest ship, and desiring me to engage the next in strength. This noble example inspired every person with confidence of success, and each ship steered for her opponent; but the enemy determined to evade an action, and bore away under a press of sail, the smallest ship making off to windward."

At nine in the morning "they found themselves in a close bow and quarter line," and continued to run before the *Unicorn* and her consort in that position, the largest ship being under easy sail. They were fast being overtaken, and supposing they would soon be brought to action, Captain Williams signalled to clear away for battle; the hammocks were brought up and stowed, the bulkheads sent down in the usual fashion, the ports and magazines opened, the fire put out in the galley, and then the drums beat to quarters.

Nearer drew the chase, and the corvette, which detained the other ships, hauled, as we have said, to windward, and passed the weather-beam of our frigates in long-shot range; but afterwards she steered in the same course with her consorts, evidently to afford support to whichever might need it most.

At one p.m. the two frigates hoisted French colours gates in long-shot range; but afterwards she steered in proud defiance, as ours had already done the crosses of the Union. The largest ship showed a commodore's pennant, and at the same moment commenced a well-directed fire with her stern-chasers. The French corvette at this time, greatly to the surprise of Captain Williams and his crew, brought-to, for the purpose of boarding a sloop that was passing on the contrary tack.

The largest vessel was now discovered to be the *Thames*, 36 guns, and 320 men (formerly one of His Majesty's ships),

View of Cadiz.

251

now commanded by Citoyen Fraden; and the craft of which the *Unicorn* was in chase was *La Tribune*, 44 guns and 320 men, bearing the broad pennant of Citoyen Moulston, commander of a division. On her main deck were twenty-six twelve-pounders, on the fore and quarterdeck sixteen long sixes and forty-two-pound carronades. She had just been launched. The corvette to windward was *La Légère*, 24 guns (nine-pounders) and 180 men.

As Commodore Moulston continued to wait for the *Thames*, the *Unicorn* approached them both, but was retarded in her progress by the effects of their fire. At four p.m. the *Thames*, being the stern-most ship, bore round to avoid the fire of the *Unicorn*, and to pour a broadside into the bows of the *Santa Margarita*, while Captain Martin, manoeuvring his ship with the greatest judgment, laid her alongside his antagonist.

The superior and well-directed fire from Captain Martin's guns soon put the *Thames* in his possession; as he silenced her battery, her colours were struck, and a prize-crew put on board. On seeing his consort captured, the commodore made all the sail he could, hoisting royals and running out his studding-sails, and, by a very sudden and injudicious movement, sought to gain the weather-gage of the *Unicorn*, which at that time was pursuing him towards the entrance of the Irish Channel; and both vessels soon passed close to the Tuskar Rocks, a group off the coast of Wexford, consisting of four great and dangerous masses, about two furlongs in extent, on one of which a lighthouse now guides the mariner to the southern entrance of St. George's Channel.

The parity of sailing in the two ships, aided by the good judgment of the French commander, kept them engaged in a most exciting running fight for two entire hours. During this period the *Unicorn* suffered considerably aloft, as the French directed most of their efforts to cripple. "We were for some time," says her captain, in his dispatch to the;admiral, "unluckily deprived of the use of our maintopsail; but on its falling to less wind after dark, we were enabled to use our super and royal steering sails, which, by slow degrees brought us so near his weather quarter as to take the wind from his canvas, when, at half-past ten at night, after having pursued him two hundred and ten miles, we shot up alongside of our antagonist, gave him three hearty cheers, and commenced close action, which continued in that position with great impetuosity on both sides for thirty-five minutes, when, on the clearing up of the smoke, I observed that the enemy had dropped on our quarter, and was close-hauled, by a masterly manoeuvre, to cross our stern and gain the wind."

This, however, Captain Williams prevented by instantly throwing all his sails aback, and thus giving his frigate strong stern-way, by which he passed the Frenchman's bow, regained his situation, and once more poured- in his round shot and musketry. The effects of the fire soon put an end to all further manoeuvring, by completely dismantling the enemy's ship; her resistance gradually ceased, and her crew called out that they had surrendered.

The commander of the *Tribune* proved to be John Moulston, an American, who had been sixteen years in the French navy; and when brought on board the *Unicorn*, he was found to be severely wounded. The squadron he commanded, consisting of *La Tribune*, *La Proserpine*, the *Thames*, and *La Légère*, had only left Brest two days before. The second-named ship had parted from the rest in a fog.

"I will not attempt to find words to convey to you, sir," concludes Captain Williams, "the sense I feel of the conduct of the officers and ship's company under- my command, for if it was possible to say anything that could add to the glory of the British seamen, I have ample field for doing so in the situation I held this day. Indeed, nothing less than the confidence of the most gallant support from them, and the high opinion I entertain of our second, the *Santa Margarita*, could induce me to risk an action with a force apparently so much our superior; and while I congratulate myself upon the happy effects of their valour in the capture of two of the enemy's frigates that have done so much mischief to our commerce during the war, and on their present cruise were likely to do so much more, you may easily conceive what my feelings are, when I inform you that this service is obtained without the loss of one of the brave men under my command. My happiness will be complete if I find that the *Santa Margarita* has been equally fortunate."

Palace of Justice, Bruges.

The losses of the *Tribune* were thirty-seven men killed and seventeen wounded; thirteen of these severely.

The losses of the *Santa Margarita* in capturing the *Thames* were only two seamen killed, the boatswain and two seamen wounded; while the latter had thirty-two killed and nineteen wounded, many of the fatter so severely that they died.

The little squadron of Commodore Moulston was a very unlucky one, for, five days after the capture of those two ships, Captain Lord Amelius Beauclerk, in His Majesty's ship *Dryad*, when cruising, with Cape Clear bearing west by north, twelve leagues distant, at one in the morning discovered a strange sail standing towards him from the southward; but, on nearing, she hauled her wind and tacked, making off with a press of sail, and the sea whitening in foam under her bows.

Lord Beauclerk instantly bore after her in pursuit; all day the chase continued, till nine in the evening, when he brought her to close action, and in forty-five minutes compelled her to strike, when she proved to be the missing frigate *La Proserpine*, carrying twenty-six eighteen-pounders, twelve long nine-pounders, and four thirty-two pounders, with 348 men, under Citoyen Pevrieu; and in this instance, as in the other two, the disparity in casualties was very great, for Lord Beauclerk had only seven men killed and wounded, while *La Proserpine* had lying on her deck thirty slain and forty-five severely injured.

For his services in this naval campaign, Captain Williams was knighted, though no reward seems to have fallen to Captain Martin. Lord Beauclerk died an Admiral of the White, and G.C.B.

NAVAL EXPLOITS, 1796-7

ON THE 15th of July the *Glatton*, 54 guns, commanded by Captain Henry Trollope, sailed from Yarmouth Roads, in order to join a squadron under Captain Savage, then cruising in the Texel. The *Glatton* had only 350 men on board, and was one of those Indiamen which had been purchased by the Government, and armed with sixty-eight pounder carronades; and these were a species of gun with which Captain Trollope had been particularly successful during the war.

Next day, at one o'clock p.m., when four leagues off Helvoet, he descried a squadron with its topsails barely visible at the horizon; and owing to light winds and calms, it was seven in the evening before he was near enough to make out that it consisted of six frigates, one of which, the commodore's ship, appeared to mount fifty guns, two others about thirty-six guns, and the three smaller twenty-eight guns. There were also a very fine brig and cutter with them. As they did not reply to his signals, Captain Trollope suspected they were enemies, and, heedless of their numbers and strength, he cleared away for action, beat to quarters, and bore down on them.

From their manoeuvring, it was ten at night before he got close alongside the third ship of the enemy's line, which, from her size, he supposed must be the commodore. He hailed her, and on-being replied to in French, ordered her colours to be struck. In reply to this, fire flashed from all her port-holes, and her broadside came crashing into the *Glatton*, whose guns repaid her with interest, at twenty yards' distance. The action now speedily became a general one.

The two headmost ships of the enemy tacked, and one of the largest placed herself alongside the *Glatton*; the other on her weather-bow; and the sternmost placed themselves on her lee-quarter and stern, literally surrounding and sweeping her by a terrible cross-fire of cannon and musketry.

"In this manner," reported Captain Trollope to Admiral Macbride, commanding at Yarmouth, "we were engaged on both sides for a few minutes, our yard-arms nearly touching those of the enemy on each side, but I am happy to acquaint you that in less than twenty minutes we beat them off on all sides; but when we attempted to follow them we, much to our regret, found it impossible. I have no doubt, from the apparent confusion the enemy were in, we should have gained a decisive victory; but unfortunately, in attempting to wear, we found every part of our running rigging cut to pieces, and the major part of our standing rigging also."

Except the mizzen, every stay in the ship was cut through, thus endangering the fall of the masts, which, with the yards, were severely wounded; but every unwounded officer, seaman, and marine, were soon at work, knotting, splicing, and refitting, during the entire night; but it was seven in the morning before the ship was in tolerable enough order to engage again. The enemy, who had suffered but little aloft, though severely in their hulls from the smashing sixty-eight pounders of the *Glatton*, appeared in the morning in a close line; yet though the disabled state of the *Glatton* must have been plainly apparent to them, they did not care to come within range of her again, but bore away towards Flushing.

Until nine o'clock on the morning of the 17th, the *Glatton* followed them till they were within three leagues of that port, Captain Trollope having hope, as he tells us, of meeting with some of our cruisers to enable him to destroy them; but as it came on a tough gale from the west, and his battered ship being in bad working order, he was forced to haul off shore and seek the offing. He then bore back to Yarmouth Roads.

"I cannot conclude this report," he states, "without recommending to your notice in the strongest manner, Robert Williams, my first lieutenant, who gave me every assistance in his power on the upper deck; as also Lieutenant Schomberg, second lieutenant, and Third Lieutenant Pringle, who commanded on the lower deck; and also Captain Strangeways, of the marines."

The latter was severely wounded by a musket-ball in a dangerous part of the thigh; and though it could be extracted, and a tourniquet was put upon him, he insisted on ascending again to the main deck, where, sword in hand, he remained at his post encouraging his men, amid all the uproar of that midnight battle, till he grew faint from loss of blood, and was again carried below.

It is a very remarkable circumstance that in this hot action, in which so many guns were turned upon her, the *Glatton* had not one man killed, and besides the captain of marines, only another wounded, Corporal William Hall, who also received a bullet through one of his thighs. "Our small loss," says Captain Trollope, "can only be attributed to their firing totally at our rigging to disable us, in which they too well succeeded; and as H.M.S. *Glatton* was unfit to keep the sea from the damage she has received in her masts, yards, and rigging, I have thought fit for the good of his service to come to Yarmouth Roads."

Captain Strangeways died soon after his wound. The merchants of London presented Captain Trollope with a piece of plate valued at a hundred guineas, and he was afterwards knighted by the king.

On the 13th of January in the following year, 1797, the *Indefatigable*, 44 guns, commanded by Sir Edward Pellew, Bart., and the *Amazon*, 32 guns, under Captain Robert Carthew Reynolds, when about fifty leagues south-west of Ushant, at half-past twelve in the day, discovered a large vessel, in the north-west quarter of the horizon, steering under easy sail towards the coast of France.

The wind was westerly, and blowing hard. The atmosphere became thick and hazy, making the sails and outline of the stranger loom very large to the eyes of the watch on deck. Sir Edward signalled to the *Amazon* for a general chase, and followed it by the signal, "An enemy in sight."

By four in the afternoon he had gained upon the stranger sufficiently to make out that she had two tiers of guns, with her lower-deck ports closed, and that she was flush-built, without a poop. At a quarter to six Sir Edward brought her to action - a close one, that was well supported on both sides for fully an hour, when the *Amazon* came up under a press of sail, but unavoidably shot ahead of the enemy, who very nearly ran on board of her, and seemed to be very full of men from the terrible musketry fire she maintained, from both of her sides at once.

As soon as some repairs necessary on the rigging had been effected, and the *Amazon* had reduced her canvas, both ships commenced a second attack on the two-decker, placing themselves, after some raking broadsides, on each of her quarters, within pistol range; and thus they fought, in the dark, without a moment's intermission, for five consecutive hours.

The two British frigates then sheered off a little way to secure their masts, which were damaged; but the battle was resumed at a quarter to six a.m., and did not close until half-past four p.m. that day. Ten hours of greater fatigue were scarcely ever experienced by seamen than were endured by those of the *Indefatigable* and *Amazon*. The, sea was high, and rolling around them in foam, so that the men on the main deck frequently were fighting up to their waists in water, as sea after sea was shipped through the port-holes.

Some of the guns, by the rolling and pitching, broke their breechings four times over; some of them tore out the ringbolts, immediately after they were loaded. All the spars were wounded, and the maintopmast of the *Indefatigable*, which was totally unrigged, was only saved by the alacrity of her officers.

At twenty minutes past four in the morning, the clouds which partially obscured the moon passed away. She shone out more brightly than usual, and Lieutenant George Bell, who was looking out on the forecastle of the *Indefatigable*, reported "land in sight." He had scarcely gone aft to tell Sir Edward, this, when the white foam of breakers become visible to the look-out The ship was then under the enemy's starboard bow, and the *Amazon* as near her on the larboard.

Not an instant was to be lost, every life now depended on the prompt execution of Sir Edward's orders; the ships crippled, close in on an enemy's coast - a lee shore - and a French prison before all who might escape death among the breakers. The exact part of the land could not be ascertained in the moonlight; but it was supposed to be Ushant, or some portion of the Bay of Brest. With incredible alacrity, the tacks were hauled on board, and sail made to the southward.

Before day broke, breakers were again visible to leeward, so the two frigates wore to the northward, on the other tack. The officers were then satisfied that the land they had seen could not have been Ushant, and all waited the approach of day with the most intense anxiety.

When it stole in and lit the winter sea, the frigates were in twenty fathoms water, and their crews beheld, with generous commiseration, as Sir Edward relates in his dispatch to Mr. Evan Nepean, the enemy, who had so bravely defended herself, lying on her broadside, and a tremendous surf beating over her. The miserable fate of the brave but unhappy crew was, perhaps, the more sincerely lamented by us, from the apprehension of suffering a similar misfortune."

The *Indefatigable* could yield the drowning Frenchmen not the least assistance. She had at that time four feet of water in her hold; and had, after the battering she had undergone from the strange ship, to encounter a wild sea with a strong wind dead on the shore. But Sir Edward now ascertained by the chart his situation to be that of Audierne Bay, and that the fate of all on board depended on their being able to weather the Pen-march Rocks, near Point l'Abbé, in Finistère, which, "by the blessing of God," Sir Edward tells us, they did by eleven in the forenoon, exhausted though all were with the long chase, the battle, and the events of the subsequent night

While his ship had hauled her wind to the southward, the *Amazon* hauled hers to the northward. Captain Reynolds, notwithstanding every effort to save her, found her masts, yards, rigging, and sails so miserably cut up that, with three feet of water in the hold, it was impossible to work off a lee shore, on which she struck fatally at five in the morning. The crew- - all save six, who went off in the cutter and were drowned - were saved by making rafts of the wreck; but immediately on landing they were made prisoners.

The loss sustained on board the *Indefatigable* was only nineteen wounded, chiefly by splinters. Among these was Mr. Thompson, the first lieutenant. The *Amazon* had three killed and fifteen badly wounded.

The enemy's ship proved to be *Les Droits des Hommes*, 76 guns, commanded by Captain the *ci-devant* Baron le Crosse, manned by 1,600 seamen and soldiers, of whom 170 perished among the breakers, exclusive of those who fell in action.

- C H A P T E R   X X X   -
CAMPERDOWN, 1797

BRILLIANT THOUGH our navy campaigns were, they occurred in a season of gloom and distress. Holland had deserted her alliance with Britain; the latter stood alone against all the powers of Europe; and when the Bank of England stopped cash payments, and the ill-paid navy became mutinous, the distress and gloom seemed to deepen.

The French had a large army and powerful party in Holland, from whence it was determined to fit out an expedition against Ireland; which, in revenge for the succours afforded to the Royalists in Bretagne, was either to be severed wholly from Britain, or subjected to the ravages of war. The Directory gave orders to embark a body of troops on board a fleet, under the command of General Daendels, and no doubt was entertained that many of the discontented Irish would flock to his standard; but the chief difficulty was to have it unfurled on Irish soil.

On the first intelligence of these preparations, the Board of Admiralty sent a powerful fleet to the North Sea, with orders to intercept the enemy. During the whole summer the Texel, where the Dutch armament lay, was successfully blocked up by Admiral Adam Duncan. This celebrated seaman, was an officer of great experience and resolute bravery, who, by his tact and address, prevented the dangerous spirit of mutiny from spreading in his ship, the *Venerable*. The second son of Duncan of Lundie, in Forfarshire, he had entered the navy so far back as 1747, and had served with honour in many battles, particularly in the glory won by Rodney over the Spaniards off Cape St. Vincent, where his ship was the first in action.

Although he assumed such a position off the Texel as enabled him to discover all the motions of the enemy, yet, in- consequence of repeated procrastination and delay, no occurrence took place till autumn, when he was compelled to return to Yarmouth and refit; leaving, however, Captain Trollope, with a small squadron of five sail, to watch the Texel, the entrance to which is the south channel, then well fortified by many batteries, among which there was one mounting thirty-six thirty-six-pounders, and another twenty-four twenty-four pounders.

No sooner was his departure known at Amsterdam than the Dutch Government, which, in consequence of the advanced season, had brought the troops ashore, issued instant injunctions for the fleet to put to sea and achieve something. This movement was duly notified to Admiral Duncan by a signal from a vessel stationed at the back of Yarmouth Sands; so, with joyous alacrity, his whole fleet got under weigh with a fair wind, and in the afternoon the last of their sails had melted out of sight.

The Dutch fleet was under De Winter, an officer who had frequently distinguished himself as a general under Pichegru, and was supposed to be well acquainted with naval affairs. He had left the Texel with a squadron consisting of twenty-six sail, carrying 1,266 pieces of cannon, and 8,762 men

The force of Admiral Duncan amounted to sixteen sail, ranging from seventy-four to fifty-gun ships, having on board, including the frigates, 1,110 guns, and 8,916 men.

Of all the officers on board the British fleet at that time, few were more beloved than Duncan, unless we except Nelson; and certainly no man was more stately or commanding in appearance. "He was, without exception," says ah officer who met him at a public dinner, "the finest man in his person I ever beheld. Imagine a man six feet two inches in height (I think he was six feet four), with limbs of proportionate frame and strength. His features were nobly beautiful; his forehead high and fair; his hair white as snow. His movements were all stately, but unaffected, and his manner easy, though dignified. One of the most delightful traits of the nature of the gallant old man was, that he took the earliest occasion to turn towards his home and affections. 'Gentlemen/ said he, 'I give you the health of the best woman in the world - I give you my own wife, Lady Duncan !'The room shook with cheers, and I saw the veteran's eyes become moist with tears of fond recollection."

His flag was on board the *Venerable*, 74, with the starboard, or weather division; while Admiral Onslow, in the *Monarch*, 74, led the larboard, or lee division.

At nine o'clock, on the morning of the nth of October, Duncan got sight of Captain Trollope's squadron, with signals flying for an enemy to leeward. The admiral instantly bore up, making the signal for a general chase, and in less than an hour came in sight of the Dutch armament forming in line on the starboard tack to receive him, with the country between Camperdown and the three villages of Egmont and the sand-hills known as Egmond-op-den-Hoef lying about nine miles to

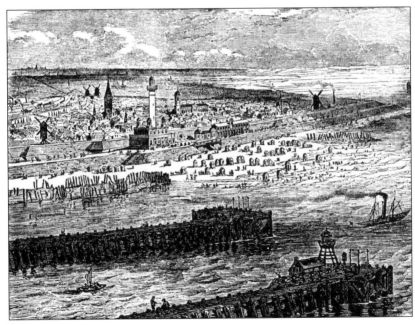

Ostend.

leeward. The coast was crowded by thousands of spectators, who, says a print of the time, "had the mortification of observing the entire destruction of their fleet, without the possibility of affording it any relief."

Fearing that the Dutch ships, which were built for their own shoaly seas, might get so close inshore that ours could not follow them, Admiral Duncan made a signal to prepare for action; to shorten sail and form in compact order; then to bear up, break the Dutch line, and engage to leeward, each ship choosing her own opponent: and by these means he got between them and the land, which they were fast approaching. In clearing away for action, all the bulkheads, and even the cabin chairs, were flung overboard, "with everything that might be in the way of working the guns, or occasion splinters."

His signals were obeyed with remarkable promptitude. Vice-Admiral Onslow, in the *Monarch*, bore down in the most gallant manner on the enemy's rear, followed by the whole of his division, the *Russell*, *Montague*, and *Powerful*, all ships of seventy-four guns, and four of sixty-four, the *Director*, *Veteran*, *Monmouth*, and *Agincourt*.

The Dutch were drawn up in two lines, the three admirals, De Winter, Story, and Reyntier, with their special flags flying, and all with their topsails aback. A little after twelve Admiral Onslow broke through the enemy's line, and passed under the stern of the Dutch Vice-Admiral Reyntier, engaging him to leeward.

Meanwhile Admiral Duncan, intending to engage the Dutch commander-in-chief, was prevented by the *States-General*, a seventy-six-gun ship, under Rear-Admiral Story, bearing a blue ensign at her mizzen, shooting close up to him; but the dreadful fire of the *Venerable* soon drove Story out of the line, after which Duncan fell alongside De Winter, in the *Vryheid*, 74. Each admiral was nobly supported by the ships of his division.

"At twelve," says an officer of the *Ardent*, 64, "our fleet was closely engaged with the enemy. The roaring of cannon was tremendous, and lasted two hours and a quarter, when we had the pleasure of seeing one of the Dutch ships with her poop all in a blaze, and one of their admiral's ships totally dismasted. In about ten minutes after, several of them struck their colours to us, the remainder making off as fast as they could; we being now within six miles of the land, and the wind blowing fresh. If we had not been so close to the enemy's coast, I have no doubt we should have brought the whole to England. Our loss is great; we have 140 killed and wounded on board of us. One of the men's wives insisted on firing the gun where her husband was quartered, though frequently requested to go below; but she could not be prevailed upon to do so, till a shot carried away one of her legs and wounded the other."

At the beginning of the action it is said that De Winter, on perceiving the movements of Duncan, had also hoisted the signal for his fleet to take close order, but that, owing to the thickness of the smoke, it was seen by only a few of the captains.

Captain Schomberg states that by one o'clock the action was general, and that every ship was engaged save two or three of the enemy's van, which slipped off without the smallest apparent injury, and returned quietly to the Texel next day. With unabated fury the battle went on for two hours and a half, by which time all the masts of De Winter's ship had gone by the board. However, she was defended for some time after in a most gallant manner. At length, finding further resistance vain, Admiral De Winter, being, it is said, the only man left on the quarter-deck who was not killed or wounded, struck his colours to the *Venerable*. About the same time the Dutch vice-admiral, dismasted and dreadfully battered, struck to Admiral Onslow.

A Scotch paper states that by this time the Dutch ships "presented a shocking spectacle in the inside, being covered with blood and brains." With these ghastly memorials the shrouds and rigging were literally clotted.

At one time the *Ardent*, whose captain was killed, had no less than five Dutch ships upon her at once; and she must have been sunk, had the *Venerable* not come to her assistance. The latter had many of 'her men killed by their crowding to the portholes and cheering whenever they saw any of the enemy strike.

The two first broadsides of the Dutch are described as having been terrible; but after they were received, on an average we fired three guns to their one.

Admiral Duncan, on finding himself in only nine fathoms of water, and but five miles from the land, had his attention so much occupied in getting his crippled ships off shore, that he was not able to distinguish die number which were actually captured; and as the wind blew constantly from the seaward, our fleet was much dispersed.

The ships secured were seven sail of the line, two of fifty-six guns, and two large frigates; the *Delft*, 56 guns, Captain Veerder, foundered. One of the frigates was also lost; the other drifted to the Dutch coast, and was retaken.

A conflict more bloody had not been as yet recorded in the naval annals of Britain, since the old Dutch wars at least. The loss sustained in killed and wounded on board of only nine ships of Admiral Duncan's fleet was upwards of 700; but the only officer of note killed was Captain Burgess, of the *Ardent*. The carnage on board the Dutch ships must have been terrible, if we are to judge by that on board the two which bore the admirals' flags, each having not less than 250 killed and wounded. Among the latter was Vice-Admiral Reyntier, whose injuries were such that he died soon after in England.

Admiral de Winter was a man of considerable bulk and stature; and it is said that when he came on board the *Venerable*, after the first exchange of compliments, he said in French -

"It is a matter of some surprise to me how two such gigantic objects as Admiral Duncan and myself have escaped the general carnage of the day." He lamented bitterly that amid that carnage, which, says Captain Brenton, "literally flooded the decks of the *Vryheid* in blood, he alone should have been spared."

After the action Admiral Onslow passed under Admiral Duncan's stern, three hearty cheers being exchanged between the ships. The former officer was then publicly thanked by the latter for his gallant conduct from the stern gallery. All the other ships then passed in succession, their crews saluting with those hearty triple cheers which Britons alone give, and never so well as in such a glorious hour as that.

After the cessation of the contest, the admiral mustered the crew of the *Venerable*, and, kneeling on the deck in their presence, "returned thanks to the God of battles for the splendid victory with which he had crowned their arms." The same authority adds that he and De Winter played a friendly game of picquet together on the night after the latter came on board the flag-ship.

The action was not over until half-past three in the afternoon, according to an officer of the *Belliqueux*, 64, whose crew, like those of other ships, spent the subsequent night in knotting, splicing, and refitting rigging and spars, and bending new sails, the old being torn to ribbons. At half-past twelve, he adds, all hands were called to bury the dead.

"The purser read the burial service over one lieutenant, a midshipman, and nine brother tars, who were immediately launched into the deep, tears streaming from all our eyes."

We are told that at the beginning of the action, the captain of the *Belliqueux*, John Inglis, a veteran Scottish seaman, on becoming perplexed by some of the admiral's signals, closed his telescope, and shouted to the sailing master -

Surrender of De Winter.

"Hang it, Jock! doon wi' the helm, and gang richt into the middle o't!"

Few events caused more ardent demonstrations of joy in London and elsewhere than the battle of Camperdown; and the excitement of the audience at Drury Lane was beyond all description when, on the curtain rising, they saw before them a model of the *Venerable*, fully rigged, floating on a transparent sea, with her rigging full of lamps.

On the 16th of October, the admiral anchored with his prizes at the Nore. On the following day His Majesty created him a peer of Great Britain, by the titles of Baron Duncan of Lundie, and Viscount Duncan of Camperdown, with augmentations to his coat-armorial, one of his supporters being a sailor bearing a Union Jack. His eldest son was created Earl of Camperdown in 1831; and at his new family mansion in Forfarshire (bearing the name of that old Dutch village near Alkmaer) there is still preserved the standard which Admiral de Winter struck when the *Vryheid* lay dismasted under the guns of the *Venerable*. There also is the sword of De Winter, as a letter from the present Earl of Camperdown informed the author.

The veteran admiral retained the command of the North Sea Fleet till 1804, when he retired into private life. Four years subsequently he offered his sword and his services to Government; but being struck by apoplexy, he had to hasten home to Scotland, and died at Kelso, in his seventy-third year.

- C H A P T E R   X X X I -
THE NILE, 1798

ENGAGING IN a fruitless attempt to open a path to the conquest of India, Napoleon spent two campaigns in Egypt and Syria. With a great fleet and army he sailed from Toulon, took Malta on his way, and landed at Alexandria. Passing onward to Grand Cairo, he defeated the Mamelukes in battle near the Pyramids; but his armament had been closely followed by Admiral Nelson.

Napoleon's movements in the East attracted the attention of all Europe, but particularly that of the British Government. Positive instructions had been sent to Lord St. Vincent, then stationed off Cadiz, to select a sufficient number of line-of-battle ships, the nomination of which was left entirely to his own choice; but the name of the commander to whom they were to be entrusted was specifically pointed out. This proved to be Sir Horatio Nelson. The latter was already in the Mediterranean, with a flying squadron under his orders, his flag being hoisted on board the *Vanguard*; but this force was insufficient to cope with an armament so powerful as that commanded by the French Admiral Brueix. Ten sail were detached, under Captain Trowbridge, the moment that a reinforcement from the Channel Fleet enabled Lord St. Vincent to spare such a force; and when these joined Sir Horatio Nelson, then Rear-Admiral of the Blue, he found himself invested with a command of fourteen sail, thirteen of which were seventy-fours, and one a fifty-gun ship, which he admitted into the line of battle. This fleet carried in all 6,968 men when he sailed in quest of the enemy.

Repairing to Naples for information, he next steered for Sicily, where he first heard of the surrender of Malta. He took on board expert pilots, and was the first admiral who ever passed the Straits of Messina with a fleet. On seeing his armament off their coast, the London papers allege that the people who crowded on its headlands shouted -

"God save King George and La Madonna!"

Having learned that after the delay of a week only the French had left Malta, he steered for Candia; and on being assured that their destination was for Egypt, he sailed for that coast, and reached the mouth of the Nile three entire days before the arrival of Napoleon. After an interview with the British consul, supposing his information to be incorrect, he sailed to Rhodes, and from there to Syracuse, from whence, on receiving undoubted intelligence that the French had been for some time in Egypt, he steered again for that coast, and ere long discovered thirteen sail of the line and four frigates at anchor in the Bay of Aboukir, on the 1st of August, and the tricolour flying on the walls.

Their presence there was first communicated by a signal from Captain Hood, of the *Zealous*. Nelson immediately hauled his wind, a movement followed by the whole fleet with the greatest alacrity. The signal was also made to prepare for battle.

For many days previous to this Nelson had scarcely taken either sleep or food. He now ordered dinner to be served; and when his officers rose from table to repair to their various posts, he said -

"Before this time to-morrow I shall have gained a peerage or Westminster Abbey !"

The French fleet, under Admiral Brueix and Rear-Admiral Villeneuve, lay moored in the form of a crescent, as near as possible to the island of Aboukir, and protected towards the west by a battery of cannon upon it. The whole of the west side of the bay abounds in rocks and shoals. On the east there are nine fathoms of water. The fleet of Brueix consisted of his own

The Battle of the Nile.

ship, carrrying 120 guns, three of eighty guns, nine of seventy-four, and four frigates, ranging from forty-eight to thirty-six guns, carrying ill all 10,110 men.

It was Nelson's intention to attack this squadron in the van and centre, as it lay at anchor, according to a plan which he had previously communicated to the captains under his command. His idea in this disposition of his force was, first to secure the victory, and then make the most of it, as circumstances might permit. A bower cable of each ship was got out abaft, and bent forward; the fleet carrying sail and standing inward in a close line of battle for that of the enemy, whose line, describing something like a crescent, or, perhaps, obtuse angle, was flanked by numerous gun-boats, four frigates, and the guns and mortars of the battery already mentioned, on the island.

According to Admiral Brueix' own account, his headmost vessel was moored as close as possible to the north-western shoal, "and the rest of the fleet forming a kind of curve along the line of deep water, so as not to be turned by any means in the south-west."

By Bonaparte's desire, says Southey, he had offered a reward of 10,000 livres to any pilot of the country who would carry the squadron into the ruined harbour of Alexandria; but none could be found who would venture to take charge of a single vessel drawing more than twenty feet. He had therefore made the best of his position in the open bay; the commissary of the fleet assuring him that they were moored in such a way as to bid defiance to any force, even were it double their own strength. Every way the advantage, in numbers, in shipping, guns, and men, lay with the French; but the - moment Nelson saw their position, the intuitive genius with which he was endowed displayed itself. He knew that where there was room for an enemy's ship to swing, there was also room for one of ours to anchor. The plan which he intended to pursue, therefore, was to keep entirely on the outer side of the French line, and, so far as he was able, to station his ships one on the outer bow and another on the outer quarter of each of the enemy's.

"If we succeed, what will the world say?" exclaimed Captain Berry, with exultation in his tone.

"There is no 'if in the case," replied the admiral. "That we shall succeed is certain; but who may live to tell the story is a very different question."

The sun was about to set - the red, hazy sun of Egypt - and darkness about to follow, before there was a possibility of putting his scheme in practice. The fleet bore on, and at thirty-one minutes past six, just as the sun's broad disc began to dip, the action began with an ardour and vigour that baffle description.

As our ships advanced, they were assailed by a shower of shot and shells from the batteries on the island, while the enemy opened a steady fire from the starboard side of their whole line, within half gun-shot distance, full into the bows of our leading ships. The wood splinters flew about in showers; the smoke curled high amid the masts and rigging. Many British seamen fell, but the survivors received this terrible fire in silence. On board every ship the men were out on the yards aloft, handing the sails, or ahead making ready to let go those anchors that had been brought forward and bent to the rope cables. This was a miserable sight for the French, "who, with all their skill," says Nelson's best biographer, "and all their courage, and all their advantages of numbers and situation, were upon that element on which, when the hour of trial comes, a Frenchman has no hope. Admiral Brueix was a brave and able man; yet the indelible character of his country broke out in one of his letters, wherein he delivered it as his private opinion that the English had missed him because, not being superior in force, they did not think it prudent to try their strength with him. The moment was now come in which he was to be undeceived."

A French brig had been instructed to mislead the British, by manoeuvring so as to decoy them towards a shoal lying off the Isle of Bekier; but Nelson either knew the peril or suspected some deceit, and so the lure proved unsuccessful. Captain Thomas Foley led the way, in the *Goliath*, 74 guns, outsailing the *Zealous*, which for some minutes disputed the post of honour with him. He had conceived that if the enemy were moored in a line with the land, the best plan of attack would be to lead in between it and them, as the guns on that side would most probably neither be manned, shotted, nor in any way ready for action.

Intending, therefore, says Southey, to fix himself on the inner bow of the *Guerrier*, he kept as near the edge of the bank as the depth of water would admit; but his anchor hung, and while opening fire he drifted to the second ship, the *Conquérant*, before it was clear or ready to be let go. He then moored by the stern inside of her, and in ten minutes shot away one of her masts. Hood, in the *Zealous*, perceiving this, took the station he intended to have occupied, and from the port-holes of his seventy-four poured such a tempest of shot upon the *Guerrier*, that in twelve minutes he riddled and totally disabled her. The third ship which doubled round the enemy's van was the *Orion*, Captain Sir J. Saumarez. Passing gracefully and swiftly to windward of the *Zealous*, she fired her larboard guns so long as they could be brought to bear upon the *Guerrier*, then passing inside the *Goliath*, by a single broadside she shattered and sunk a frigate, *La Sérieuse*, which annoyed her, sending her to the bottom in an instant with all hands on board, 250 men, and all her spars standing; then hauling round towards the French line, and anchoring inside, between the fifth and sixth ships, she took her station on the larboard bow of the *Franklin*, 80 guns, Admiral Blanquet, and the quarter of *Le Peuple Souverain*, a seventy-four, receiving and returning the fire of both ships.

By this time the sun had set. The *Audacious*, under Captain Gould, was pouring a crashing fire into the *Guerrier* and *Conquérant*, as she moored on the larboard bow of the latter; 'and when that ship struck she weighed, and then turned her guns upon the *Peuple Souverain*. The *Theseus*, Captain Miller, following next, swept away the remaining masts of the *Guerrier*, and then anchored inside of the *Spartiate*, the third ship of the French line.

While these advanced ships doubled on the latter, the *Vanguard* was the first that came to anchor on the external side of the enemy, within half pistol-shot of the *Spartiate*. Nelson had six colours flying in different parts of his rigging, lest they should be shot away - "that they should be struck no British admiral considers as a possibility" - but Schomberg states that no colours were hoisted on either side, nor was a gun fired, till the ships of the British van were within half gun-shot.

Nelson veered half a cable's length, and immediately opened a fire alike heavy and terrible, and under cover of it the other four ships of his division, the *Minotaur*, *Bellerophon*, *Defence*, and *Majestic*, gliding like mighty phantoms through the gathering gloom, passed on ahead of him. In a few minutes every man stationed at the first six guns forward on the *Vanguard's* main deck lay killed or wounded; and three times the reliefs at those guns were all shot down in succession ere Captain Lewis, in the *Minotaur*, by anchoring just ahead, drew off the fire of the *Aquilon*, the fourth ship in the enemy's line.

Captain Darby steered the *Bellerophon* ahead, and her stern anchor was let go close to the starboard bow of *L'Orient*, 120 guns, the ship of Admiral Brueix, on board of which Casa Bianca was captain, and the weight of ball from the lower deck of which alone was equal to the whole broadside of the *Bellerophon*. As the ships anchored by the stern, the whole line became inverted from van to rear.

Captain Peyton, in the *Defence*, took his station ahead of the *Minotaur*, and engaged the *Franklin*, the sixth in the line, by which judicious movement ours remained unbroken. Captain Westcott's ship, the *Majestic*, got entangled with the main rigging of a ship astern of *L'Orient*, and was dreadfully battered by the three-decker's triple tier of guns ere she swung clear, and closely and fiercely engaged the *Héreux*, the ninth ship on the starboard bow, exchanging fire also with the *Tonnant*.

The battle now presented a scene of unexampled grandeur and terror. By seven the darkness was complete, and there was no light, save that which came from the flashes of the hostile cannon, and the red, rolling fire of musketry from poops, or tops, or forecastles; but by this time, on a signal from the admiral, the British had hoisted out their battle-lanterns, or distinguishing lights - four hung horizontally at the mizzen-peak.

Four ships of the British squadron, having been detached previous to the discovery of the French, were at some distance when the battle began.

Captain Trowbridge, in the *Culloden*, then foremost of the remaining ships, was six miles astern. As all the others had done, he came on sounding with the lead; but as he advanced the darkness increased the difficulty of navigation, and after having found eleven fathoms of water, ere the lead could be hove again his stately seventy-four was fast aground, nor could all his exertions get her off in time to bear a part in the action, which he could hear and see raging with unremitting fury.

The *Culloden* served, however, as a guide to the *Alexander* and *Swiftsure*, under Captains Ball and Hallowell, which must inevitably have perished on the reef; but entering the bay in safety, they took their stations in the darkness in a manner that was long remembered with admiration. Captain (afterwards Sir Alexander) Ball was one of the first naval officers who wore epaulettes, then deemed by the sea-service military foppery. As Captain Hallowell bore down, he fell in with what seemed a strange ship, and without the required lights, but he would not permit her to be fired on.

"If she is an enemy," said he, "she is in too disabled a state to escape; but as her sails are loose, and from the way she lies, she may be a British ship."

The vessel proved to be Captain Darby's ship, the *Bellerophon*, whose lights had gone overboard. Nearly two hundred of her crew lay about the decks killed or wounded; her masts and cables had been shot away, and she was drifting helplessly out of the line to leeward, so her station was at once occupied by the *Swiftsure*, the guns of which opened instantly on the bows of the French admiral, whose towering stern was raked by the *Alexander* in passing. Captain Ball then anchored the latter on his larboard quarter, pouring a dreadful fire of small-arms on his upper deck.

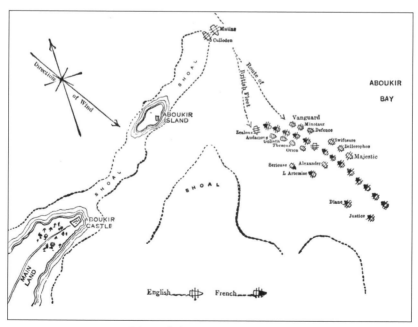

Plan of the Battle of the Nile.

279

The last ship which arrived to complete the destruction of this formidable enemy was the *Leander*, 50 guns, which Captain Thomson anchored in such a manner athwart the hawse of the *Franklin* as to be able to rake her and the *Orient* too.

Within a quarter of an hour after the action commenced, the two first ships of the French line had been dismasted, and all the rest had been so terribly mauled that a victory seemed certain; and by half-past eight the third, fourth, and fifth were in our possession.

It was about this time that Nelson received a severe wound from a piece of langridge shot, which struck him on the forehead. Cut from the bone, a flap of skin had fallen over one eye, and as the other was blind, he was in total darkness. As he was falling backward, Captain Berry caught him in his arms; and so great was the effusion of blood that all thought the wound was mortal. When carried below, where the horrors of the cockpit far exceeded those of the upper deck, the surgeon came to him at once, relinquishing a seaman who was under his hands.

"No," said Nelson; "I shall take my turn with my brave fellows."

Nor would he suffer his wound to be attended to until his time came. From its severity he was certain that he was about to die, and desired the chaplain to bear his last remembrance to Lady Nelson; but a burst of joy resounded through the cockpit when the surgeon pronounced the wound to be merely superficial. And now Lieutenant Galway, of the *Vanguard*, appeared with the sword of the captain of *Le Spartiate*, which had struck and been taken possession of by a party of the Royal Marines. The surgeon ordered the admiral to remain quiet in his cabin; but he could not rest, says Southey. "He called for his secretary, Mr. Campbell, to write the despatches. Campbell had himself been wounded, and was so affected by the blind and suffering state of the admiral that he was unable to write. The chaplain was then sent for; but before he came Nelson, with his characteristic eagerness, took the pen, and contrived to trace a few words, marking his devout sense of the success which had been already obtained. He was now left alone, when suddenly a cry was heard on deck that the *Orient* was on fire. In the confusion he found his way up, unassisted and unnoticed, and, to the astonishment of every one, appeared on the quarter-deck, where he immediately gave orders that the boats should be sent to the relief of the enemy."

It was at nine o'clock in the evening that this catastrophe occurred to the great three-decker. Admiral Brueix was dead. He had received three wounds, and stood gallantly on deck till a fourth shot nearly cut him in two. Even then he had strength left to entreat that he might be left to die where he lay. The devouring flames soon mastered the ship, which had been so recently painted that the oil jars and paint buckets lay yet upon the poop.

The mighty glare she shed on all sides, as she became a pyramid of flames, enabled the men on board the two fleets to see each other distinctly. Their different colours were distinguishable; the dismasted hulks of France, and the shot-riven sails of the British.

At ten o'clock the fire reached her magazine, and she blew up with a dreadful shock, that made every ship in the bay vibrate to her keel. Her officers and men sprang into the sea in hundreds and were seen, some helplessly drowning, others clinging thick as bees to spars and pieces of floating wreck. Many were picked up by our boats and many even dragged in at the lower-deck ports of our ships, at the very moment the guns were run back to be reloaded many of her crew stood the danger to the last, and continued to fire from her lower tier of guns while the ship was a mass of flame overhead.

A silence that seemed awful followed this tremendous

explosion. The firing, as if by mutual consent, instantly ceased on both sides, and no sounds were heard but the wild cries of the drowning and wounded, and the splash of the burning brands as they fell hissing into the bay from the vast height to which they had been blown.

Seventy of her crew were saved by our boats; but among the many who perished (she entered the action with 1,010 officers and men) were her captain, Casa Bianca, and his son, a boy only ten j years old. She had on board the plunder of Malta, amounting to £600,000 sterling.

Among the ships to leeward the work of death and destruction re-commenced, and continued till about three; and by five in the morning, when the sun shone again on the Bay of Aboukir and the towers of its Turkish castle, the two rear ships of the enemy, *Le Guillaume Tell* and *Le Généreux*, were the only French ships of the line which had their colours flying. At fifty-four minutes past five *L'Artémise*, frigate, struck her ensign, after firing a farewell broadside; "but such was the unwarrantable and infamous conduct of the French captain, M. Estandlet, that after having thus surrendered, he set fire to his ship, and, with part of the crew, made his escape on shore."The poop of *La Sérieuse* alone was visible above water.

The victory was ours; the loss to the French was terrible. The *Guerrier*, *Conquérant*, *Spartiate*, *Aquilon*, *Souverain Peuple*, *Franklin*, *Tonnant*, *Héreux*, *Timoleon*, *Mercure*, all seventy-fours (with 700 men on board each when the action began), were taken; *L'Orient*, 120, and *L'Artémise*, 36, were burned; *La Sérieuse*, 36, dismasted and sunk.

Four of their vessels alone escaped.

The British loss in killed and wounded amounted to 895 of all ranks. Westcott was the only captain who fell. Of the French, 3,500 were sent ashore under a flag of truce and 5,225 perished in various ways.

During the action the whole shore was covered by crowds of Arabs and Mamelukes, who beheld with exultation the destruction of their invaders; and, to demonstrate their satisfaction, the "European Magazine" of January, 1799, states that they illuminated the whole coast and country, so far as it could be seen, for three successive nights. On the morning of the subsequent day, the following memorandum was issued by Nelson: -

"Vanguard, off the Mouth of the Nile,

"2nd day of August, 1798.

"Almighty God having blessed His Majesty's arms with victory, the admiral intends returning public thanksgiving for the same at two o'clock this day; and he recommends every ship doing the same as soon as convenient.

"To the respective captains of the squadron."

The solemnity of this act of gratitude to Heaven seemed to make a deep impression upon the prisoners, who were Republicans and infidels, or worshippers of the Goddess of Reason, and so forth; and some of them remarked "that it was no wonder we could preserve such order and discipline, when we could impress the minds of our men with such sentiments after a victory so great, and at a moment of such seeming confusion."

When the event became known at Constantinople, the Sultan sent Nelson a superb aigrette of diamonds, taken from one of his imperial turbans, with 2,000 sequins to be distributed among the seamen. The sultana, his mother, sent the admiral a rose set with diamonds; the island of Zante presented him with a sword and cane; but the most singular gift he received was his celebrated coffin - an unpleasant memento that stood long in his cabin, and which was made from the mainmast of *L'Orient*, and sent on board by order of Captain Hallowell, of the *Swiftsure*.

Long after the British fleet had departed with its prizes, innumerable bodies were seen floating in the Bay of Aboukir, despite the exertions that were made to sink them, from dread of pestilence as well as from the natural loathing such objects presented. Most of these ghastly relics of the contest were cast upon the Isle of Bekier, and after an interval of three years they were seen by Clarke, the traveller, who assisted in the interment of numbers of them, which the waves had flung ashore to fester and decay under the hot Egyptian sun; while for no less than four leagues the whole coast was covered with wreckage.

The great admiral was now in the zenith of his glory; and he was created Baron Nelson of the Nile and of Burnham Thorpe, with a pension of £2,000 yearly for his own life and those of his two immediate successors. A grant of £10,000 was voted to him by the East India Company; the City of London presented a sword to him and to each of his captains; and the first lieutenant of every ship was promoted.

TRAFALGAR, 1805

W E HAVE now to relate the story of the most glorious and decisive victory ever won by the British navy - Trafalgar - the name of which must ever stir a chord in every heart; and yet, with all its glory and renown, a name fraught with sadness; for there, in the zenith of his fame, fell our gallant and immortal Nelson, the idol of our sailors - he who had so often led our fleets to battle, but never to defeat.

After the somewhat indecisive action between our naval force under Sir Robert Calder, and the combined fleets of France and Spain, sixty leagues off Cape Finistère, on the 22nd of July, they had refitted at Vigo; and, effecting a junction with the Ferrol squadron, had entered the harbour of Cadiz in safety. Nelson was appointed to command the fleet destined to extinguish this allied force of France and Spain; and Lord Barham, on handing him the list of the Royal Navy, desired him to choose his own officers.

"Choose them yourself, my lord," was the noble reply of Nelson; "the same spirit actuates the whole profession - you cannot choose wrong !"

The exertions made to equip the ships he had selected were unremitting, more especially the *Victory*, which was chosen as his flag-ship. Before leaving London, he called at an upholsterer's, where he had deposited the coffin given him by his old friend Captain Hallowell, saying that it might be wanted on his return; for he seemed to be impressed with an idea that he should die in the coming battle.

On the 14th of September he reached Portsmouth, and endeavoured to elude the populace by taking a by-way to the beach; but crowds collected, pressing forward to obtain a sight of the one-armed and one-eyed hero. Many were in tears, and many knelt down and blessed him as he passed. "England has had many heroes," says Southey; "but never one who so entirely possessed the love of his fellow-countrymen as Nelson. All men knew that his heart was as humane as it was fearless; that there was not in his nature the slightest alloy of selfishness or cupidity; but that, with perfect and entire devotion, he served his country with all his heart, and with all his soul, and with all his strength; and therefore they loved him as truly and fervently as he loved England."

Hence, as he now entered his barge for the last time, never more to be on English ground as a living man, they pressed about him in such numbers that the marines had to threaten them with the bayonet; but the enthusiastic people were heedless, and Nelson returned their cheers by waving his hat as the barge's crew shoved off to the stately old *Victory*.

The 29th of September saw him off Cadiz, with a fleet ultimately consisting of thirty-three sail; the *Victory* leading the van, the *Royal Sovereign* the rear. Fearing that the combined fleets of the enemy might know his force, and thus might be deterred from quitting the shelter of the batteries of Cadiz, he kept out of sight of land; he desired of Collingwood, the vice-admiral, that no salutes were to be fired and no colours hoisted; and he wrote to Gibraltar to request that the strength of his fleet should not be inserted in the *Gazette* of that place.

When Admiral Villeneuve received orders to put to sea he hesitated, as he had heard that Nelson was again in command. He called a Council of War; and some doubts that were expressed as to whether Nelson was actually at sea were confirmed by an American skipper, who had but lately left Britain, and who maintained that it was impossible, "for he had seen him but a few days before in London; and at that time there was no rumour of his going again afloat."

While Villeneuve was consulting his officers, Nelson was hovering sixty miles westward of Cadiz, near Cape St. Mary, where he hoped to decoy out the enemy, while guarding against the danger of being caught by a westerly wind and driven within the Straits of Gibraltar. Theatrical amusements were performed every evening in most of the ships; and "God Save the King," was the hymn with which the crews, standing afoot, with hats off, concluded the sports.

Nelson complained much of the want of frigates, "the eyes of the fleet," as he often called them.

His order of sailing at sea was to be the order of battle; the fleet in two lines, with an advanced squadron, consisting of eight of the swiftest-sailing two-deckers. The second in command, having the entire direction of his line, was to break through the enemy about the twelfth ship from their rear. He would lead through the centre, and the advanced squadron was to cut off three or four that were ahead of it, i.e., the centre. This plan was to be adapted to the strength of the enemy, so that they should always be superior to those whom they cut off.

The admirals and captains knew the precise object of Nelson to be close and decisive action, which would supply the place of any deficiency of signals. "In case signals cannot be seen, or clearly understood," he wrote, "no captain can do wrong if he places his ship alongside that of an enemy." Among his last orders was one directing that the name and family of every officer, seaman, and marine, who might be killed or wounded in action, should be as soon as possible returned to him, in order for transmission to the chairman of the Patriotic Fund, for the benefit of the sufferer or his family.

On the 19th, at nine a.m., H.M.S. *Mars*, which formed the line of communication with the in-shore scouting frigates, signalled that the fleets were leaving Cadiz. At two o'clock came the signal that they were at sea. All night our fleet kept under sail, steering south-east. At daybreak the fleets of France and Spain, the former under Villeneuve, and the latter under Don Ignacio Maria d'Aliva and Don Baltazar Hidalgo Cisternas, were distinctly visible from the deck of the *Victory*, formed in close line of battle ahead, about four leagues to leeward, and standing to the south.

Our fleet consisted of twenty-five sail of the line and four frigates; theirs consisted of thirty-three, and seven frigates. Their force in weight of metal and number of men far exceeded ours. They had 4,000 troops on board, and among these were a select force of riflemen, the best that could be procured from the Tyrol, scattered by detachments in every ship. And now (to quote Clarke and M'Arthur's Memoir) we come to the great and terrible day of the battle, when, as it has been so well expressed, "God gave us victory, but Nelson died !"

He came on deck soon after daylight on the 21st of October, which was a festival in his family, as on that day his uncle, Captain Suckling, in the *Dreadnought*, with two other line-of-battle ships, had beaten off a squadron consisting of four French sail of the line and three frigates.

The wind was now from the west, and the breezes were light, with a long rolling swell upon the sea. Nelson signalled to bear down on the enemy; and then retiring to his cabin, penned that fervent and well-known prayer, in which he committed the justice of his cause and his own safety to the overruling providence of God.

He next, in writing, bequeathed Lady Hamilton, whom he loved with a devotion so singular, and his daughter Horatia to the generosity of the nation. "These are the only favours," concludes this remarkable document, "I ask of my king and country, at this moment when I am going to fight their battle. May God bless my king and country, and all those I hold dear !

My relations it is needless to mention; they will, of course, be amply provided for."

He had passed a restless night, and was evidently impressed by the conviction - by a presentiment not uncommon to soldiers and to sailors - that he was to fall. He put on the full uniform which he had worn at Copenhagen. Upon its breast were the many decorations he had won, and among them was the Star of the Bath.

"In honour I gained them," said he, when remonstrated with on the peril of this display, "and in honour I will die with them."

Next his heart he placed a miniature of Lady Hamilton, his romantic passion for whom amounted to superstition. On leaving his cabin, he went over the different decks, conversed with the seamen with his usual affability; and as he ascended the quarter-deck ladder, three cheers burst spontaneously from the lips of the crew.

"I was walking with him on the poop," says Captain Blackwood, in his interesting Memoirs, "when he said, 'I'll now amuse the fleet with a signal;' and he asked me if I did not think there was one yet wanting. I answered that I thought the whole of the fleet seemed clearly to understand, and to vie with each other who should first get nearest to the *Victory* or *Royal Sovereign*. These words were scarcely uttered, when his last well known signal was made -

"'England expects every man to do his duty.'

"The shout," continues Blackwood, "with which it was received throughout the fleet was truly sublime.

"'Now,' said Lord Nelson, 'I can do no more. We must trust to the great Disposer of events, and the justice of our cause; I thank God for this great opportunity of doing my duty.'"

And in this spirit did Nelson, whom the sailors were wont to say "was as mild as a lamb, yet brave as a lion," bear on towards the enemy. When Blackwood turned to leave him, saying he hoped soon to return and find him in possession of twenty prizes -

"God bless you, Blackwood!" he replied; "I shall never see you again."

A long swell was now setting into the magnificent Bay of Cadiz; under a press of canvas bellying out before the south-west breeze, our stately fleet moved on. The sun shone full on the snowy sails of the enemy \ and their well-formed line - their many three-deckers, with all their ports triced up, and their decks glittering with the weapons of the troops and marines at their quarters - though formidable, was also grand; and our seamen could not but admire the beauty and splendour of the spectacle; and, in the full confidence of winning the battle, many of them were heard to say, "What a fine sight those ships will make at Spithead!"

According to Collingwood's despatch, "the enemy's line consisted of thirty-three ships, of which eighteen were French

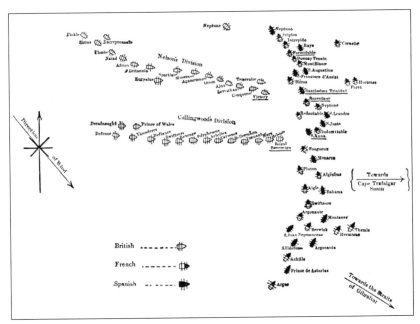

Plan of the Battle of the Nile.

and fifteen Spanish." Admiral Villeneuve was in the *Bucentaure*, in the centre; and the *Prince of the Asturias* bore Gravina's flag, in the rear: but the French and Spanish ships were mixed without regard to nationality. With us, Nelson led the weather column, and Collingwood the lee.

Nelson's squadron steered two points more to the north than that of Collingwood, in order to cut off the enemy's escape into Cadiz; the leeward line was therefore first engaged.

"See," cried Nelson, exultingly, pointing to the *Royal Sovereign*, as she cut through the enemy's line astern of the *Santa Anna*, a Spanish three-decker, and engaged her at the very muzzles of her guns, on the starboard side; "see how that noble fellow Collingwood carries his ship into action!"

And at that moment it would seem that Admiral Collingwood was saying to his captain -

"Rotherham, what would Nelson give to be here ? "

After the *Victory* was engaged, the enemy continued to fire a gun at a time at her, till they saw that a shot had perforated her maintopgallantsail, when they poured their broadsides at her rigging, in the hope of disabling her. Nelson, as usual, had many colours flying, lest one should be shot away. The enemy, however, never hoisted colours during the action, until they began to feel the necessity of having them to strike.

In the first heat of the action, Mr. Scott, Nelson's secretary, was killed by a cannon-ball, while conversing with Captain Hardy. Captain Adair, of the Marines, who fell soon afterwards, attempted to remove the mangled body, but it had already attracted the notice of the admiral.

"Is that," said he, "poor Scott who is gone ? "

Afterwards, when in conversation with Captain Hardy near the quarter-deck, while a shower of musket-balls, mingled with round and cross-bar shot, swept the poop, one of the latter missiles came across and killed eight marines. Captain Adair was then directed by him to distribute his men about the ship. In a few minutes after, a shot passed between Nelson and Hardy, drove some splinters about them, and bruised the foot of the latter. They mutually looked at each other; when Nelson, whom no peril could affect, said, with a smile -

"This work is too warm to last, Hardy."

The *Victory* now became totally shrouded in smoke, except at intervals when it partially dispersed; and, owing to the want of wind, was surrounded by the ships of the enemy. Among these was the *Santissima Trinidad*, Nelson's "old acquaintance," as he used to call her, a gigantic four-decker, and towards her he ordered the *Victory* to be steered. By this time the latter had fifty of her men killed or wounded, her mizzen-topmast, her studding-sails, and all her booms had been shot away; without a shot having left her ports, till four minutes after twelve, when she opened fire on both sides, with all her guns at once.

As the enemy's line could not be broken without running foul of one of their ships, "Which shall I take, my lord?" asked Captain Hardy, to which Nelson replied -

"Take your choice, Hardy; it does not matter much."

The helm was then ported, and the *Victory* run with terrible force on board the *Redoubtable*, at the moment that her tiller-ropes were shot away. Seeing her coming, the crew of the French ship let fly a broadside from their lower-deck ports, and the instant after closed and lashed them, for fear of being boarded between decks. She used them no more during the engagement, but her crew betook them to small-arms; and, like all the other ships of the enemy, her tops were filled with riflemen, who maintained a murderous warfare, by picking off individuals, especially officers, in the intervals when the smoke cleared a little.

On the other side, Captain Harvey, in the old *Téméraire*, 98 guns, fell on board the luckless *Redoubtable*; but another ship of the enemy fell on board the *Téméraire*, "so that those four ships formed as compact a tier as if they had been moored together, their heads lying all the same way."

This compelled the crew of the *Victory* to depress the guns of the middle and lower decks, and fire with lessened service of powder, lest their balls should pass through the *Redoubtable* and injure the *Téméraire* beyond. As there was great danger that the former ship might take fire from the lower-deck guns of the *Victory*, the muzzles of which touched her side when run out, the fireman of each gun stood by with a bucket of water, which he dashed into the hole made by the ball. From both sides of the Victory the cannonade was unremitting; her larboard playing upon both the *Bucentaure* and the towering *Santissima Trinidad*.

Twice had the gallant and humane Nelson given orders to cease firing upon the *Redoubtable*, as he supposed that she had struck, because her guns were silent and she carried no ensign; and it was from this ship, which he twice spared, that he received his death-shot.

During the action *L'Achille*, a French seventy-four-gun ship, after having surrendered, by some mismanagement on the part of her own crew, took fire and blew up; only 200 of her men were saved by the tenders. A circumstance occurred during the action, says Admiral Collingwood, which strongly marks the invincible spirit of our seamen when engaging the enemies of their country. The *Téméraire* was, by accident or by design, boarded by the French on one side and the Spaniards on the other. The conflict was fierce and deadly; but in the end the combined ensigns were torn from her poop, and British colours re-hoisted in their place. Such a battle, continues the vice-admiral, could not be fought without sustaining a great loss of men. "I have not only to lament, in common with the British navy and the British nation, in the fall of the commander-in-chief, the loss of a hero whose name will be immortal, and his memory ever dear to his country; but my heart is rent with the most poignant grief for the death of a friend to whom, by many years of intimacy, and a perfect knowledge of the virtues of his mind, which inspired ideas superior to the common race of men, I was bound by the strongest ties of affection."

A ball fired from the mizzentop of the *Redoubtable*, only fifteen yards distant from where Nelson was standing, struck the epaulette on his left shoulder, about a quarter after nine, during the greatest heat of the action. It passed through the spine, and lodged in the muscles of the back on the right side. Nelson fell on his face, and on that part of the deck where there yet lay a pool of his secretary's blood j and Captain Hardy on turning round, saw three men - a marine sergeant and two sailors - raising him up.

"Hardy," said he, faintly, "they have done for me at last."

"I hope not," replied his old shipmate.

"Yes - my backbone is shot through."

As Sergeant Seeker and others bore him down the ladder, he saw that the tiller-ropes had been shot away, and ordered new ones to be rove. He then covered his face and his stars with his handkerchief, that the crew, who loved him so well, might remain ignorant of his fate. Through the horrors of the cockpit, which was crowded by the wounded and the dying, he was borne with difficulty to a pallet in the midshipmen's berth, where it was soon discovered that the wound was mortal; and though aware, by the gush of blood every moment in his breast, that no human skill could avail him, he never lost his presence of mind for a moment. Nothing could be done to lessen his agony, and all his attendants could do was to fan him with paper and give him lemonade to alleviate his intense thirst; and there lay "the mighty Nelson," weaker than a child, with the roar of his last and greatest victory in his dying ear.

Great though his sufferings, he expressed much anxiety for the fate of the struggle. As ship after ship of the enemy's fleet struck her colours, the crew of the *Victory* cheered; and at every hearty hurrah, as it ran along the echoing decks, a gleam of joy came into his eyes. In much that followed, we cannot but quote Southey, whose authorities seem to have been Captain Blackwood, Stanier, Clarke, and M'Arthur.

He became impatient to see Captain Hardy; and as that officer, though often sent for, could not leave the deck, Nelson feared that some fatal cause prevented him, and repeatedly cried :

"Will no one bring Hardy to me ? He must be killed - he must be dead !"

After more than an hour had elapsed, the captain came down, and Nelson pressed his hand in silence, and then said -

"Well, Hardy, how goes the day with us ?"

"Very well," replied Hardy, striving to repress his emotion; "ten ships have struck; but five of the van show an intention of bearing down on the *Victory*."

"I hope none of our ships have struck."

"There is no fear of that," was the confident reply.

"I am a dead man, Hardy - I am going fast - it will all be over with me soon. Come nearer to me. Let my dear Lady Hamilton have my hair, and all other things belonging to me."

With a bursting heart Hardy returned to the deck, where, amid the smoke, the wild work of carnage went on. Upon Dr. Beatty asking the sufferer if his pain was great -

"So great that I wish I was dead," said he; and then added, in a lower voice, "Yet one would like to live a little longer, too !"

In fifty minutes more, Hardy returned, and taking the clammy hand of his old friend and commander, congratulated him on obtaining a complete victory, and that some fifteen of the enemy had struck.

"That is well! "exclaimed Nelson; "but I bargained for

twenty." Then, with something of his old voice of authority, he said, "Anchor, Hardy, anchor!" for he knew that the fleet would be in some peril,, many of the ships being shattered, dismasted, and near the shoals of Trafalgar. Hardy hinted that the vice-admiral would now take upon him to give orders.

"Not while I live - do you anchor !" As Hardy turned to leave, he called him back, and desired that his body - unless the King wished otherwise - might be laid by the side of his parents. He then asked Hardy to kiss him; and kneeling down, the captain kissed him on the forehead.

"Who is that ?" he asked, for his only remaining eye was dim now.

"It is Hardy, my lord."

"God bless you, Hardy! I wish I had not left the deck. I shall soon be gone !"

His voice then became inarticulate, and after a feeble struggle these last words were heard distinctly.

"I have done my duty - I praise God for it!"

He then turned his face towards Mr. Burke, and at thirty minutes past four expired.

Meanwhile, terribly had the strife been waged above where his shattered body lay; and it was not long before there were only two Frenchmen left alive in the mizzentop of the *Redoubtable*. One of these was the man who had fired the fatal shot. An old quartermaster, who saw him fire, recognised him by portions of his dress - a white frock, and a glazed cocked hat. The quartermaster and two midshipmen (Collingwood and Pollard) were the only persons left alive on the poop of the *Victory*. The last two continued to fire shot after shot at the top, while the former supplied them with cartridges. One of the Frenchmen, when attempting to escape down the rigging, was shot by Mr. Pollard, and tumbled like a bloody heap on the poop. The other came forward to fire again.

"That is he!" cried the old quartermaster. "That is he!"

Both the middies then fired together, and the slayer of Nelson fell dead in the top. One ball lodged in his head, and the other in his breast.

Twenty minutes after the fatal shot had been fired, the *Redoubtable* was the prize of the *Victory*; but she afterwards sank, when in tow of the *Swiftsure*. Our two ships the *Prince* and *Neptune* afterwards sank the *Santissima Trinidad*. Some of the Spanish ships fought with great bravery. The *Argonauta* and *Bahama* were defended till they had each lost 400 men; the *San Juan Nepomuceno* lost 350. Five of our ships were engaged muzzle to muzzle with five of the French. In all five the Frenchmen deserted their guns, and shut their lower-deck ports; while our men continued resolutely to fire and reload, till they made the victory secure.

The sound of the last cannon that had reached the dying ear of Nelson were those fired by the flying van of the enemy, from ships under Admiral Dumanoir. In their flight, they fired not only into the *Victory* and *Royal Sovereign* as they passed; but, with a cruelty that was infamous, poured their broadsides into our Spanish prizes, actually laying their topsails to the mast that they might point with greater precision. "The indignation of the Spaniards at this detestable cruelty from their allies, for whom they had fought so bravely and bled so profusely, may well be conceived."

Our total loss in this battle, which took its name from the low sandy cape on the south-west coast of Andalusia, was estimated at 1,587 of all ranks. That of the enemy, which was never revealed by Bonaparte, has been stated by some at nearly 16,000, including many officers of high rank. Twenty of the enemy struck to us; but it was not possible to anchor, as Nelson had enjoined. A gale came on from the south-west. Some of the battered prizes went down, some drifted on the lee shore,

An incident at Nelson's funeral.

one escaped to Cadiz, others were destroyed by order of Lord Collingwood. Only four were saved. Among the prisoners was Admiral Villeneuve, who, when released, is said to have destroyed himself when on his way to Paris.

According to an anecdote which appeared in the London papers for October, 1872, an old marine of the *Bellerophon*, who was then alive at Charlesbury Tring, when asked by the incumbent of his parish how soon the fleet knew of Nelson's death, related it thus: -

"We were lying pretty close to the *Victory*, and about four or five o'clock, I think, in the evening, we saw the admiral's flag half-mast high; and then we knew too well what had happened. Besides, soon after the action, we had a batch of French prisoners sent on board of us; and as they passed along the deck they mocked and jeered, and pointing with the thumb over the shoulder at the admiral's flag, cried -

"Ah, where your Nelson - where your Nelson now?'"

As an example of the grand and pious spirit which animated our officers and seamen, we may be pardoned when quoting the General Order issued by Vice-Admiral Collingwood to our victorious fleet, and given on board the *Euryalus*, off Cape Trafalgar, on the 22nd of October: -

"The Almighty God, whose arm is strength, having of His great mercy been pleased to crown the exertions of His Majesty's fleet with success, in giving them a complete victory over their enemies on the 21st of this month; and that all praise and thanksgiving may be offered up to the Throne of Grace, for the great benefits to our country and mankind:

"I have thought proper that a day should be appointed of general humiliation before God, and thanksgiving for this His merciful goodness; imploring forgiveness of sins, a continuation of His divine mercy, and His constant aid to us in defence of our country's liberties and laws, without which the utmost efforts of men are nought; and direct therefore that (date blank) be appointed for this holy purpose.

"C. Collingwood, Vice-Admiral."

To describe the sorrow of the entire nation for the fall of Nelson is superfluous here. Suffice to say that a public funeral was decreed, and a public monument; while statues and memorials sprung up in every city of England and Scotland. The leaden coffin in which he was brought home was cut in small pieces and distributed as relics.

At his interment in the crypt of St. Paul's, when his flag was about to be lowered into the grave with him, the sailors who formed the most interesting feature of that solemn ceremony, and who had so often seen it waving amid the smoke of battle, simultaneously and with one accord rent it to shreds, that each might preserve a fragment of it as long as he lived.

His uniform, with its orders on the breast, and the epaulette, left as it was, shattered by the fatal shot, his white vest stained with his blood, his drinking glass, and the glass of Lady Hamilton, with his watch, and other mementoes of him, are preserved in the Great Hall of Greenwich Hospital.

MORE FROM THE SAME SERIES

Most books from the 'Military History from Original Sources' series are edited and endorsed by Emmy Award winning film maker and military historian Bob Carruthers, producer of Discovery Channel's Line of Fire and Weapons of War and BBC's Both Sides of the Line. Long experience and strong editorial control gives the military history enthusiast the ability to buy with confidence. The series advisor is David McWhinnie, producer of the acclaimed Battlefield series for Discovery Channel. David and Bob have co-produced books and films with a wide variety of the UK's leading historians including Professor John Erickson and Dr David Chandler.
Where possible the books draw on rare primary sources to give the military enthusiast new insights into a fascinating subject.

The English Civil Wars

The Zulu Wars

Into Battle with Napoleon 1812

Waterloo 1815

The Anglo-Saxon Chronicle

Medieval Warfare

Renaissance Warfare

1914-1918

Sea Battles in the Age of Sail

Sun Tzu - The Art of War

Recollections of the Great War in the Air

Soldier of the Empire

For more information visit www.pen-and-sword.co.uk